MANGO ELEPHANTS IN THE SUN

MANGO ELEPHANTS IN THE SUN

How Life in an African Village Let Me Be in My Skin

SUSANA HERRERA

Shambhala Boston & London 2000

Shambhala Publications, Inc.
Horticultural Hall
300 Massachusetts Avenue
Boston, Massachusetts 02115
www.shambhala.com

9 8 7 6 5 4 3 2 1

First Paperback Edition
Printed in the United States of America
⊗ This edition is printed on acid-free paper
that meets the American National Standards Institute
Z39.48 Standard.
Distributed in the United States by Random House, Inc.,
and in Canada by Random House of Canada Ltd.

The Library of Congress catalogues the hardcover edition of this book as follows:

Herrera, Susana.
    Mango elephants in the sun: how life in an African
village let me be in my skin/Susana Herrera.—1st ed.
        p. cm.
    ISBN 1-57062-376-7 (cloth)
    ISBN 1-57062-572-7 (pbk.)
    1. Guidiguis (Cameroon)—Social life and customs. 2. Herrera,
Susana. 3. Peace Corps (U.S.)—Cameroon—Guidiguis. 4. Guidiguis
(Cameroon)—Description and travel. I. Title.
DT581.G85H47 1999   98-41764
967.11—dc21   CIP

To my love, my soul mate, John David Guillory
whose faith and love nourished this book
to wholeness and joyful awakenings.
I love you always. Promise.

For my family in Africa
who opened my eyes to
the miracle of each breath
and taught me to celebrate
being in my skin.

CONTENTS

Lizard dreams are sacred ground,
A holy land of chanting and dancing
In ceremony circles around
Africa's ancient fires.

—"The Lizard"
  Cameroon, West Africa
  427 BC

1. AWAKENING

> Mango trees,
> Banana leaves,
> Elephants, zebras, giraffes, and snakes.
> A huge black and orange lizard,
> painted dancing and breathless drumming;
> tangerine sunrises and ripe moons
> that I can reach and pluck from the sky.
> Ah—Only a dream. . . .
> No.
> I'm in Africa.
> No.
> Africa is in my dreams.
> Wait. . . .
> That sound is real.
> What is that sound?
> It's the call from the mosque for prayer.
> I *am* in Africa!

I chant it out loud—Africa; again—Africa. The sound resonates within, as if I am a bell being struck—a call to my soul to awaken.

The fragrance of the African desert permeates the air, and I drink it in. I'm savoring the tangy sweetness of morning's juicy breeze and the bitterness of dust being stirred by children leaving footprints behind their song. The rays of sun tickle my lips even before my eyes open. From my bed outside in front of my house, I look up at the stars in their slow-fading flicker. I know I'm no longer dreaming because, with each inhalation, Africa's essence fills my body. I exhale and linger in a sacred silence for which my heart has hungered.

The villagers awake with a merciless bang. Cows holler as they pass along the dusty, brown road next to my little cement house, which is standing out in sharp contrast to the surrounding mud huts. Hot peanut oil sizzles, frying the *beignets* in my neighbor's outside kitchen. Roosters join the Islamic prayers ringing out across Guidiguis. The desert sand awakens and circles us all in its embrace. Women clang their buckets, filling them at the water well, chattering of village news. Even with my few words of Fulfulde, I understand that the villagers are talking about the new white woman. "*Nasara, nasara,*" they say, and my ears hurt. Their voices frighten me, for within that word meaning "white man," I feel separated from the hope I have of belonging to the community.

I don't want to be an outsider; I don't want to be full of fear; I don't want to resist this adventure. I want to become part of this desert, this village, these people, these laughing children. My body is filling with Africa's spirit.

Out of the corner of my eye, I see a huge orange and black lizard, and I turn my head for a better look. The lizard was in my dream! Was it a dream? Or perhaps it was one of those moments when the spirit is somewhere between two worlds. The lizard sits very still, in deep meditation. He observes the village from high up on a tree branch, the eyes of God watching our every move, hearing every thought, and witnessing our dreams.

Now that my eyes have fixed on him, he moves suddenly, flashes across the branch and down the tree. I rub my eyes, yawn, stretch, and gaze at the rising sun.

I discover that my mind has become fixed on loving this moment.

I call upon my soul to come and see.

And my soul comes.

Gently at first, but growing brighter, the warmth of my soul's light is like the sun rising higher in the sky, expanding out into forever.

I smile as I hear my neighbors opening their house to put their stick beds back inside and setting up the outside latrine for washing. Yves, Clotilde, and their four-year-old son, Alex, are natives of Cameroon but are also foreigners here in what is called the extreme north. With food, cool water, and smiles, they had awakened in the middle of the night to greet me, the newest newcomer.

I get out of bed, step onto the cool sand, and pull on a brightly decorated red and orange African dress. I walk around the side of my yard to my front door to unlock it. The children stop walking to the well when they see me. They're surprised to see a white woman. Didn't anyone know I was coming? My light brown skin is white to the neighbors who are approaching to welcome me, to see how

I've survived my first night. Later I will tell them about my Navaho and Spanish origins. Maybe they'll be able to explain to the villagers in Fulfulde and Tapouri that I'm really not *nasara* at all. But for now, I'll accept *nasara* as a name for a Peace Corps volunteer and English teacher at the high school.

I hear Alex coming closer, singing in French. Other children are racing tin cans with sticks, the cows are grazing near my latrine, roosters are pursuing the hens, and termites are chewing on my bed.

Oh no! Termites chewing on my bed?

I approach the wooden stick bed. I lift the side, where I hear a tapping and crackling as if someone were eating a bowl of crunchy cereal. I hesitantly lift my bed on its side and immediately drop it: a swarming sea of termites is feasting on the tasty wooden sticks of my bed.

So this is West Africa!

The lizard comes down from the tree to welcome me. He nods, inviting me to come along on this unknown adventure. What can I do but giggle and follow?

2. LIZARD SPEAKS

At dawn, my dreams are chased away
Like rocks thrown at children
Playing on trespassed property.
A thundering truck shakes awake
Heads drenched with night's perspiration.
Black eyes snap open as if the end
Of the world were pounding on the door.

The driver and passengers are Tapouri,
Workers from the bush
Whose leather hands crack like
The splitting bark of a tree.
They've dug, planted, and picked
In desert fields of cotton and millet.
A bushman's hands
Now grip the rubber of an unfamiliar wheel
Behind a windshield missing glass.

The truck swerves along the dirt road
Where dusty children march to the water well,
Carrying empty morning buckets on their heads.
The barefoot children scream
And race off the road
As the truck skids to a stop
And dumps its load of sand,
Burying my land as if a
Pyramid tomb were being
Raised for the dead.

This one empty field is all that
Remains of my desert kingdom
Of sun, sand, and stone.
Now the Tapouri have taken
This plot of land to build
A house for a foreigner.

But in the beginning, it belonged to
Lizards and snakes, peanuts and millet.
At the end of a great war,
An imaginary boundary was drawn,
Like a child coloring beyond the lines,
Creating countries and nationalities.
The Tapouri were forced to leave,
Walking across new borders,
Their houses on their backs,
To a land without footprints or voices.

I welcomed them,
Gave them insight and quests.
Now they invade my field with cement
To build a home to give away to an American.

They've traded me in for a stranger,
Someone who doesn't know who she is,
Someone who will not guard the Tapouri path
Nor hear their hearts' aching voice.

Now I roam this dry, barren field
Like a betrayed, hollering ghost,
Taken too soon,
Without a body to go back to
And no future destination,
In a cemetery without names or flowers
Where the sudden dead are neither heard nor remembered.

What can a lizard do?

I have no voice to wail my sorrow,
No tears to mourn my loss, no wings to fly away
Or to enfold my body in sleep.
I only have dreams and visions to give away.

But the Tapouri no longer hunger for these.
They want a world of shrieking machines,

To build a country different
From the one expanding out
To the desert horizon
Beyond the wasteland,
Which they call "nothing."

But I am not nothing.
This desert is a place of life;
We live here crouched between time and space,
Where we long to dance.

To them, I am only a reptile.
They don't know that I am
A healer,
A shaman.

I have been here from the beginning,
And it is I who will last.

I will survive another stranger on my land.
Perhaps this stranger will hear me.
I will speak to her.
If she listens, I will give her my dreams.

3. BECOMING AN ELEPHANT

I'm sitting on a cement brick on my front porch, leaning against the wall, watching the children playing in the dirt road near the side of my house. Many children are naked, their swollen bellies bouncing up and down as they laugh, chasing each other and shouting in their Tapouri language.

The smallest naked boy is of the darkest black I've ever seen, making him almost blue. His head is shaved, as are all the other boys', his calloused feet spotted with white, cracking skin—feet that have never known the inside of a pair of shoes. Something in the field of dry weeds catches his eye, and he skips quickly to it. He bends over, and his eyes squint at it. He shouts at the others to hurry. The children stop their chasing game and race to the small, naked boy. As they arrive, he jumps out of the grass like a smiling, radiant Buddha, holding the shiny tin can he's found. The children surround him as he displays his treasure. They now have a key piece of equipment needed for a new game. The children laugh together. Excitement ripples from the group like stones skipping across water, and I'm aware that I've become affected by their wave of laughter. I wish someone would come over and invite me to play.

A little girl, about the age of five, with sweet dimples and de-fined muscles, is retying a falling sarong around her naked tummy, when she spots another piece of the puzzle. As she picks up a long stick, the boy immediately throws the can to the ground. He smiles, stops as if bestowing a blessing on everyone, and then, as a signal, he claps his hands. The dimpled girl yells out a message, and the game begins. The children form two groups and begin chattering among their teammates. The teams begin racing, one handing off the stick to the other, pushing the tin can down the dirt road.

What would they do, I think to myself, if I got up, went over, snatched the stick, and ran down the road pushing their tin can?

Would they play with me? Would they be my friends? I fumble with a loose thread of my skirt. I'm too scared to go out and try to play their game with them.

I notice that my legs are covered with flies. It won't do any good to chase them away. They just come back. Like an elephant, I don't even bother to shoo them anymore.

The game with the tin can is heading toward my compound. I stand and stretch and realize I'm feeling a bit hungry. Out of the corner of their eyes, the approaching children must notice my pale figure, because they abruptly stop playing. Then, as if sharing one mind, they all take a simultaneous step toward me. They wait, then take another step, then another. They hold each other's hands and giggle, then become a single team huddled in discussion for their next play.

I slip inside under the mosquito net I've hung over my doorway and reach for the bag of fresh raw peanuts my neighbors brought me the first night I arrived. When I step outside again, the children are even nearer, standing very close in a pack, laughing and talking nervously. The oldest girl with the dimples grabs the younger ones by the neck and pulls them back far enough to be safe from me.

They stare as if they've never seen a white person before.

I feel like an enormous elephant in a zoo.

I return to sitting on my cement brick and lean forward, setting the bag of peanuts on the sand. I crack a peanut open, eat it, and toss the shell aside. The children come a step closer.

One little boy takes a step away from the group and smiles at me. Mucus runs from his nose, down to his chin and onto his belly. Another child, wearing a *bu-bu* robe with a huge hole exposing his buttocks, also steps forward. The dimpled girl doesn't smile. She stares, unblinking and unimpressed. She pulls her curious-cat brother and the smiling-Buddha brother back to her. She wraps her sarong tighter around her waist again and thrusts a thumb in her mouth. With the other hand, she puts her arm around her smallest naked brother, who tightly squeezes her hand.

The children continue to stare. They don't breathe. They just gawk at what must look like a strange white elephant.

Deciding to break the ice, I stand up to welcome them.

They scatter farther away.

Glancing at my peanuts, I get an idea that might make them laugh and feel more comfortable. I crack several open, toss them high in the air, and leap suddenly from my seat to catch them in my mouth. The children scream and run away. The smallest boy shrieks and cries hysterically as his older brother pulls him, both running as fast as they can away from me.

I didn't mean to frighten them. I only wanted to play.

But then, who would want to play with an elephant?

I stare out the window, across the dirt road, and beyond the field to where a circle of women are washing clothes at the well. I watch, but they can't see me. I hide here alone. I am dressed in their traditional clothes—a sarong of green, blue, and bright yellow with a top cut from the same cloth. I feel as if I'm made up for a costume ball. Even my expression is a cleverly designed mask so they can't see my longing, so they won't be able to tell that I'm terrified they'll reject me or make me feel like I don't belong.

I hear the women laughing, and they don't hold anything back. Their shoulders rise and fall like wings of birds. One woman playfully whacks another on the shoulder with a wet, twisted cloth, and they burst out laughing. They are the most beautiful and graceful women I have ever seen. In their sarongs and matching blouses, their lovely skin is the darkest black, and my hand aches to touch their velvet cheeks.

I yearn to sit with the women upon a decorated stool cut from a tree trunk and made for women's work. I'd like to sit beside them finely dressed in a bright Cameroonian cloth while my hair is combed and braided by the young girls whose lightning fingers whip and tie strands of African hair. I long to understand their native tongue, to laugh with them, to throw my head back in surrender to their joy.

It's been so long since I've laughed with someone until my cheeks hurt. Although I haven't spoken to anyone in English for five days, it feels like years. Time in the desert is endless, without bounds. I have so much to say to anyone who will listen about what I'm witnessing out here in the bush.

The women scrub fervently, creating more suds than any American washing machine. At the opposite end of the circle, a woman finishes her bucket of laundry and pushes it aside. She scoots her stool closer to the woman sitting next to her and eagerly dives in to help her finish. Another woman finishes and gathers her own bucket and a few of those of her friends and gets in line at the well to fill them for rinsing.

The women go back to their laundry but continue to tease each other. Another woman throws a wet garment at a friend, who shrieks with delight and throws it back. Their playful voices make their language sound like a sun-drenched song.

What are they so happy about?

Here I am, dying of thirst, and I dread going out there among them. I've been using water sparingly, afraid of looking like a *na-sara* fool at the well in front of the women. I've never pumped water before, and I certainly don't know anything about carrying a bucket on my head. What I wouldn't give for a Peace Corps post with a water faucet, a toilet, and shower.

The lizard is here again, crawling toward my windowsill.

"I'm going to die out here," I say to him. (He's the only friend I've made so far.) The lizard nods and returns to his push-ups, seeming to agree that I'd better do something.

I watch the women and children across the way doing their daily routine so easily, washing clothes and dishes, pumping water, and carrying buckets effortlessly back home on their heads.

I can't do that. There's no way I can do that!

They've been balancing water buckets on their heads since they were children, and suddenly, at twenty-three years old, I'm going to attempt it? I really don't think I can do any of this. How do I mount the water pump and pressurize it so that water will pour out? What if I slip off the pedal and look like an idiot trying?

They have old metal buckets for a specific reason I don't yet understand. What will they think of my new blue plastic buckets that no one else has?

They'll laugh at my buckets. They'll laugh at me.

What did I really imagine the Peace Corps would be like?

Not like this. Nothing like this.

I feel white. Naked. A foreigner without the skill to survive out here in their desert, their millet fields, their world without water, their world that I know nothing about. I am supposed to be a teacher here? I don't even know how to take care of myself, to fulfill my basic need for water and food. Where do I begin to learn how to live their way?

I stare out the window again. My neighbor Clotilde has arrived at the well. She has the warmest eyes in Cameroon, like chocolate melting in the sun. From the jungle, she stands out as different from the others. With her high cheekbones and a longer forehead, she seems almost white. Clotilde is diminutive, much shorter and more slender than Tapouri women. Her husband, Yves, a science teacher, will be my colleague for two years. Clotilde has made peace with the women and has become a part of their daily lives. From them, she has learned to survive in the desert. She knows she cannot do it alone.

Clotilde greets every woman in the circle by raising both hands open-palmed in front of her chest and asking, "*Jam bah doo nah?*"

It means, "Are you in your skin?" Or a better translation would be, "Is your soul in your body?" The Tapouri women all say, "Yes. Oh, yes, we are alive," they say.

They receive her greeting by offering their right wrists for her to shake instead of their wet hands and exclaim, "*Jam core doo may!*" I am in my skin!

I watch their exchange and repeat to myself, "*Jam bah doo nah? Jam core doo may!*"

The circle opens up, with the women pushing their buckets and stools back so Clotilde can sit among them. Clotilde first helps the woman sitting next to her with her laundry. Another woman brings a fresh bucket for Clotilde to wash her clothes.

Now would be the time to go, I say to myself, because someone I know is there and can help me. I pick up my buckets, and move across the room in a hurry before I change my mind. I didn't come all the way to Africa to die.

I am alive.

I am in my skin!

"*Jam core doo may!*" I say to myself as I take the first step out my door. Now everyone can see me. Everyone is curious. Everyone stares at the white woman coming out of her house like Lazarus from the tomb. The children stop playing to look. The students living in the hut next door stand up from their washing and stop to watch me. The neighbors, bending over in their peanut fields, hands deep in soil, wave, and wipe away the sweat from their foreheads and necks. I wave back as I head toward the well.

As soon as the women see me, they stop laughing.

They stop playing, and they stop washing. They don't do anything. They just stare at me.

I stare back. I have suddenly forgotten all the greetings I know in their language.

It would be easy to run, to give up right here, to call this a mistake, to take the first bush taxi out of Guidiguis tomorrow morning and go straight to Peace Corps headquarters, a three days' journey away. It would be easy to race back to the land of indoor plumbing, bottled water, and pizza deliveries.

After a long, still, and silent moment, Clotilde jumps off her stool and wipes her hand on the back of her skirt. She offers her wrist for me to shake, and I do. "*Jam bah doo nah?*" she asks.

"*Jam core doo may!*" I say.

I am in my skin like never before. I am in my skin like I hadn't thought possible. I am aware that my soul is in my body. I am here, fully present—and frightened to death.

I want to hug Clotilde tight and to tell her that she's just saved my life, to say that, without her, I had wanted to die of thirst all alone in my house. Even if I had the words, I'm not sure she'd understand if I was joking or serious. So I remain motionless, like an animal crouched in between the moment of hiding and discovery.

Clotilde takes one of my buckets and smiles at me. I relax and smile back. The women begin to wash again, and I follow Clotilde to the water pump. I know the women are speaking about me. I hear "*nasara,*" but it doesn't bother me this time. I understand that it's not so much my skin color that they are referring to by using "*nasara*" but everything about me that's different or other or doesn't fit in. It's the quick steps I take, how my long hair sways when I move, my tentative smile, my nervous hands, the way I don't know how to survive in the desert. Everything says that I don't belong.

But I'm here to try.

Clotilde heads straight to the front of the line and replaces the bucket underneath the water pump with my blue one. The young girl who is pumping nods at Clotilde. Then she smiles at me, melting away my fears with the compassion revealed in her steady gaze.

I'm afraid that cutting in front of everyone is rude, and I search the eyes of those in line—but Clotilde, by reaching out and touching my arm, assures me that everything is fine. The girl pumps the pedal twice, then pulls it up high with her foot. Next she jumps on the pedal, riding it up and down. With one hand, she wipes her forehead and the front of her neck while, with the other hand, she holds on tightly to the pump handlebars. It doesn't look so hard. It's like riding a bike standing up and with only one pedal. I can do this!

When the bucket is full, Clotilde replaces it with my other one. The girl finishes pumping that bucket, and then the next in line puts hers underneath the spout and the girl continues pumping.

"*Oh say ko, oh say ko jour,*" thank you very much, I say to the girl.

"*Mon amie, c'est le temps d'apprendre comment tu vas porter l'eau,*" Clotilde says. My friend, it's time to learn how you're going to carry water.

I nod and agree. But how?

Clotilde tells me that it's in the hips that one balances, it's in the center of the body that we find our balance. It's not the head that does the work but a place in our belly that knows where to take the next step. Clotilde demonstrates. She bends her knees, lifts the bucket, and places it perfectly on her head. She smiles, then sets the bucket back on the ground.

I can feel everyone watching. "I can do this," I say to myself.

I am in my skin.

I bend my knees. My hands grab each side of the bucket while Clotilde holds the handle.

"*Un, deux, trois,*" she says, and we lift together. As I lift the bucket, I stand up straight. She doesn't let go, and I'm glad because I don't yet have a sense of balance. I try to find it in my hips, in my center, but I'm not quite sure if I have it or not. Clotilde lets go, and I hold the bucket up on my head with two hands. Clotilde puts her hands on my hips and looks into my eyes.

"You need to find your center here," she says. I close my eyes and concentrate. I remember the first time I learned to ride a bicycle. My father kept telling me to find my balance, and I didn't know what balance was until somehow I just felt it. I try to find it now—to remember what it felt like to find it for the first time as a child on my bike.

And there it is. I can feel it. Balance is a focused pulse in my belly that frees me to move my body with ease. The bucket rests perfectly on my head. I open my eyes. Clotilde is looking directly at me. So are the women. So are the children. I take another step. The water laps against the sides of the bucket and spills over. Still no one moves. I take another step and drop one hand to my side. I take a few more steps. I relax. More water spills over the side. I can hear rustling behind me as the women resume their work.

I'm walking slowly now, feeling proud of myself, still not daring to release the other hand from the bucket. I look toward my little cement house and smile; I'm almost there. And then my foot slips, and my ankle twists. I try to maintain the balance, but the bucket is tilting too far. I try to keep up with little, quick steps; water splashes over me.

My ankle gives way. I see the sand swirling around me as the bucket topples. I fall hard and land sprawled in the middle of the dirt road. For a moment, there is silence. And then the women laugh like wild hyenas.

I can't get up. I'm caught in my sarong.

I wipe my face and brush back my wet hair. The laughter stings, and I can hear my ankle screaming for attention. I finally find the opening of my sarong, untangle the long cloth from my legs, and retie it. As I stand up, I'm surprised to hear my own voice cry out.

I fall again, and the women laugh even harder. How can they keep laughing like that?

Clotilde approaches and squats next to me. She gently turns my ankle. I clench my jaw so as not to show weakness. Clotilde pushes further, and I cry out. She shakes her head and reaches out to help me up.

The young girl comes and picks up my bucket and returns to the well to fill it. Clotilde puts her hand around my waist, and I put an arm around her shoulder. We walk to my house. The young girl soon arrives carrying a bucket full of water.

When we get to my door, she opens it for me and helps me

inside. She asks again, as if reminding me of what's really impor-tant, "*Jam bah doo nah,* Suzanne?"

"*Oho,*" I say. "*Jam core doo may!*"

The experience didn't kill me.

I am in my skin.

I am alive!

A cool wind whips through green millet fields and ripe corn stalks. Clouds grumble and swirl in dark shadows. The desert hasn't decided whether it's going to rain or not. The animals remain unconvinced and wait, hidden in secret homes, stocked for the approaching wet season.

I've lingered on my front porch for hours, my sprained ankle keeping me from walking beyond the straw walls of my compound and into the village, where people are planting and harvesting life.

I wait for someone to visit, to check on me, but no one comes.

I hear the clanging, pounding, scrubbing, splashing, and sizzling of village life all around me. Will my life burst through the cracks in the walls and set itself free like a newborn butterfly?

Nothing is happening here with me. No water is being poured into barrels. No seeds are being planted, no gathering in the fields, and no storage of grains. I can only sit and wait where time doesn't tick, in the spaces between the notes of the Muslims' chanting to the East at sundown. Their song awakens a yearning that I can't name. I savor nature's songfest, too, and drink in the desert essence like fine red wine. The birds sing and chase, swooping down in the cooling air, sighing in relief that the sun is going to bed. The crickets, having just awakened from heat's hypnotic trance, fiddle to the tune of the children's buckets.

When I look up to the evening sky, there's a setting mango sun, peeling its skin and melting into a river of thick, sweet juice, trickling onto the desert horizon. Wings stir in my heart wanting to lift off to a distant place, far from this one. But now I'm caught somewhere between two stages. Part of me is neither here nor there. I was becoming a part of this village, but now I can't return to the well. I wanted to be in Africa; now I don't. For a moment, I was present, but now I'm not.

Nothing seems to be happening on the outside, yet I feel something taking place within.

I think of the caterpillar becoming a butterfly.

What happens to the caterpillar inside a cocoon?

The caterpillar becomes a glob of goo.

Not the sweet goo of cookie dough but the messy, sticky, smelly goo of an insect's guts being torn apart by nature's design.

I want wings and to fly, but I don't want to suffer in the confining darkness of a cocoon and go through the process of becoming a butterfly. I want to skip a step and move my wings—or even crawl back into my caterpillar's body.

Anything would be better than this.

In this in-between stage, I can no longer rush back to my old body in California. And I don't yet know how to become a part of this village of Guidiguis.

My skin has become the cocoon and my soul a caterpillar. I am metamorphosing; my entire molecular structure is melting down. There's nothing I can do to speed up the process. I'm stuck with this goo form I have become.

But somewhere within the goo is the coding of what's coming next. So I wait for the place I can finally reach inside myself that I can call home.

I'm bathing underneath a noon sun in the desert and washing away the layer of heat on my body, the soap spread over me like icing on a piping hot cinnamon roll. The bathwater quenches my skin's thirst and, for a moment, I've cooled off. But then the sensation of heat rises again as water beads race down my legs and instantly evaporate. I feel my shoulders burning underneath the shampoo that slowly slides from my hair and down my neck, chest, belly, and on down to my toes, burning places along the way never before touched by the sun's rays.

"You must be Suzanne," I hear a deep voice say.

The voice comes from behind the straw wall of the outdoor latrine, which hides my soapy body and sudsy hair from his eyes. I'm startled to hear a voice speak to me at the back of my house while I'm bathing; a red alarm flashes above my head, telling me something is very wrong and to scream if he gets any closer.

But then it hits! This man speaks English!

I slowly peek around the straw wall and spot shiny black shoes bought somewhere far from here. My eyes move upward, and I notice his creased blue jeans. A green and white European polo shirt fits snugly across broad, relaxed shoulders. This man is Cameroonian but from a different tribe than those of the extreme north. His light brown skin tells me he's from the south. The man smiles and melts the red plastic alarm above my head and makes it ooze over my skin like the hot wax of a candle. His grin is wide, as if we've shared laughter before and he remembers what it was that left us with a smile.

"Hello," I say, and pull a towel around my body even though he can't see me.

"I apologize for approaching without an invitation, but I knocked, then waited for your return. As I was leaving, your neighbors assured me you were home. Usually, I don't make house calls, but I heard about your ankle and thought a doctor's visit would be a good way to welcome you."

"I appreciate your time, Doctor."

"In your world, they say time is money."

"Yes, well—"

The doctor interrupts, "My time is yours; no money necessary."

He turns and walks away without waiting for a response. I stand still, reassuring my frantic heart that it's not a fight-or-flight situation. I loosen my grip on the ends of the towel. As the doctor backs off, he begins to hum a familiar song. The music enchants me to whistle along while my fears swim up my chest like migrating salmon and dive into the bucket of bathwater. They leap wildly about, their eyes open and staring at me. Then they dive under the suds, their tails splashing me, and disappear when the doctor begins to sing the lyrics.

It's "Stand By Me." I begin to hum along, swaying my hips to the rhythm. I throw my towel on the straw wall and lift the clean bucket of water over my head and then pour it like a shower over my body.

The doctor is singing to himself as if he's his own best friend. Here in the desert, his spirit creates an oasis of laughter and music. As he reaches the front of my house, he sings the chorus, and I begin to sing along, slowly feeling more comfortable with my rusty vocal chords. Since being in Guidiguis these last ten days, I hadn't thought to sing to myself; the awareness of how long it's been since I'd enjoyed my own company makes me reflect upon my past. I have been unaware of my own melody. Instead, I searched for others to sing to me, to fill my empty spaces with their musical notes.

I wipe the suds out of my ears and hear the children laughing with the doctor on my front porch.

How did he do it? How did the doctor get the children to come close? I hurry and dry off, wrapping the sarong around my waist, pulling on a loose T-shirt. I brush my hair as fast as I can, but I can't wait until the tangles are out. I rush toward the laughter with my brush while trying not to put too much weight on my ankle.

The doctor is singing with Southern soul, as if he'd grown up in the French Quarter of New Orleans, entertaining on the streets for a living. The children dance, jumping and swaying in circles on the sand. They move their bodies to his rhythm, giggling as they fall to the ground and lean back on their elbows with long sighs.

They're wiggling their toes and catching their breath, waiting for the next reason he gives them to wave their banners of joy.

When the children spot me, there is silence. They squint up in my direction.

The doctor stops singing and tilts his head, examining me like an X-ray in front of the light but not giving a diagnosis. He turns again to the children with his melody, and they erupt like volcanoes, with warm love spilling out of their smiles. The children hold their aching bellies and look back at the doctor with sly grins.

"Please sit down, Suzanne," invites the doctor in a voice reassuring that he'll heal what's ailing me. "I want to check that ankle."

I limp across the porch like the hunchback of Notre Dame, feeling embarrassed by my whiteness. As I sit on the stool, the doctor scoots his chair behind me. My hands fidget with the bristles of the brush like I'm four years old. The children stare at the brush as if they'd like to play with it.

"May I?" The doctor asks as he takes the brush from my hand, knowing I won't say no, but being polite in order to iron out the wrinkles on my forehead.

I nod, too choked up to speak, the salmon returning, fiercely swimming upstream, and leaping against the rocks in my throat. The doctor leans forward, winking at the children, who now plop down on the sand to watch. He starts the brush at the top of my head and combs the long strands of hair so gently that my heart is squeezed by the pain of so much tenderness.

The children are mesmerized. Their eyes are like bees that flutter back and forth from one flower to the next following the movement of the brush, but the doctor's got the sweetest honey, and their eyes linger on him as he begins his song where he left off.

When he comes to a tangle, his fingers press softly against the back of my head, holding the hair at the scalp and easing the brush slowly through. He puts his hand lightly across my forehead and caresses my loud and raging thoughts into tiny whispers.

I close my eyes. The sensation of his breath on my neck ignites a longing for someone who can hold me.

When I open my eyes, the doctor's hand is outstretched to the five-year-old girl with the smiling dimples. She gets up and takes the brush from the doctor. He moves his chair aside, and she stands behind me, putting one hand on my shoulder as she moves the brush from the top of my head to the middle of my back. The children's eyes follow the brush from my scalp to the ends. The girl takes the brush and pulls my hair up and out away from my ears until my hair falls to my shoulders. She brushes all the tangles out until my hair is nearly dry.

She is shy and curious as her gentle hand reaches to the top of my head. She holds a strand of my hair between her thumb and index finger, twirls it and smoothes it as if touching satin for the first time.

The children are now more interested in my hair than in my skin color, and I'm tickled inside. I meet their eyes, and for the first time, they really see me, not as an elephant or anything else. The children and I look at each other. We are all people here.

The smallest boy jumps up and stands in front of me. He cautiously reaches out and touches my cheek with an index finger. He pulls his hand back, then touches from my ear to my chin as if painting with a brush. He giggles. I giggle. The doctor giggles. The children laugh shyly with me, and the doctor sings again. Then the boy reaches out and touches my hair. He lets his fingers slide all the way down to the ends. He giggles again and then runs back to the group.

The radiant Buddha boy reaches out his right hand to shake mine. I shake his hand; then he runs back to the group and sits down. Moments later, the same boy runs back to me, shakes my hand again, and then returns to his place on the sand. One by one, each member of the group approaches me. They touch my cheek or my hair or my eyelashes or my forehead, or they shake my hand, or they just come up close and stare directly into my eyes.

I feel my bones sewing themselves back together in the spaces between the cracks. There are now five children standing behind me, and the doctor chuckles. They are touching, combing, pulling, twirling, and brushing my hair with their tiny and curious hands, all the while laughing and exchanging glances with me.

The doctor picks up my hand in both of his and says softly, "I'm glad God sent you to Guidiguis." He takes my swollen foot and then examines my ankle.

The Buddha boy pinches my nose, and once again we laugh together.

Girls won't answer.

When I call on them for an example of the present continuous in English, they obediently rise from their seats, hands trembling as they lean on their desks, and stare at the ground, as is the custom. Their voices are silenced by tradition, as if shame were a man with a gun to their heads threatening to rape their minds.

Only four girls sit in this unfinished classroom; they hide in the back from the 107 male students. The boys are dressed in hand-sewn blue shirts and pants with their names written in red thread over their hearts. The girls wear simple blue cotton dresses that are short-sleeved and reach one inch past the knee, as specified by the school. The Tapouri girls in the other classes wear only their blue dresses and cheap Nigerian plastic flip-flops, but the Foulbe girls in my class walk elegantly in their leather sandals. They wear solid pastel sarongs over their uniforms to conceal their ankles and wrap scarves around their heads to protect themselves from a man's eyes, as required by the Koran.

There are only twenty deteriorating wooden desks in the room, table and bench attached, made from the cheapest wood possible. The tops are covered with scars from termite trails made over summer vacation. The desks are meant to accommodate two students but are occupied by five, each one fighting for every inch. One hundred students are seated this way. The other eleven students are squirming on cement bricks, leaning over their laps, writing in notebooks on their knees. The cement bricks are dispersed throughout the room, making it impossible for me to move through the aisles. The four girls sit in the back every day, and from where I'm standing in front of the class, I can barely see them.

Three Foulbe girls exclude the fourth girl, Lydie, and sit squished together on a bench they must share. The girls give over half of the bench to two boys, as if embarrassed to take up any space at all.

Lydie's been pushed to the very edge of her seat by four boys, but she sits up straight in her seat, commanding the space beneath. She doesn't sit next to the other girls because she, too, is referred to as *nasara*. Since coming to the extreme north from the southern province, Lydie's been a foreigner in her own country. Solidarity among women of different tribes is not practiced in Guidiguis.

Lydie is sixteen and shy like the other girls, but she stands out as different. It's not only her lighter skin color and Westernized manner, but there is something else—a fire within her that yearns to burn brighter. It's in her eyes, which dare to defy custom and look straight into mine. When I speak of America, she stares as if wanting to be in my skin; her mind tiptoes through a forbidden door to travel to faraway lands. Upon returning from her adventure, she leans forward, eager to ask questions but afraid of the names boys call brainy and curious girls.

Lydie knows more English than any of my students, even the boys, although after what happened yesterday, she won't ever again show it. After I told a funny story, Lydie laughed like a thief running away with stolen jewels. The boys made fun of her because, from their point of view, her timing was wrong. To set the record straight, I thanked Lydie in French for being the only one who got the punch line of my story. But Lydie only covered her mouth and lowered her head to become invisible.

Like a pack of wolves, the boys followed Lydie home, singling her out from the other girls and calling her names. I watched from my window as Lydie buried her head in her notebooks, hugging them tightly to her heart.

Lydie and the other village girls are fortunate they can go to school; the others, immediately married off to monogamous or polygamous husbands, or working in their parents' fields, aren't so lucky. Lydie has a chance to finish school, and I have a feeling she'll do whatever it takes to reach her dream.

But the classroom is suffocating, and today my only goal is to make it to lunch break, when I can go home and rest for three hours. I'm struggling with my lesson, and the students are ready to collapse from heat exhaustion. The sound of donkeys braying outside makes me shout to be heard. Giving up the competition with the animals, I turn to the chalkboard and write, "I am writing on the chalkboard now." Facing the class, I wonder how we'll make it until noon.

When I write on the chalkboard again, small pieces of it crumble and fall to the sand and cement, where a floor should be. How will I teach in Africa for two years? I write the sentence again, losing more of the surface of the board, then turn and look at my students.

Slightly irritated, I say, "I am writing on a chalkboard now. Repeat."

The students repeat, like mechanical robots, and I look at them, wondering why they are learning English at all. What is a Peace Corps volunteer doing in this bush village teaching English to students who will never need it? Even if a student did get accepted to the university, he would never have the money to travel across the country to attend. How would a Cameroonian student pay for tuition? Why do they even bother going to school?

I wipe the sweat from the front of my neck and look up at the metal roof, which covers and heats up this unpainted cement brick classroom. The room has only three small holes where windows are supposed to be and one doorway without a door. If the temperature is 115 outside, it must be at least 130 degrees in this small tin oven with 112 bodies in it.

I'm blessed to be standing, not sitting at a desk and sharing it with four other bodies. I am able to move three feet away from sweaty students and breathe the outside air seeping through the windows. Barely able to continue my lesson, I'm amazed that my students have more concentration and stamina than I do. I take a sip of water from my canteen, and it's steaming hot.

I call on a student waiting patiently in the front row for me to continue: "What are you doing right now?"

"I am writing on the chalkboard now," he says.

"No," I say. "You are answering the teacher right now."

"No, you are answering the teacher right now," he says.

This is supposed to be an advanced English class in a grade equivalent to eleventh. They can read and write in English but can hardly speak or understand it. I realize that my accent must be hard for ears accustomed to a Cameroonian teacher's British accent from schools in the southern province.

"Class, listen." I hold my hand up to my ear, then jog around the classroom and say, "I am running in the classroom right now."

The students laugh at me, and while they take their time settling down, I'm debating whether to walk out and call it a day. When I try to make them laugh, they just stare. And when I'm being serious, they think I'm funny. It's been two weeks, and I still don't have a sense of my students or how to really get through to them. Maybe if I knew the *why* for being here as a teacher and Peace Corps volunteer, I could find the *how* to help them learn English.

I borrow a notebook and a pen from a student in the second row. He's as tall as I am, and he's sitting down on a low bench.

"Class, repeat, 'notebook.' "

"Notebook," they all say slowly and shyly.

I gesture as if I'm writing in the air. "Writing," I say. I wave my hand in a large buoyant circle as if directing an orchestra.

"Writing!" all 107 male students shout enthusiastically. I'm discovering that choral responses are popular with the class, but wish I could get the girls closer so I could hear them and stand near for support.

I write on the chalkboard, "I am writing in my notebook right now."

I point to them, and they write it down.

We hear a bat screech in the space between the cement wall and the tin roof. I jump, and the students laugh at my surprise. The small black piles that have fallen from the roof in all four corners of the classroom must be from the bats. And at the back of the room, on the loosely packed cement bricks of the wall, termite sand tunnels are being constructed from the ground up, like roots of trees.

Why am I in this forsaken classroom in Africa, anyway?

Didn't I think I'd find a better way of life here? I ran as far away from home as possible, only to find a place worse off than where I was. And the pain of my divorce and bitter childhood memories are not fading away like I'd hoped. Instead, these memories creep up on me like ghosts at moments when I'm not looking.

I let out a loud sigh and try to focus on this moment.

I guide my students to say as we write, "I am writing in my notebook right now."

As they copy from the board, I see them smiling and nodding as they softly repeat the sentence to themselves.

I ask for another example in the present continuous. A student raises his hand, and I call his name. He stands up, grabs the hand of his neighbor, and says, "I am shaking Mousa's hand right now."

"Yes!" I say. Now we're getting somewhere.

I ask for another example, and many hands go up. I smile and relax but wait until there is silence to call on a student because there are young cowboys outside yelling in Fulfulde as they guide their herd straight through the school grounds and past our window. The boys are taking the cows to the dry riverbed, where they will dig underneath the sand for drinking water.

I call on a student who gets up and walks to the door. "I am walking across the classroom right now," he says.

"Very good, Abbo. Thank you."

I call on another student when suddenly I see Lydie raise her hand.

The boy smiles and says, "I am smiling right now."

"Yes," I say, and smile back. "You are smiling right now."

I call on Lydie and move as far as I can toward the back, stopping in front of a student stretching and shifting on a cement brick. I'm surprised that Lydie raised her hand but pleased she'd want to give me an example.

"How are you?" I ask.

"I am fine today, Miss, thank you," she says.

"What is your name?" I ask her.

"My name is Lydie."

"How old are you, Lydie?"

"I have sixteen years," she says.

"What are you doing right now?"

"I am being now."

All the boys laugh at her sentence. I ask the class to be quiet, but this makes them laugh even harder. Lydie sits down, crosses her arms, and lowers her head, disappearing inside herself. When the class settles down, I explain that, in English, we don't say "I am being" unless we're explaining how we're being.

"For example," I say, "we can say, 'I am being silly' or 'I'm being ridiculous' or 'I'm being shy,' but there always has to be an adjective after 'being' to describe how you are."

I don't see Lydie's eyes. I'm afraid she'll never raise her hand or speak in my classroom again. I think of the Cameroonian customs, the restraints, and about how the boys constantly taunt and tease the girls. Then there's Lydie, who stands up to participate, despite it all, and I don't let her know how brave she is. Then I get it—like understanding a joke days after you've heard it.

"I am being," she had said.

I am being.

Lydie meant what she said. She was *being*—fully alive, fully present, fully in her skin.

And I wasn't.

I wasn't being; I wasn't in the moment; I wasn't at all present.

Some of me was flying back home to the States and counting down the minutes until lunch break. Part of me was hating teaching and the wretched heat. Another part was sickened by poverty and how people suffer just to survive. And there was also a place inside that was judging the Peace Corps and wondering why I signed up. I was irritated with donkeys, bat shit, and the termites who are eating up everything everywhere.

No wonder I didn't really hear what Lydie had said.

I wasn't in my skin.

"*Me eedee maco*," I say in Fulfulde.

I'm bargaining with a Foulbe woman for a handful of peanuts on the edge of the busy Sunday market swarming with aggressive merchants and local buyers. The old woman sits on a faded green sarong spread out under the shade. In front of her are a hundred small tin cans heaping with freshly roasted peanuts. Although busy making a deal with me, she continues to call to passersby. She claps her hands, laughs now and again, and wipes the sweat rolling down her bare breasts, which sag past her belly and sit on her lap.

"*Me eedee maco. Me whalah cheday. Me janghee no woh pukarajo hah Guidiguis. Hokee am bon prix, sobajo am. Tamerayjoy?*" I want to buy it, but I don't have any money. I'm a teacher in Guidiguis. Give me a good price, my friend. Twenty-five CFAs? (A franc issued by the Communauté Financière Africaine—African Financial Community.)

To say, "I want to buy this," you say, "*Me eedee maco*," but a direct translation would be "I buy it." *Maco* means "it," "him," or "her." *Ma* means "you." *Me eedee ma* means "I love you" or "I need you." It can also mean "I desire you." But in the market, "*eedee*" is used for the verb *to buy*.

The woman shakes her head while smiling at me, revealing orange-stained teeth that are thought to make a woman's mouth look lovely. She claps twice and then throws the palms of her hands out, suggesting I add more money.

"Give me a good price, my friend, give me 125 CFAs, my friend," she says in a high-pitched voice as if an old, creaking door were stuck in her throat and opens when she speaks. The woman is asking for five times the price. She knows all whites are wealthy.

I offer her a twenty-five-CFA coin, but she only laughs and waves her hand in the air, dismissing me. She says that she'll give me what I want when I give her what she wants.

The tantalizing aroma of her roasted peanuts appeals too strongly to bargain any further. When my stomach yells for something to eat, the woman hears it and takes pity. She lowers the price by twenty-five CFAs, asking only four times the price instead of five.

I *hokkee* her some *cheday* and *diddlee* to *la marche*. My thoughts are getting mixed up in three different languages. English, French, and Fulfulde are spinning in my head and out my throat. What will happen after two years?

As I walk toward the market, I recognize the king of Guidiguis, known as the Lamedoh. He graces his seat, sitting high and pretty in the back of his old white Mercedes Benz. As the car passes two feet in front of me, the Lamedoh spots me. He rolls the window down; a blast of cold air kisses my face. But the Lamedoh doesn't speak; he only stares, licking his lips and rubbing them together as if looking at a feast.

I want to squawk like the chickens carried to the market by their feet. I have a feeling someone is thinking about tearing the skin off the breast and sucking meat from the bones.

The car stops fifty yards in front of me, and the driver opens the door for the Lamedoh. He steps onto the ground as if it all belonged to him and everyone who didn't pay a toll was trespassing. He's elegantly dressed in the finest fabric, a royal blue *bu-bu* embroidered with white satin thread swirling around the sleeves and from the collar down to his large stomach. The blue cap covers only a small portion of his fat, bald head. His skin is light brown, and from a distance, I can see that his eyes are an unusual aqua color.

The children crowd around the Lamedoh offering pledges so he'll choose one of them to guard his car. They squeeze their hands together and clap, standing on their tippy toes to get his attention. But the king looks out beyond their heads, not hearing the pleas that echo down to the dark cave of their empty bellies.

Without meeting their eyes, the Lamedoh throws a coin at the nearest child, who smiles at the others he beat out. The boy stands on his only leg, and with grace and speed, he circles the car by leaning on a long stick used as a crutch and hops around his prize.

As I pass the boy with one leg, he looks up at me and smiles. "*Bonjour*, Miss! *Bonjour!*" He's not afraid, so I introduce myself. His name is François, and he'd like the rest of my peanuts, please.

He holds out his hand and flashes such a lovely smile that I forget my own hunger and give him what's left in my hand.

He says, "*Merci, merci, merci,* " and I can hear *merci* even after I've walked off a few yards.

I'm strolling behind the Lamedoh when he shoos the children away like flies. His long, manicured fingers point in the direction of the two dead cows being stripped of their skins. Cow heads, tails, and hooves are lying in pools of blood underneath a table. The bloody carcass on the table is black with flies until the butcher is told what part of the cow to cut. As his knife draws closer, the flies buzz off the cow and circle overhead. Then they return like black rain to feast on the blood.

As I walk through the market, nearly everyone grabs or pulls at my arm, my hand, or hair. The children give up on the king and follow me. They tug at my clothes, singing out *"nasara"* and asking for money in three languages. But if I give them each a coin, I won't have any money to buy the food I need. I have just enough money to ration until payday, less than a month away, when I'll journey to a bank in Maroua.

I didn't expect this much hassle. I foolishly hoped I'd be welcomed at the market, but when I try to explain that I'm a volunteer teacher in order to gain some understanding and a fair price, then translate this into Fulfulde, the Tapouri and Foulbe look at me with disbelieving eyes. The merchants stick to their outrageous prices, wanting as much as they can get. They've only translated my words into tourism: I'm seeing the sights and will be leaving soon.

I give up and move on to see if anyone will show a little mercy today. The village is now packed with locals and merchants selling goods on wooden tables underneath metal roofs. The shouting of competitors squabbling over each potential customer is giving me an aching head. The things I used to complain about—the long lines at Safeway, the mindless magazines, the elevator music, the beeps as the checker rings up groceries, and the annoying question, "Paper or plastic?"—wouldn't even bother me now. I still haven't seen anything I recognize as food. Instead, I see gigantic brown roots, leaves, yellow and red spices, rocks of salt, live ducks, squawking chickens, and enormous sacks of millet. The Peace Corps should have given us a market in-service, or at least a cookbook, before sending us off to our posts.

Tapouri women enter the market carrying huge clay water pots on their heads. The married ones wear an enormous wooden button in between their nose and upper lip. If a woman takes the button out, there's a huge hole through which she can stick her tongue—a disfigurement meant to keep other men away. Around her ankles, she wears heavy and thick silver bracelets. How does she walk while carrying a water pot on her head and wearing bracelets that look like shackles around her ankles?

The local male merchants ride their bikes off the paved road and down to the market. A few men carry rolled walls of straw used to make a fence around a compound or latrine. A Foulbe man struggles on a bike carrying his son, who holds a chicken under each arm. Another man slowly wobbles down the road on his bike with a huge sack of millet on the back. I haven't seen a single woman on a bike.

As I turn the corner, passing a row of plastics, I see Lydie, her sister, Hervine, and her older brother bargaining for a duck with a Foulbe man. But the merchant turns and walks away.

"*Puis-je vous aider?*" I ask, hoping I can help.

"Thank you, Miss."

"How are you, Lydie?"

"I'm fine, thank you, Miss. Have you met my big brother?" Lydie asks.

"No, I haven't, but I've seen you at school. You're the math teacher?" I ask.

"*Oui. Je suis Monsieur Mfoumba. Bienvenue.*" He shakes my hand, but there isn't any warmth.

"Where is your bicycle, Miss?" Lydie asks.

"I walked today."

"I've seen you bike through the village. Your bicycle is very nice."

"Yes, I like it. I can get to places fast."

Mr. Mfoumba says slowly in English, "Time is money."

Lydie is surprised he made a joke and laughs with me.

"True. Americans are always in a hurry," I say.

The Foulbe man wants to continue bargaining and waves the duck by the feet to get our attention.

"*Noy indee ma?*" What is your name? I ask, stepping forward.

"*Ah! Nasara! Ah whadee nah? Ah donne nah?*"

I don't understand what he's saying, but he's excited that I speak Fulfulde.

Bargaining with this man, who I finally discover is named Saidou, is like a game you play to win but mostly to have fun. When we finally agree on a price, Lydie grabs the duck with one quick swoop. When we say good-bye, I'm feeling more confident I'll be able to survive in Guidiguis.

A young man sells clothes donated by an American charity. He sells jeans, shorts, dresses, and blouses. He's even selling a Burger King uniform and a Domino's Pizza jacket. Each is going for five dollars, an amount of money that could easily buy groceries for a student for a month.

I turn into a long row containing tools, spices, and glass dishes. There are Nigerian-made batteries, soaps, and cloth. I find sugar, flour, beans, rice, and peanut butter. I bargain for hours with merchants for a fair price. Women are harder to bargain with than men.

I spot the Lamedoh again, and he sees me, too. He stops, I'm assuming to buy me a gift, since he keeps looking up at me and then at the object on the merchant's table, but I can't see what it is. He again lifts his eyes toward me; they sparkle as he smiles, romantically, then pays the young man wrapping the present. The Lamedoh is walking toward me now like a prince holding a glass slipper.

I move away. The king follows. But I'm curious to see what my present is. What would an African king give to his princess?

Although I'm interested in opening the gift, I don't encourage him. I turn down two aisles, then find myself in the dried fish section. I stop. The stench of the fish makes me nauseous. I cover my nose and mouth and try not to breathe, but the contents of my stomach are defying gravity.

The Lamedoh taps me on the shoulder; startled, I spin around. He shakes my hand and tickles the middle of my palm. I snatch my hand away, knowing the light caress means he's just made a pass at me. He smiles.

I stare at the package his driver is holding and guess at what's inside: lovely jewelry, a wooden carved mask, an African basket, mangoes?

How I wish it were chocolate!

The driver hands him the paper-wrapped present, and then the Lamedoh hands it to me.

"*Oh say ko, oh say ko jour.*" I say thank you and accept the gift.

The Lamedoh says, "*Me eedee ma.*"

What exactly does he *mean*? Does he love me? Need me? Desire me? Want to buy me? How confusing.

I open the package. Staring up at me is a bloody goat head.

I drop it and scream.

Was that supposed to be a bouquet of flowers?

I turn away from the goat head, lean over, and vomit. I see that I've ruined a pile of dried fish, and the owner is yelling at me. She shouts in Fulfulde, but the Lamedoh quickly pays her for the pile of fish. She quiets down but mumbles insults under her breath as she rearranges her piles of fish and throws one away.

The driver offers me a handkerchief to wipe my mouth, and a woman offers a calabash of water. I drink as I'm guided to the king's car. The driver explains that the Lamedoh has more shopping to do and has offered me the use of his Mercedes so I may get home quickly. I'm thinking only of air-conditioning and getting home and not what the consequences might be.

As I sit in the back seat, the Lamedoh knocks on the window. I roll it down wondering what price I'll pay for accepting his gifts. He gallantly asks me a question in Fulfulde and then waits. When he sees he won't get a response, he returns the unwrapped goat head and walks away.

I wrap the head, put it on the floor of the car, and then lean back in my seat. The driver laughs at me in the rearview mirror. "The king said that he wants to marry you."

What? I'm only worth a goat's head!

Women are usually bought from their fathers by their fiancés for a certain price, a dowry, and usually it's a *large* number of cows, goats, bags of millet, and some calabashes of wine. But this is an insult!

"I'm worth more than a goat's head!" I say to the driver, but he's not listening, since from his perspective that was an entirely correct marriage proposal. He only laughs and drives like a speed demon down the dirt road.

Looks like prince charming has at long last arrived.

Dear Mom,

I'm thinking of you while sitting in front of my house on a traditional wooden stick chair, sent as a gift by the king of Guidiguis. He has proposed marriage every day this week. I'm sure he'll be in contact with you shortly to negotiate a price for my dowry. So far, it looks like you'll only get a goat's head, a stick chair (termites not included), and possibly a few cows. If I were you, Mom, I'd ask for more, since you taught me the true value of things. At least ask him to throw in another goat and a calabash of sweet millet wine.

I'm sure the king's thinking I'm playing hard to get, because he won't take no for an answer. Why wouldn't I want to be his African queen? Yesterday he sent his Mercedes to chauffeur me wherever in Cameroon I wanted to go. I must confess, I couldn't resist the offer. Those few precious moments of air-conditioning are worth putting up with a couple more of the king's advances. How hot is it, Mom? It's so hot you can dry a pair of cotton underwear on the clothesline in two minutes. No kidding. Both sides are even extra crispy. And sheets only take five.

The driver suggested we travel to Nigeria, six hours away, to do some shopping, but I wanted to go to Kaele's market, only twenty miles away, where my friend Vann lives. In my last letter, I wrote you about our meeting during Peace Corps language training in Batia, and that she nicknamed me Suzi-Monster because of my love for chocolate chip cookies, but what I didn't mention is how similar our pasts are. Vann is Cajun and has faced discrimination and obstacles just as we mixed-bloods have. I don't have to explain to her how it felt for me to grow up Spanish and Navaho. Those feelings have been passed down to her from previous generations like hand-me-down clothes that have never fit anyone.

Vann and I were excited to see each other and to finally speak English. We talked until our tongues were flabby and we could only lift our fingers to wave good-bye. I'm glad to have a Peace Corps friend nearby, although in the bush, it's not so much the distance but the lack of access to transportation that makes getting there so hard.

The only possible time you can reach me at the number of the Peace Corps house in Maroua is on the date I gave you. The telephone is a six-hour journey from my village. Since I have to wait for a bush taxi to appear out of nowhere in the desert in order to get out of Guidiguis, there's no way of telling whether I'll even be able to travel to the phone. If the lines are busy again, I'll wait at least four hours at the phone. If we don't get to talk, I'll send a message the following month with another volunteer's parents with the date and time I'll be in Maroua.

Mom, I wish you could come for a visit, but I understand that you wouldn't call a trip to Africa a vacation. But what do you think you'd see right now if you had a glimpse into my life in Guidiguis? You'd see children playing in the dirt road in front of my house. They're stopping and coming my way. They plop down on the sand and sit in a circle and watch me. The girl with the dimples is Adele. She's the oldest child from the mud huts surrounding my house. She stands up and signs "brush" to me. Our made-up signs are the only language the children and I use to understand each other. She takes the brush through my hair as if sensing my need for tenderness. And then if you looked out on the horizon, you'd see elephants the color of ripe mangoes leaving their footprints across the sun as they migrate through the desert in search of water.

My neighbor Clotilde is coming with a plate of food since I'm having a hard time finding anything I recognize and know how to cook. Please send more Kool-Aid, music tapes, and batteries. But don't send any more chocolate: it melted. Thank Grandma for sending Mexican spices, but what she expected me to do with a check for fifty dollars and a packet of microwave popcorn, I'm not certain.

I miss you, Mom, and I miss everything about home.

Love,
Suz

10. LIZARD SPEAKS

She won't tell you everything.
She weaves her story like a spider's web
So that you, the reader, will get caught in it.
She doesn't want to kill you—
But she'll spin and guard you
Until she's hungry enough
To nibble on your ear.

I know. I watch her.
I see what she wants to hide,
The memories she'd like to squeeze from her brain
Like pus from a swollen wound.

She watches me, too.
She sits there on the sand
With pen and paper,
Gazing now and again
Into my eyes when I crawl closer.

I lead her to the edge of a desert cliff,
Where she lifts off and meets her spirit soaring.

And she soars,
Capturing in words
The view high above this African land,
Appearing as a quilt of millet fields,
Cotton farms, desert sand, and mud huts.
She embroiders her poems
Upon the colorful tapestry
She has sewn together
In her letters home.

She longs only for sugarplum dreaming
And the opening of her letters,
With exotic stamps of Cameroon,

To be ripped open like a
Long-awaited Christmas gift.

She does not venture beyond the
Threads of the web she has spun,
Nor does she quest for
Nourishment of her spirit
Beyond the fabric of her creation.

I sigh and crawl across the dead tree lying along the horizon.
It makes a bridge between two naked tree trunks
That hold the woven ceiling of straw above her head,
Protecting her dreams from the radiance
Of the sun and the moon.

11. DISCIPLINE

Journal, October 1992

MONDAY

Aïssatou was late for school and forced to kneel where the vice principal saw her enter the school grounds. He hit her across the shoulders and back with a stick the size of a baseball bat. The class and I heard Aïssatou scream as she rolled her long, thin body into a tiny ball. She protected her head with her arms and her uniform with the pink and gold sarong that was wrapped around her shoulders.

I did nothing.

I could only bite my lip and stand at the door like a frightened child, wanting to defend her but unable to do or say anything.

The boys laughed and watched as if what was going on outside was a well-loved sport. Hervine looked away from the door and closed her eyes. I asked my students to focus on the lesson endless times, but this class was refusing to cooperate. The other classes respect my rules, but I do need to find more ways to discipline. Although I've seen my colleagues bringing sticks to school, I've never thought to use violence to control behavior.

TUESDAY

Doing nothing yesterday is haunting me. I feel guilty of a crime and wait for a conviction. I tell myself that there's nothing I could have done. My mind won't accept it. I see her pain-stricken face over and over again. My heart hurts, and I wonder if there isn't something else going on.

The Peace Corps is here to help. We're not here to change a system, custom, or tradition. We are not here to judge or condemn. Nonetheless, corporal punishment is wrong, and I must do something.

But what can I do? Can I continue to work for a school that inflicts pain for punishment?

WEDNESDAY

I took roll exactly at 7:00 AM as requested by the principal and pronounced most of my students' names wrong, throwing them into fits of hysterics every time I made a gross mistake. The class is showing little respect for me, and I feel I'm losing them more every day.

When I finished roll call, I counted 109 students. One student was absent—Aïssatou again. I passed back tests and began my lesson on adverbs, but they wouldn't listen. I asked them to settle down several times. The louder my voice yelled "quiet," the noisier they became.

When Aïssatou finally entered the school grounds, the principal eagerly walked toward her while tapping one hand with the stick. The class completely lost control and rushed out of their seats to stand and watch. They spoke their patois and thrust their heads out the doorway and windows, taunting Aïssatou for being late again.

They mimicked my words as I tried to restore order. I don't know how to discipline.

I pushed the students aside and walked out the classroom door not knowing whether I was quitting the Peace Corps or not. I rushed across the grounds to where the principal and Aïssatou were standing, but before I could even get close enough to stop him, he struck her on the thigh. She fell to the sand, and as I approached, the principal kicked her and told her to get to class. Before I could say anything he spun around and walked away.

I offered Aïssatou a hand to stand up. When she took mine, she lowered her eyes and turned her head away. Her hand felt as if it were on fire. I touched her forehead and confirmed that she had a high fever. I told her that she needed to go home and rest, but she shook her head and said nothing. As she lifted herself to her feet, I felt her gathering strength from deep within her body.

She stood with her head high and proud. I held her hand tightly in mine, and we walked together to class. The students clapped for Aïssatou as if thunder had two hands. They pointed through the windows at us, mocking me by pouting and imitating crying noises.

Their stabs of cruel laughter made me want to cry. Why couldn't Aïssatou have stayed home this week? Why was I teased by my students for showing my feelings? Compassion must be a weakness forbidden at school.

As Aïssatou brushed off before entering the classroom, I wondered why she even bothered coming to school. If I were a Cameroonian woman in the extreme north, what would I do?

THURSDAY

Aïssatou was not at school today. Part of me thought she'd be late again, so I frequently looked out the window for her arrival; this time, I was determined to rush out and stop anyone who tried to punish her.

During the exam, I looked out the window and over and over relived Aïssatou being hit. This happened until I was ready to walk out of my own skull.

Then I saw myself in the corner of my classroom: I looked like a scared five-year-old. I felt removed from the image—as if it belonged to someone else. When I had heard Aïssatou scream, it had reminded me of something long forgotten. The sound crept its way down my ear and through a dusty tunnel into my memory. Since being in Africa, I've tried to forget my childhood, but this time, I was unable to keep the memories from coming, one after another.

Like a moving picture I see my younger brother and myself crouched in a corner, crying and clinging to each other. My father roars at us and turns the dinner table over; plates and glasses are smashing on the floor. Then my father grabs my mother and puts her in a headlock as he stands behind, choking her.

Then I think I screamed. Or maybe it was my brother. I can't quite remember.

What happened after that—just the feeling that the weight of my father's love would soon crush us.

I squeezed my eyes shut to force the memory out of my brain.

My students were still busily working at their English tests. I looked at my watch. It was 7:45, and time was up for the test.

I felt relieved that Aïssatou didn't come tardy and was glad that she hadn't come to school. I hoped she was at home resting and taking care of her fever.

I called time and collected the tests. My students stood up and walked over to their friends and started chatting.

I asked them several times to get back in their seats and to listen, but no one heard me. I stood in front of the class and used a commanding voice in French to tell them to be quiet, but all I got was more noise.

On the verge of tears, I shouted at my students, "Why won't you listen to me!"

One very young and shy student raised his hand. I called on him, and he stood and said, "You don't beat us, Miss."

"I will not beat you," I said.

"We respect a teacher who beats us," another student said.

"I'm not going to beat you," I said firmly.

I've got to find a solution.

FRIDAY

I stopped at the water barrel in front of the office building for a sip before going to prepare lessons for my seven o'clock class. I dipped the dried-out melon half into the barrel and filled it to the top and drank. A lightbulb went on. What if I bring buckets to school and, as punishment, send students out to get five buckets of water at noon for lunchtime detention? They'd certainly hate that. Noon is when everyone naps; it's too hot to do anything else but sleep.

At once, I raced home to get my water buckets. I decided that anyone causing discipline problems would pump five buckets of water and bring them to school.

I got another idea when I saw the women washing clothes at the well. I saw one mother carefully washing her child's uniform by hand. A mother doesn't smack, scrub, or wring a uniform like she washes her sarongs, towels, and sheets. She washes her child's uniform as if it were fragile. One mother lovingly rinsed the uniform while a friend arrived at the well. The woman proudly showed off the uniform to her friend, who looked at the fine work she'd done. Students are proud of what their parents worked hard to buy and sew. Then I remembered what a departing Peace Corps teacher had told us new volunteers about a family's dignity and honor. She made the students kneel in front of the classroom for punishment.

When I returned to school, I knew that I'd do things differently.

As I walked into the room, my seven o'clock class didn't even sit down. They paraded around the room as if they were Mardi Gras floats, flinging paper to the crowd. A student yelled out a window at a tardy student. I told him to kneel in front of the class or go out and face the consequences with the administration.

Regretfully, he walked up to the front of the class, placed his notebook on the hard, rugged cement surface of an unfinished floor, and kneeled on it. I shook my head and told him to give me the notebook. He stood up and hesitantly handed it over.

I pointed for him to kneel again. He looked at me as if it were worse than death.

"But it will tear my uniform!" he protested.

"I know," I said coldly.

"It will shame my parents!" he replied.

I just nodded my head.

When he kneeled on the floor, the class fell silent, and students sat in their seats.

At 7:10, two boys sneaked past the administration and climbed through the classroom windows. I handed them each a bucket and told them to bring back ten buckets of water and dump them into the school barrel.

They looked at the faces of the others in the classroom and knew I meant business. The water pump is a quarter of a mile away, and within the hour, the temperature will hit 100 degrees.

The first student kneeled throughout the entire period but didn't make a sound.

As I began my lesson, I heard everyone listening. I could even hear them breathe.

12. SUFFERING

Doc and I are walking by flashlight down the dirt road on our way to a mud hut that sometimes doesn't sell out of cold French drinks. Doc is in a festive mood tonight because he's spent twelve hours in intensive surgery and his patient is going to live. And I'm thrilled to be out of my 450-degree-Fahrenheit house, where a sneaky rat and a screaming cricket have been driving me nuts.

"Doc operates, and nobody dies!" I shout out to the starry night.

Doc laughs with me and takes my hand in his for the first time. Our laughter has broken the barrier of the well-built wall that stands between us. I squeeze his hand and let his fingers gently caress mine like the sweet strumming of a guitar.

"That makes seventeen patients I've operated on in Guidiguis, and every one has lived!" Doc says.

"Let's celebrate the lives of your patients!" I say enthusiastically.

Something moves under my feet, and I nearly jump out of my skin. Doc notices my body tense and shines the flashlight into the bushes to calm my fears of snakes and scorpions. He drops my hand and puts an arm around me. He pulls me close and rests his cheek against mine.

"I won't let anything happen to you while you're in Cameroon, Suzanne. You're under my protection now. In two years, you'll return to your mother in the States, and you'll be perfectly healthy. Promise."

"Could you speak to my mom?" I ask. "She thinks Cameroon is going to kill me."

"Tell her I'm making her a promise," Doc says, and winks at me.

We reach the mud hut, where the electricity has been cut and where more than twenty men are drinking in the darkness. There isn't even moonlight.

I recognize two of my colleagues, who look up and stare at me walking into the bar with the doctor. I raise my hands together and say *"Bonsoir"* to the English teacher, a short, chubby man with glasses and moustache, and to the history teacher, Mr. Ndo, a man of the same height who is muscular and clean shaven. Everyone in the bar raises his hand to greet us; they all know my name even though they may not have met me. For some reason, the theme song from *Cheers* pops into my head: "You want to go where everybody knows your name."

Like a true gentleman, the mayor of Guidiguis stands to greet me and shakes my hand. We remain standing as a sign of respect. He offers to buy us a drink, but Doc politely refuses. The mayor tells the bartender, a ten-year-old boy with a foot that faces in the opposite direction, to bring us two of whatever we want. We order beer and then the mayor invites us both to his house for dinner next Saturday and to watch TV, since *Dallas* will be on and everyone is eager to find out who shot J.R.

We gladly accept his invitation, though I'm surprised to learn that someone in Guidiguis actually has a TV. I'm aching to watch current world news, but I'll settle for repeats. I don't dare tell the mayor that he's watching reruns and that I *know* who shot J.R. He says that he loves American TV and wishes Cameroon had more than one channel. Should I tell him that America has hundreds of TV channels and entertainment around the clock? Better not. When the mayor excuses himself, saying that he has to meet with the new military commander of Guidiguis, I notice Doc's eyebrows go up, but I don't ask why.

When the mayor leaves, Doc and I finally take a seat. Doc sits close to me on the same bench. The bartender limps out with four drinks, but he never meets our eyes. He uncaps the warm bottles, then offers them to us. Doc and I toast to the generous mayor.

"I had hoped for a cold drink today," says Doc, "but the electricity seems to be off more than on."

"I've resigned myself to thinking that I don't have electricity. That way, I'm always delighted when I do," I say.

Doc nods and says, "I like that idea."

He takes a long drink and finishes half the bottle while I only take a sip. Hot beer is terribly bitter. Then, with a pretty handkerchief, Doc wipes the sweat off the front and back of his neck, then off his forehead.

"We're in hell, aren't we?" Doc says glumly.

"Sometimes it feels that way."

"What sin did you commit to get here?"

"I only wanted to be a teacher and experience a better way of living," I say.

"What could be worse than this?" Doc asks.

How do I tell him about my ex-husband's fists, fashioned like the ancient stones of emerald Ireland? I laugh and change the subject. "What sin did you commit?"

"I only wanted to practice medicine," Doc says. He sighs, then adds, "and they sentenced me to what may turn out to be a lifetime away from my family and friends."

"Who is 'they'?" I ask.

"The government."

Discussing politics usually leads to an argument, so I don't ask how they're responsible.

"I keep thinking the real reason I'm here is to meet you," Doc says.

For a moment, it feels as if I remember a place we knew each other long ago.

"They're speaking about us," Doc says about the other patrons and laughs.

"I haven't paid attention," I lie. I know that people are always talking about me and watching everything I do. Still, it's beginning to hurt less and less.

"Should we give them something to fuss about?" Doc asks, as he plays with his car keys inside of the beer cap.

"What do you mean?"

Doc leans over and kisses my cheek while taking my clenched hand in his underneath the table. He plucks my fingers open and places my hand on top of his. His thumb caresses my fingers as if they were strings meant to be played. I can hear the silent music he makes racing wildly from my heart through my veins. The melody invites butterflies to dance in my belly. I try to look him in the eyes, but I can only stare at his soft lips, craving them to brush against mine.

My face is now flushed, and I'm certain my cheeks are cherry red. I never thought I'd say this—but thank God for no electricity. In the dark, Doc doesn't even notice his effect on me.

"I thought Cameroonians never show affection in public," I say as I take my hand from his and gently push Doc away. A vibration lingers on my palm where I felt his heart pounding as fast as mine.

I don't hear what Doc says. He chuckles as if he knows something that I don't. He moves a strand of hair out of my eyes, his fingertips moving down through my hair until I have to really concentrate in order to say, "I'm sorry, what did you say?"

"Why worry what the villagers say about us if it's the truth?" Doc smiles and finishes the rest of his drink.

How am I supposed to guard my reputation when Doc is already spoonfeeding the villagers gossip about us? It matters what people think of me after hearing that the former African-American volunteer in Guidiguis quit after only one year. The story was that she didn't have a good rapport with the villagers. They either made up stories about her or exaggerated them. After only a few months, she went to live at the Italian Catholic Mission on the outskirts of the village to protect herself from gossip and theft.

Doc finally gets the plastic off the bottle cap and discovers a symbol indicating that he's won the drink of his choice.

"I was hoping it would be a million CFAs," he says.

"What would you do with that kind of money?"

I notice that my colleagues are arguing loudly now and turning their heads to look at us. I hear them speaking of the "rich American," and I shift uncomfortably in my seat.

"I would buy a trip to visit you in the United States," Doc says as he toasts to our friendship. He starts on the other bottle while I toy with my own bottle cap. I look up at the stars and wonder what's in store for Doc and me. Have our lives been written by fate, or does life simply take its course? Who decides how it will all turn out?

"Have you ever thought about practicing medicine overseas?" I ask.

"Only studying," Doc says, and my heart sinks. "My soul is

African. I belong here. Besides, I want to someday return to my village and take care of those who are fighting for our freedom."

I've heard about the revolution in the southwest, but I'm not looking for any new information. I want to ask questions, but then again, do I really want to know?

Mr. Benito and Mr. Ndo stand up and move toward their motorcycles—but then stagger back into the bar and toward our table.

"Miss, buy us a beer," Mr. Ndo says.

"I'm sorry, but I don't have any money," I say.

My eyes plead with Doc for help. He waves the bartender over, but the two drunken men haven't noticed the boy coming to our table.

Mr. Benito moves closer and thrusts his face in mine.

"Miss, you are American. You are rich. Money grows on you."

"I'm sorry, gentlemen, but you are mistaken," I say.

Doc stands and indicates the bench on the opposite side of our table.

"Please, gentlemen, sit down with us awhile," Doc says invitingly.

"You have money to buy as many beers as you want," Mr. Benito says to me.

"Do you know what it feels like to want something and not be able to have it?" Mr. Ndo asks, and sits down next to Doc. Benito sits next to me and starts picking the plastic off my bottle cap without asking.

"Yes, I do," I say. "I'm a volunteer. I'm not working for money."

"But you came with money, isn't that so?" Mr. Ndo asks.

"No—" I say, but am interrupted.

"Now I know you are lying. No one works for free, and an American would never leave his country without money."

My fingernails are digging into the wood underneath the table, picking off the bright blue paint.

"In the United States, some struggle to survive, and some are poor. My family is Spanish and Indian—" I stop myself, for they'd never believe my story. I'd like them to know about the poverty and discrimination families struggle with all their lives. And anyway, an

American with a low income has at least a toilet, running water, and glass windows, which is much more than a Cameroonian has in the extreme north.

"Miss, what do you know of the suffering we endure? You haven't experienced pain," Mr. Ndo says.

I want to spit in his face.

How dare he say something he knows nothing about? No one knows what kind of brutality I endured as a child. Only I know that it's a miracle I'm still here.

"I'm still here," I say to myself over and over like a mantra until my breathing becomes relaxed. My soul must be listening because I hear a loving response inside that says,

"We made it. It will be all right."

I begin to say something to my colleagues, but I stop. Doc nods, encouraging me to speak. I look in the eyes that are tempting me to tell him what's inside me, but I can't seem to move my lips.

I've never let anyone know my pain, and that's how I've survived. I swallowed my childhood without digesting it. Now for the first time, I ache to get the past out of my system so that my heart can move on and learn to love and trust again.

The bartender arrives with two beers for my colleagues. They swing their heads back so that the beer flows quickly into their mouths.

"You're only tourists here," Mr. Benito says to Doc and me. "You'll be leaving Guidiguis soon."

"When you look at the pain of a Cameroonian, it's as if you're observing a monkey behind a cage," Mr. Ndo says, and then spits out a swallow of beer that has come back up his throat.

I stand and lean my hands on the table for support.

Doc takes my hand and pulls me down again. He leans over and whispers that I should never take drunken words seriously. He says he'll take me home in a moment. He raises his beer to make a toast with them.

"To suffering," they say.

I don't drink with them. I sit next to Doc. I reach for his hand under the table and he squeezes mine tightly.

"She has no idea what suffering is," Mr. Ndo says, and drinks from his bottle.

"True," I say, "I have no idea."

"Will you teach me to ride a bike, Miss?" Lydie asks. She is so shy, almost shaking, and her eyes are squinting as though she's afraid I'll slap her for merely asking the question.

"When do you want to start?" I ask.

"*Jeudi*," she says.

"What time?"

"Four-thirty." Lydie steps back, her eyes drifting to the ground while she inhales, then holds it.

"I can't. I have a faculty meeting," I reply.

"In the morning," Lydie says.

"Four-thirty in the morning?"

"*Oui*, Miss. *C'est mieux*." Lydie's eyes flutter as if there were a butterfly trapped inside and longing to be set free. "No one must know, Miss. Please don't tell anyone I want to learn. *Pardonnez-moi. S'il vous plait.*"

I nod and smile, extending a hand to Lydie, motioning for her to come inside my home for private conversation.

"I promise, Lydie."

Lydie exhales.

I don't understand why Lydie is asking me to teach her to ride a bike. Why doesn't she know already? I learned how to ride when I was six, the Christmas I received my first girl's bike. I remember being happy that it was purple and that it didn't have that bar across the center. Being a girl felt special that winter.

Instead of sitting across from me in one of the wooden chairs, Lydie sits cross-legged on the mat on the floor. She looks up to where I'm sitting and whispers, "Promise?"

"I promise, Lydie, but why?"

Lydie's eyes shift away from mine to show her respect. I don't like this custom, as I often feel that people aren't listening if they're not looking into my eyes.

"Women don't ride bikes. They say we won't be able to make babies. And nobody would want to marry me if he knew I could ride a bike across the village and get into trouble."

I feel ignorant. I don't understand what it means to be an African woman.

"Miss," Lydie goes on, "I need to draw water at the well at five-thirty. We only have an hour. *Ça va?*"

"OK, but how much work must you do before school?" I ask.

"My little brothers help me with the water. Then I make *beignets* for breakfast and bathe the children. After I wash dishes, I'll start the laundry or, if I have time, begin the midday meal. Then I'll sweep the compound just before going to school."

"I didn't realize, Lydie. I'm sorry I was so hard on you for being late to class."

Lydie shrugs. "You have high hopes for me, Miss. I'm grateful you push me hard to do my best."

"Now I understand why you've been late recently."

"Girls are usually the ones who are tardy, Miss. Boys don't work in the morning. They start for school as soon as the sun comes and study their notebooks as they walk. They pick peanuts for their empty stomachs along the way."

"Are you able to have breakfast before school, Lydie?" I ask.

"No."

"Is that why you've fallen asleep during class?"

Lydie stares blankly at the door and beyond it.

"Perhaps, then, it's time for some tea and American animal crackers." Lydie hugs her legs to her chest and smiles softly as she lays her chin on her knees. She stares out the window at the sky.

The morning before the scheduled instruction, I open my door for a run, to discover Lydie sitting just outside in the silent darkness.

"Isn't it tomorrow?" I ask. "I thought we said—"

Lydie interrupts, "Miss, I want to run with you."

It's still dark as we begin. We're running side by side as the sun comes up beyond the mango trees and spills across the desert like molasses.

"I want to be strong, Miss," Lydie says, and then clears her throat of the smoke beginning to fill the air as women light their garbage on fire in the road as we pass.

We turn down a small dirt path. Lydie's breathing is now hard and frequent, in contrast to my measured rhythm. As we turn past a compound of mud huts, we can hear a Muslim family chanting morning prayers. Our feet ease over the hardened sand of the trail that runs through the millet fields. I smile at Lydie, honored to have been chosen as a friend to this blossoming young woman.

"Have you told your brother about our bicycle lesson?" I ask.

"No. He'd be very angry, Miss. You promised not to tell anyone."

I feel a sense of rising danger, like the sly desert winds that begin softly, then rip apart the worn-down, shabby bits and pieces of our habitat, which then need to be reformed.

"Miss, last market day, you were running toward the bridge, and I saw the muscles in your legs. They are so developed. If you want, you can ride your bicycle all the way to Nigeria!"

"Thank you, Lydie. Perhaps I could, but I might die of thirst before I got there. I seem unable to take a trip, even only to Maroua, without running out of water."

"Miss, would you take me to the capital? To Maroua? I want to see a big city."

"Sure. If it's OK with your family," I say.

"First, I have to get an identity card."

"You don't have one?" I ask.

"I don't know. Perhaps I do, but I don't own it. My brother must have it," she says, and sighs.

Lydie stops running, shades her eyes, and looks at the rising sun. Light on the sand has turned the molasses to a sea of honey.

Then Lydie starts running again, but faster, and I can hardly keep up. What's gotten into her all of a sudden?

"Maybe it's different in Nigeria," she says.

"Every country is different."

"What is Dzigilou like?"

"I've never been," I say.

"When you teach me, could we ride to Dzigilou?" Lydie asks.

"Sure we can."

"I have heard they have the biggest and sweetest mangoes."

"What direction is Dzigilou?" I ask.

"Just past the market, over the bridge, toward Touloum. It's only thirty kilometers." She pauses, then says, "I have watched you cross that bridge so many times."

I look at Lydie, running next to me. Her eyes are fixed on the horizon. Here, women learn to put their secret hopes in the distance and wait for the wind to change and blow their dreams closer.

"I'm imagining riding my bike, and my friends wave to me as they walk to the millet grinder," Lydie says. "The children sing out my name and chase me as they do you. I imagine being a Cameroonian citizen and that the *gendarmes* allow me to pass the checkpoint because I have an identification card and a receipt of purchase."

Lydie stops running and squats in the sand. She dumps pebbles out of her shoe, then looks up at me and smiles.

"How far is it to Nigeria?" she asks.

I think to myself as I hear Lydie breathing beside me that there's a reason women aren't allowed to ride a bike or own their identification card. It's much more than being able to get into trouble and make a baby. A woman on a bicycle could be dangerous. If she began steering and pedaling, she could go where she wanted. Then she might start doing whatever she pleased. What good would a woman be then?

The next morning, Lydie arrives exactly on time. She insists on guiding the bike through the darkness toward our remote destination. We hear the call to prayer, a chant on the loudspeaker from the mosque, and the rustle of devoted Muslims awakening. Lydie's shoulders are high and tense as we head out from the village.

Even with a flashlight, it's still pitch-black, and Lydie stumbles and falls, stifling a scream by covering her mouth. She is so nervous and serious that I slowly begin to understand that this is something we'd better not be caught at.

"Any snakes around here?" I ask, turning my flashlight on the bushes.

"No," Lydie whispers.

"You sure?" I start whispering, too.

"Yes."

I sigh in relief. Lydie knows better than I, since she's far more afraid of snakes than I am.

"Have you ever tried to ride a bike before?" I ask.

"No."

"When I started to learn, I was sure it couldn't be done. I fell many times and thought I'd broken every bone in my body. My father made me get back up and do it again. He said if my bones were broken, I'd know it. So I kept getting back on."

"Do you think I'll learn, Miss?" Lydie asks.

"Yes, and you'll fall. You need to allow yourself to make mistakes. In class, you try to speak English too perfectly, which causes you to make more mistakes. If you allow yourself to make some, you'll get it a lot faster."

"I don't want to fall," she says, and she's serious about that.

I shrug. Lydie takes a deep breath, swallows hard, and wipes the sweat from her brow. Then she clenches her teeth, fists, and her entire body. I can see the doubts and dreams racing across her face like storm clouds across the sun. She lifts her head high and, for the first time, swings her right leg over the bicycle.

"OK," I say. "You pedal, and I'll push."

"Don't let go, Miss."

I don't say a word, I just begin to push. She glides along for twenty yards or so without doing a thing.

"Pedal, Lydie, pedal!" I say.

As I push, she begins to pedal, gently at first, until I encourage her to pedal harder. I start running faster, trying to maintain the balance myself, while increasing the speed so she can gain momentum. But Lydie is steering wildly and twists the bike from my grasp. I'm forced to let go and fall backward onto the ground as she sails through the air for a split second. Then she crashes.

Lydie lies sprawled on the sand as I quickly get up and run to her.

"Miss! You let go!"

"The bike was swerving, and I couldn't hold on," I say.

"I will never be able to steer!"

"Steering will come. Try to keep your arms still. Hold on more lightly," I say, trying to comfort her.

"You said, 'Do what comes naturally.' I did that," Lydie says angrily.

"Yes, but let your body loosen up. The worst that can happen is you'll fall again. And the sand isn't too bad."

"Do you think I will ever learn?" she asks, dusting off her clothes.

"How does a child learn to walk?" I ask.

"But maybe I just can't."

"Lydie, you will learn!"

She takes another deep breath, then gets up and climbs onto the bike again, more determined than before. As I push again, running behind and steadying her with both hands, Lydie pedals furiously. Her steering is improving.

"That's it, Lydie, that's the way!"

"Don't let go, Miss!"

When she has a rhythm, I let go. But this time, she falls hard, screams on impact, then quickly throws a hand over her mouth in panic. We both look around to see if anyone is nearby. We wait. No one.

Lydie looks up at me bitterly.

"I'm sorry, Lydie, but it's the only way."

"I can't do this."

"Sure you can."

"I can't! When I look down and see how fast I'm going, I get scared," Lydie says, and she sounds as if she's given up.

"That's it, Lydie! Don't look down!" I say.

I haven't yet told Lydie about needing to find a balance. Here I am trying to find the balance for her, and it doesn't matter how she pedals or how she steers if she doesn't have a sense of balance of her own.

And then I realize, African women grow up learning that skill. I think back to my experience at the well, when I tried to find a balance.

"Lydie, imagine carrying a bucket of water on your head. You don't look down when you're carrying water. You look at what's in front of you. This time when you pedal, imagine carrying water on your head."

She gets up and dusts herself off. Both knees are bleeding, and her elbows are badly scraped. Lydie winces as she slowly mounts the bike.

"Imagine a bucket of water right here." As I touch the top of her head, she looks into my eyes, and finally, she smiles.

"Imagine that you don't want to spill a drop."

We start off, and Lydie begins pedaling confidently, softly at first. Her steering is even better than before, her head is up, and she begins pedaling faster. I can feel her gaining a new sense of balance. The seat is steady in my hands now, and I'm no longer struggling to maintain a grip. I push with ease as Lydie pedals even faster. In a moment, we're gliding through the fields.

"Keep that bucket of water on your head!"

Lydie raises her chin. The imaginary bucket is there, sitting atop her head like a crown. Lydie gets it and flies with it.

And when I finally let go, she doesn't even notice. She just pedals on.

What seems like an eternity is perhaps only one triumphant minute. I hold my breath, watching Lydie flow through the desert like a graceful sailboat driven before a steady wind. Lydie has found her moment of victory. She is free.

Suddenly, I become aware that this is Lydie's moment and her achievement, not mine. I recognize that Lydie has found the door to freedom on her own. I let go of the "American hero" thinking I came to Africa with. I am no longer Peace Corps, no longer a volunteer, nor am I Lydie's teacher. I am simply a woman. And Lydie is no longer of the developing world. She's not African, not Cameroonian, and not a student.

We're only a woman and a woman, and each of us is struggling to learn something new.

It feels right, and I let out a joyful cry.

Lydie hears me and realizes that my voice has come from a distance. As she turns her head and looks back at me, she loses control of the bike and crashes.

But this time, it doesn't matter. Lydie has had a victory, and I can't wait to tell her how proud I am and how brave she is.

I run to her and lift the bike away. Then, on my knees, I lift her from the sand and into my arms. "You did it, Lydie!" I exclaim, as I rock her in my arms. "You did it!"

As the realization comes crashing down on her, Lydie begins to cry. Then she smiles. She can do it. She can do anything.

14. AN AMERICAN BICYCLE

"I have only one question," Mr. Mfoumba says. I panic and think about what he may have done to Lydie.

"Is she OK?"

"Did you ask yourself about the consequences of teaching my sister how to ride a bicycle?"

"Is Lydie all right, Mr. Mfoumba?"

His silence makes me imagine the worst. Has he beaten her?

"Please," I urge. My body is a mass of goose bumps.

"She's fine," he says coldly. "Now, I must ask a question. Do you intend to buy Lydie a bicycle?"

I have no reply. I haven't even thought about it.

"Perhaps you're going to give her your bicycle when you leave?"

"It's a Peace Corps bicycle. It doesn't belong to me."

"Then I ask again, are you going to buy her an American bicycle?"

"Mr. Mfoumba, I can't afford to buy Lydie a bicycle. That would take a month of my salary. I couldn't possibly survive on—"

"Then why teach her to ride a bike?" he demands. "Why teach her how to do something, then leave her without the opportunity to apply that knowledge?"

Again, I have no reply. I can't argue with his logic.

He goes on, "You come to Africa instilling so much desire for more in these young people's minds; then you leave them with nothing but empty dreams and no means to fulfill them."

"Maybe she could buy a bike later in life."

"Her husband would never permit it."

"Maybe she won't choose to get married. Perhaps she wants to go to college and make something special of herself."

"You're talking foolishly. How do you know what my sister wants? Do you suppose she wants to be like you? Do you think you are a great role model for young girls? Let me ask you, Miss, do you like being alone? You are isolated here. There is no one to take care of you, no one for you to love. You have nothing.

Do you suppose you're happy? Do you want Lydie to be all alone like you?"

I am fighting the tears. My arguments are melting like butter in the sun. I have no words. Mfoumba is right; I'm not really happy on my own. Sure, there are wonderful moments—but how can I want for Lydie what I am living through? Life in the bush sometimes feels like hell, and with no one to hold me, certain days are nearly unbearable. I don't want this lonely life for anyone, especially not sweet Lydie.

Finally, I say, "I just want Lydie to accomplish what she dreams of, and I'm here to help in any way I can."

"Miss, I'm sure you believe you are doing a good thing, but think again. Why are there signs in your zoos that say, 'Don't feed the animals?' Animals can't digest food that humans eat. It will only make them sick, even die. Be careful to whom you feed knowledge, Miss. Not everything you know is good for everyone who wants to know it."

"What about Lydie?" I ask, uncertain about what exactly it is I'm asking.

"Let her live the life she was born to live. Don't put desires in her head for things she can never have."

With that, Mr. Mfoumba turns and walks away.

I watch him for several moments, tears welling up again. Then I bolt for my house, tear open the door, run in, and flop on the bed, bawling like a child.

As the tears subside, I begin to think. Who the hell am I, the patron saint of bicycles? Have I taught Lydie in order to magnify my own sense of purpose? Have I thought of Lydie at all? Isn't this what foreigners have been doing since first coming to Africa? We think we're going to make everything "better." Are we only sweeping our consciences clean of guilt?

Do Peace Corps volunteers think we're here to perform noble acts and raise up the developing world? Are we only giving unrealistic desires for the material riches of the West?

I continue to search for answers within but find that I'm too uncomfortable asking these questions, making it impossible for me to listen long enough for their answers. But they come anyway, one by one, like birds driven by an instinctual awareness that it is the season to return home.

I sense a voice guiding me in the direction I'm to fly, but I'm afraid to show up and let nature take its course.

Where exactly would I be going?

15. AÏSSATOU

Journal, November 1992

SATURDAY

I got up at sunrise with the Muslims. Who can sleep after morning chanting? I ran thirteen miles. With all the time on my hands on the weekends, perhaps I could start training for a race. I need to find out what the distance is for a marathon.

EVENING

It's hot. Too hot to write. I'm sweating all over the paper. Why do people live in the desert?

LATE NIGHT

Clotilde came over to ask me to accompany her with a tray of food to our new neighbor's house. The woman, whose husband is the military gendarme who lives behind us, became sick during her journey from the jungle to the desert with her three children. Clotilde said she's not really sick, but it's her heart that is broken from leaving her family. We walked by flashlight to her house, on the lookout for snakes and scorpions. But we weren't able to meet the woman, whose name is Valentine and who was still sick in bed, so we left food with her family.

Lydie has not been to school since the day of the bike ride, so Clotilde and I stopped by her house to see how she is. Hervine said Lydie went to visit family in Kaele. I wonder if she'll return.

Hervine told me that Aïssatou has malaria.

She promised to take me to see her tomorrow.

SUNDAY

Aïssatou is from a wealthier family than most of my students, but her family won't take her to the hospital. When Hervine and I arrived this morning, Aïssatou's mother and sisters were on the mat kneeling in prayer next to Aïssatou's hot, sleeping body. Aïssatou didn't even look as if she were alive. Her body was still, except for her chest. Her lungs must be working terribly hard to fill themselves with air. It's only been a week since I've seen her at school, but she's lost over ten pounds.

AFTERNOON

I went back to Aïssatou's compound with a bottle of aspirin to provide help in bringing the fever down. Aïssatou's family helped me give the tablets to her and were very gracious. But when I insisted we take her to the hospital, they refused. I told them she will probably die. They weren't surprised or deeply concerned.

I nearly picked her up and took her to the hospital myself.

It's not the money. Families simply don't put as much effort into keeping girls alive as they do the boys.

EVENING

I went back to check on Aïssatou. She is dead.

I kneeled next to her body and held her hand. I thought back on the strength she had to stand up after getting beaten by the principal and to walk to class with me, her head held high.

I squeezed her hand hard, hoping she left a little of her strength that I can take with me back to school.

16. LIZARD SPEAKS

I keep the high watch
Through the night,
Guarding her dreams
And protecting her sleep
From quiet trespassers.

I keep the high watch
From the hollow of the tallest tree
Swaying above her bed in the night breeze.
I gaze up now and then at the pulsing sky,
Waiting for stars to fall
So that I can catch them on my tongue
And plant them
In the garden of her dreams.

Bring me your dreams,
My little one,
And I will give them wings.
I will raise them up—
Flinging them across the sky and
Setting them free
To fly
In their own direction.

I will hold the high watch
So that your spirit will unfold
Across the world.

17. VALENTINE'S CHILDREN

Journal, November 1992

The windows and doors are shut. I've locked myself inside the house and am only able to lie on my bed and stare at the ceiling. I am alone in the dark silence listening to the echo of my own heart beating inside my chest.

I'm hiding from my soul, rocking myself to sleep now and again hoping to disappear and not be found. When I wake up, I beg my dreams to fly back and take me away.

I've missed two days of school. I keep asking myself if I can continue teaching within an education system in which I have no confidence. Can I remain a Peace Corps volunteer in a village that oppresses women? How can I refrain from judging Cameroon harshly? My continued service feels as if it reflects my support of their belief system.

Aïssatou's beatings and her death are bringing up so much for me. My whole life is rolling itself out like a rug so that I may walk over everything that has happened. The constant, loud static of the American lifestyle is not here to drown out the memories of events long forgotten. There is total silence in the desert and sometimes nothing to do but sit and stare out at the open sky. My mind is free to turn down every corner of my life, to walk along avenues in my brain that are clear of footprints.

Now I understand why I faded out of marriage counseling. The therapist got a peek at my unhealed places and my unwillingness to do the work of forgiveness and then letting go. She pushed and I ran. All my life I've worked at keeping the pain locked deep inside the crevices of my being; in fact, that is what kept me alive. What my therapist didn't know was that by asking me to tell her my story in thirty minutes or less, she was asking me to let down the armor that had been carefully put there to protect me. Telling her what it was like to grow up being me was actually asking me to feel the sorrow. I felt at the time that it just might kill me. I had distracted myself for years from self-reflection. It's as if I ran into a church for sanctuary and hid my pain inside the golden tabernacle on the altar. I lit a candle and said my prayers to the Virgin Mary to guard my suffering, as if I wanted her to keep it breathing. Perhaps I'd hoped that I'd forget what I prayed for.

I toss and turn and try to get comfortable so I can write some more.

If I quit the Peace Corps, what would I have to go back to? I think of my divorce and the reason I fled the country in the first place—to get away from the hurt. And then I think of the people who said I'd never be able to make it in the Peace Corps. They said I didn't have what it takes to make it in Africa.

But I know that I do! I have what it takes!

I feel a sense of pride blooming within. I survived the experience of being a child. If I could do that, then anything is possible. And in spite of all that happened, I can still love and laugh and play. That is, if I allow myself to let anyone into my heart again.

I turn on my side, closing my eyes and curling into a fetal position. But how do I even begin to start the healing process? How do I take out the thorn embedded within my flesh without bleeding to death?

Someone is outside clapping his hands to see if I'm home. I'm ignoring the clapping, unable to get myself up to answer the door.

Clap! Clap!

It's not just one pair of hands clapping; it's several. I close my eyes and mumble to myself for them to go away.

Clap! Clap! Clap! Clap!

The people come nearer to the house, and now they bang on the door.

Bang! Bang! Bang!

Who the hell is that? Now there are little bang-bangs on the door.

"Coo-coo! Coo-coo!" a woman sings out like "hello."

"*Suzanne? Ça va bien? Suzanne? Suzanne!*"

I don't recognize the voice, but she sounds very concerned about me.

Bang! Bang! Bang!

Fine, you won't leave me alone, I'll answer, but I won't be nice.

Bang! Bang! Bang!

OK, I'll answer the door. Hold on. I brush my hair back and rub my eyes, then turn the key and open the door.

"*Ça va bien, Suzanne?*" asks a very tiny, lovely woman who holds her three-year-old twin boys in her arms. Adele peeks around from behind the woman's legs to make sure everything's OK before coming out and shaking my hand. The twins are looking at me as if they've seen a ghost.

"*Oui, ça va. Je suis un peu malade, c'est tout.*"

"Ah, sick?" she says in French. "That's too bad. So that's why I haven't had the chance to meet you and thank you for the good food you and Clotilde prepared. My name is Valentine, and these are my twin boys."

Valentine shakes my hand and then walks into my house without being invited. She sits down on my pillows and makes herself comfortable. The boys have enormous curious eyes that forget to blink and round bellies that remind me of the Pillsbury Doughboy. The twins leave their mother's embrace and toddle around my living room. Adele sits at Valentine's feet and sucks her thumb while watching every move I make.

"Do you have anything for me to drink?"

"Yes." I get up and head for the refrigerator for some cold water. I pour her a glass, and she drinks it quickly and then holds her cup out for more.

"People thought you were dead," Valentine says. "No one has seen you in several days."

"I've been very ill."

"It's the heat. This heat is terrible. It gave me diarrhea and vomiting all night. This is not Cameroon. I hate it already. My husband's been assigned up in the extreme north, but when I heard the news, I told him to go without me and that the children and I would stay with my mother. He said he'd die in the extreme north without me. There are no avocados, no pineapples, no cabbage, no trees, no flowers, no fields to plant, no nothing! How can these people eat millet every day?"

The boys waddle to me as if they're attached at the shoulders. They stop and stare. I reach out to pinch one of their cute, chubby cheeks. I pinch softly, but he yells for his mother. His twin screams, too, and cries. They run back to their mother, and I sit back against the wall wondering why I answered the door. Valentine ignores their crying and continues to look around my house. She sighs, disappointed that she sees nothing fine or beautiful.

Valentine clicks her tongue on the roof of her mouth and pushes the boys away. They climb onto her lap and hold on to her arms. She tries to shush them to be quiet, but they continue to cry.

"Do you want a *bon-bon?*" Valentine asks her boys, and then looks to me to deliver. "You have candy, don't you, Suzanne?"

I shake my head but then remember the caramels Mom sent. I could use a little sugar myself. I open the plastic bag of caramels, and the boys stop screaming. Adele's eyes smile, and she leans her head all the way back to look up at me while folding her hands. She opens her mouth and sticks out her tongue. I place a caramel carefully on her tongue as if it were the Eucharist.

The boys wipe their tears away and open their mouths. I offer a caramel to Valentine, and she pops it into her mouth with a smile. I sit down on the wooden stick chair across from my guests and take the wrapping off the caramel. As I watch, everyone in my living room lights up like a Christmas tree. It's amazing what a little sweetness will do for the human spirit.

I pass another caramel to everyone, and we put it in our mouths before we're even finished with the last. We sit back on the pillows and chew, laughing at how full our mouths are. Caramel sticks to our teeth, dribbles down our chins, and tickles all the way down to our bellies.

Adele gets up and reties her sarong. She runs and jumps into my arms. She puts her hands around my neck and holds me in a long and tender embrace. The boys get up and come over to hug my legs. They drool all over my bare knees and rub their sticky hands through my hair. Adele leans back to look at me, and she laughs. I pull her close and hug her tight.

I think of Aïssatou and ask her to give me the strength to live each moment as if it were the last and to give me the courage to heal and to love.

"Light the way through my darkness," I say to myself, and

Adele puts her arms around my neck. There's a feeling inside that tells me that Aïssatou already has. She's brought Valentine, Adele, and the twins to check on me and pull me out of the hole I'd fallen into. I thank Aïssatou's spirit for answering prayers before I even thought to ask.

I wake up to a motorcycle roar, so loud it sounds as if it's going to break through the straw fence and run over me in my bed outside. I jump up, pulling the sarong around my body and remember to bang my sneakers against the side of the bed in case any scorpions decided to take refuge last night. Who could be visiting me at seven o'clock on a Saturday morning?

I untie the metal gate from the straw wall and see a teenage Muslim on a motorcycle with a large box sitting between his arms. The cycle looks more expensive than the others I've seen at the *carrefour*, the center of Guidiguis on the paved road. His new shoes and dazzling green *bu-bu* robe stand out. Maybe he's the king's son come to bring me goat legs for breakfast.

"*Jam bah doo nah?*" I ask, but he's not at all impressed with my Fulfulde; his face is completely void of expression. Well, he's obviously not in his skin this morning!

"*Nasara, votre soeur est venue,*" he says.

My sister is here? But I don't have a sister.

"*Elle va arriver toute de suite.*"

She's coming right away?

He hands me the large box and tells me it belongs to my sister. I thank him but am certain there's been a mistake.

The teenager just stares, waiting to be paid. When I give him one hundred CFAs, he zooms off without even a good-bye.

As soon as the sound of his motorcycle disappears, I hear the roar of another on its way. I step out of my compound to get a better look. Another Muslim teenager on a motorcycle is approaching. I see a person on the back but can't make out who it is because of the passenger's yellow helmet.

A motorcycle helmet! This sister of mine is a Peace Corps volunteer!

The motorcycle comes into my compound, nearly running me over. Through the plastic visor, I recognize my friend Vann. She takes off her helmet, flashes me a smile, then pays the driver and climbs off. I say hello to the driver, but he only throws me a nod and takes off at lightning speed.

"It's no wonder the Peace Corps requires us to wear helmets! These kids are extremely dangerous!" Vann says in her thick Louisiana drawl. I had no idea how much I've missed her until I hold her in my arms and hug her tight.

"If you squeeze too tight, I might let out some awful-smelling gas!" says Vann.

"Evangeline," I say laughing, "it's so good to see you."

I kiss her smack on the lips, and she giggles.

"Suzi-Monster, you're amazing! How do you get so much love squeezed into that little body of yours?"

I grab the helmet, take her by the hand, and lead her into my house.

"I hope you didn't pay the other driver," says Vann.

"I did," I say, and hold the mosquito net away from the doorway so she can enter. She steps inside, and I follow.

"Jerk!" she says, "I told him not to accept any money from you. They take us for all we've got any chance they get."

I raise my eyebrows, searching her face to see if she's serious. Things must not be going well at her post. Vann sighs, drops her things on the floor, and stuffs her Peace Corps ID and money into a pocket of her backpack. She collapses onto the mat and pillows, then leans back against the wall.

"Would you like water to wash your feet?" I ask.

"That'd be great. You know, now I understand why Jesus got royally pissed off at the priests for not offering him water for his feet after he'd walked three days in the desert!"

She pulls off her sandals and rubs her toes. I bring a large empty bowl and full plastic teapot. Vann massages her heels, then pours water over her feet. I hand her a bar of Dove soap. She smiles, then puts the soap to her nose and inhales.

"I miss home," she says, and exhales.

I nod and laugh.

"Do you ever daydream about being evacuated and sent home?" Vann asks.

Trying to ignore the question, I stand up to get a towel from my bedroom.

While Vann scrubs her feet clean, I go to the kitchen and pour a packet of cherry Kool-Aid into a bottle of water. I hear Vann hum "God Bless America" and return to the living room shaking the bottle of cold, red liquid.

"Oh, yes! Cherry Kool-Aid! Yay, Mom!" Vann says, and stops humming.

I pour two glasses and we knock it down as if it were a shot of tequila. Then I put her feet on my lap and dry them gently.

"You're too much, Suzi-Monster!" she says, laughing. "Anyhow, I'm sorry that you had to pay the driver."

"That's OK. It's only 100 francs."

"He told me 200 to get to the nasara's house. Swine!" Vann's face gets instantly red.

"Next time, ask for the high school for 100."

I bunch up the pillows and wonder how Vann's experience has been these first two months and how it compares with mine. Even though the Peace Corps has been one challenge after the other, I've decided that I don't want to leave.

"How did you get here?" I ask. I've only gotten out of Guidiguis once since coming to the post and had to wait from dawn until one o'clock to catch a bush taxi.

"My principal asked if I needed to go to the Yagoua market this weekend and said he was leaving at six o'clock. That didn't sound all that bad, being that my neighbors wake me up every morning by banging their dishes clean at five-thirty. I said I needed to see my sister in Guidiguis, so he dropped me off at the *carrefour*. I didn't know he had other things in mind."

I raise my eyebrows, questioning.

"He just tickled my palm, that's all, but it gave me the heebie-jeebies," Vann says, and winces.

"The Lamedoh did that to me. It's like a man sticking his tongue out and moving it quickly back and forth, isn't it?"

"Yes! Sleazeballs, all of them," Vann says, disgusted.

"Toughest job you'll ever love," I say, quoting the Peace Corps slogan.

Vann laughs, picks up a pillow, and hugs it. I can't decide what to tell her about my experiences in Guidiguis. Do I complain about how bad it is here, or can I tell her about the adventures I've had?

Some days I struggle with just being here, but if I take it moment by moment, the days take care of themselves. I pick up the book I've just read and guess at how I can be a friend to her now.

"I just finished Toni Morrison's *Beloved*," I say. "She wrote, 'You your own best thing.' I'm trying to be that."

"I got you a present," Vann says, suddenly. She jumps up and steps outside, then brings in the other box. She places the box in my lap and smiles. "I missed you in Maroua last month. I guess you've been hiding out in your village."

"I've been doing a lot of thinking," I say, wanting to expand further on what Africa is teaching me, but the timing is wrong.

I open the box and am delighted to see ten rolls of toilet paper, two chocolate bars, vegetables, a small hunk of cheese, a loaf of bread, and a bottle of French red wine.

"Wow! Thank you, Vann," I say as my stomach growls at the familiar succulent smells. Just a slice of fresh bread and cheese now is an exquisite extravagance.

"We'll cook a fabulous dinner tonight. And I thought you'd be running low on toilet paper. Got any dysentery problems?" Vann asks.

"Always," I groan. "I never knew that diarrhea could last a week."

"Africa's gonna kill me, Suz. I'm not going to make it for two years."

"Are you going to quit?" I ask, panicked she'll say yes.

"Honestly, Suzi-Monster, I don't think any of us are going to make it. I think we'll be evacuated within three months." The tone in her voice scares me.

"What? That's crazy," I say. I stand and pick up the box, take it to the kitchen, and start unloading the edibles into the refrigerator. As Vann follows and helps by stacking toilet paper in piles of two on top of the fridge, she says, "Suz, there's a lot of political turmoil in Cameroon right now." I become uncomfortable. I look into her eyes, close the refrigerator door harder than intended, and grab the vegetables. I quickly move to the corner of the room, where I dump them into a bucket. I take the lid off the water barrel, fill a calabash with water, and rinse off the vegetables.

Vann collects two stools and sets them down at the water bucket. We sit and take the green huckleberry leaves off branches for a soup we'll make with a peanut butter sauce in silence. As we rapidly work through the tree branch, I try to calm down, waiting for the other shoe to drop. Vann takes a deep breath and continues with her news, even though she knows I don't like talking about politics.

"Remember during training when President Paul Biya's wife died? There was a lot of speculation that he murdered her in order to gain sympathy from voters. Although he won a majority, there's speculation that he rigged the elections. The southwest was hopeful and loyal to the opposition candidate John Fru Ndi. They were counting on changes in Cameroon beginning with him. The people aren't convinced that Biya's administration has won over John Fru Ndi."

We finish removing all the leaves and begin slicing them in half, then throwing them into the clean bucket.

I don't want to hear any more about Cameroon's political situation. Peace Corps volunteers are not supposed to be involved. Vann's information once again raises doubts in me about why I'm here at all.

"But there's more, Suz. The southwest province has gone mad. They want John Fru Ndi in power and Biya out. There'll be war for sure. I give it two months before it gets too dangerous. Three months, tops, before we're evacuated."

I can't believe what she's telling me. I continue to slice the leaves but cut myself across the palm of my hand. I drop the knife on the floor, clench my fist tight, and hold it in my other hand.

"You OK?" Vann asks.

"Yes, but what I wouldn't give for a cutting board," I say, as I stand up, grab a towel, and squeeze it tight over my injured hand to stop the blood flow.

"Where's your Peace Corps medical kit?" Vann asks.

"Under my bed," I say.

Vann marches into my room and returns with it. She takes out a disinfectant solution, and I shake my head.

"Give me your hand, you big baby," she orders.

I take it out of the towel, and she pours the liquid over my cut. It stings, and I hiss and stomp and fling my other hand about. She waits for the sting to subside, then gently wraps the cut with gauze, winding the tape around the palm.

"I'm sorry I've upset you," Vann says softly.

I look at her hard and say, "I really want to finish what I've started. I don't want to go home a failure."

"You your own best thing, no matter where you are in the world," Vann says, and finishes taping my hand. She squeezes my shoulder. "I've missed you, Suz."

"I hope we make it, Vann," I say.

"We will; no matter what, we'll be OK."

"Whatever happens in Cameroon, I hope we'll always be friends," I say.

"That's a promise," she says, and gives me a long, tight hug.

There must be over thirty kids and teenagers peering through the mayor's window at his TV when Doc and I walk up to the door. Several kids hold onto the bars in front of the windows to get a glimpse of Bill Cosby. Everyone laughs, and more children are arriving and climbing on top of each other to see the TV. The mayor greets Doc and me and invites us inside. He shoos the children away but in moments they return to the window.

The mayor's children walk into the room like servants, carrying trays of food for the dining room table and appetizers for the coffee table. The mayor's wife, Calixte, smiles nervously while watching her daughter and two sons closely to be sure they don't make any mistakes. The mayor disappears for a moment down the hall, then comes out with a cheer of celebration and an expensive bottle of whiskey. Calixte motions eagerly for Doc and me to sit on the couch in front of the TV, for we should eat and drink before *Dallas* begins in less than an hour.

I look away from the TV and see that there are at least ten boys standing in the doorway, peeking into the house to get a look at the way African-Americans live. Do they really believe that all black people in the United States live like Bill Cosby?

The mayor returns and pours us a glass of whiskey straight. I take my glass and knock it back. The mayor's eyes nearly pop out of his head. I don't think I was supposed to do that.

"*Ça va, Suzanne?*"

"I'm fine, thank you," I say.

Doc cracks open a handful of boiled peanuts and devours them.

The mayor calls out for cool water to the children standing like soldiers by the food table. The children scurry to the kitchen, then zip back into the living room. The youngest girl hands me the coldest glass of water in Guidiguis. Before drinking, I shake the ice cubes in the glass like a toy.

"You didn't need to go through so much trouble in the kitchen for us," Doc says.

"*Ce n'est rien.*" Calixte shrugs her shoulders.

"Nothing? This isn't a meal; it's a feast for a king!" Doc exclaims.

Calixte giggles shyly while retying her sarong as she rocks back and forth, pleased with herself and tickled by Doc's adoration.

"*Tu as pris beaucoup des poids*!" Doc says to Calixte as he flashes her a smile.

My mouth drops open.

That wasn't a compliment; he just told the mayor's wife that she's really fat!

I elbow Doc hard in his side for being so rude, and he looks at me confused. I can't believe he doesn't know what he just did! Doesn't he realize how much we both need their friendship? And why is Doc looking at me so innocently when he just ruined my chance at eating the best meal I've had in months? I'm so hungry I can hardly keep from drooling all over myself. Can't he hear my stomach growling at the smell of the familiar delicious aromas? How could he do this to me?

I remain still and wait for Calixte to throw us out or punch Doc in the nose.

"Doc!" I whisper angrily in English, "you never tell a woman she's fat!"

But then why is Calixte smiling and batting her eyes as if Doc were flirting with her? How can he tell the mayor's wife how fat she is without getting slugged?

The mayor puffs his chest out and walks gallantly to the dining table, looking extremely proud that his wife has gotten so fat. When he returns to the coffee table, he pours us another drink, and I just look at it. There's something I'm not getting here.

Calixte thanks Doc for his observation while strutting her voluptuous body across the living room as if she were showing off a trophy she had worked hard to win. With appreciative eyes, she looks lovingly at her husband, who's responsible for getting her fat. As she eases onto the couch next to her husband, she smiles and throws her head back. This is the moment she's been waiting for.

If a man told his friend's wife that she's gotten fat in the States and the husband agreed with him, there would be two dead men in the living room.

I take the glass of whiskey and knock it back. I wipe my lips with the corner of the cape tied around my shoulders. The mayor looks at me, wondering what my problem is.

The mayor is loving every minute of Doc's attention to his wife. But Doc is paying so much attention to Calixte, making her feel so sexy and desirable, that I feel like chopped liver. The mayor picks up the whiskey bottle and pours me another glass. I shoot it back again. The mayor's eyebrows raise, and he tilts his head, looking rather worried. He doesn't pour another glass. Doc looks to me and laughs.

"Be careful, Suzanne. You're so skinny the whiskey will go straight to your head."

"You've gotten too skinny!" The mayor slaps his hand on his knee.

Too skinny? It's not possible to be too thin.

"But that's good!" I say.

"That's not good," says Doc. "You look like a boy."

What does he mean I look like a boy? I look at Calixte, breasts bursting out of her bra and the dress cut so low you can almost see her nipples. Then I look at my breasts, which look like lemons instead of like her ripe papayas.

"I want to be skinny when I go back to America," I say glumly.

Doc says to the mayor's wife, "Suzanne needs to eat your cooking to fatten up."

Calixte sits up beaming, as if Doc had just presented her with an Oscar for the Academy Award for fat. The mayor sips his glass of whiskey.

"Why would a woman want to be skinny? What would a man do with a boy?"

Doc asks, "How would he know if she can bear children if she doesn't have breasts, belly, and hips?"

"When a woman's fat, then everyone knows how much her husband loves her," Calixte says, as she looks at her husband with love and gratitude for making her fat.

"So when a woman is married but skinny, then everyone knows that she's—"

"Unhappy," the mayor says.

"Why would a woman be unhappy?" I ask, wanting to continue the argument. I reach out and pour the mayor and myself another shot. I knock it back and so does the mayor. Doc smiles and does the same while the mayor again shoos the children away from the windows. This time, they don't even budge because they know *Dallas* is coming on in a few minutes.

"She's unhappy because the village would know her husband isn't working to nourish her and the children. She has a husband who doesn't take care of her and is frequently visiting other women and making them fat."

"Meat on her bones lets everyone know she's living the good life," Calixte says.

"What do people think of me? I'm unmarried, alone, and look like a boy."

"People wonder what you do with yourself," Calixte says.

"What do you mean?" I ask.

"Well, how do you manage without a man?" the mayor asks.

"What exactly do you mean by *manage*?" I ask, my face getting hot. They couldn't be asking what I think they're asking.

"Don't you need a man now and then to relieve you?" the mayor asks.

Doc sees that I'm starting to make sense of it and says to me in English, "They'd like to know if you plan on taking a lover because two years without sex is impossible."

Calixte interrupts, "You plan on having a man, don't you?"

"I really hadn't thought about it," I say, unconvincingly.

"You'd have beautiful children if you married an African. You may want to marry and take him back to the States," Calixte says.

"You'll be happier in Cameroon if there's a man in your bed," the mayor says.

"If you want a husband, you'll have to put on some weight," says Doc.

You mean I have to gain weight in order to be attractive? How strange!

All my life, I've tried to be thinner. I've been hooked on the scale to tell me how I feel about myself since I was eight years old. I've done everything possible to get thin because I couldn't accept myself as I was. I've fasted for three weeks at a time, tried every new diet in books and magazines. I've exercised beyond exhaustion and used diet pills to suppress hunger. I've lost weight, then gained it all back. Several times.

The media told me what I was lacking and that I had to work hard to attain things I need in order to be fulfilled. They told me that everything about me looks wrong. I should look like Barbie, the plastic mannequin in the store window who wears a size one, the model on the cover of the magazine, or the actress on TV.

Do American women feel good in their skin? Would they even know what *Jam bah doo nah* means? I know that right now I'm feeling awfully good and tipsy in my skin.

It makes sense that African men want their women to look like women. They want what is uniquely female to be accentuated. They want full hips, luscious breasts, a round butt, and a lovely big belly. Why do Americans want women to look like men?

For the first time, I hear that it's OK to look like a woman, to be a woman, and that I should indulge in good food to have a beautiful woman's body.

We sit down at the table and pile on the various dishes. There's fresh fish marinated in a basil ginger sauce, chicken in a succulent peanut sauce, shrimp fried rice, mashed potatoes, four different salads, plantains, ripe half avocados in a vinaigrette dressing, and plenty of fruit brought up from Calixte's recent visit to her village down south. I savor every bite of dinner as if I'd never enjoyed good food before. Doc encourages me to have seconds. I do. Gladly.

We sit glued to the TV. The music starts for *Dallas*, and everyone is tapping his feet and humming the tune. I finish my plate, and I don't feel a bit guilty.

I wonder what's for dessert.

20. WONDERFUL

Have they gone mad?

Three Foulbe men are lying on the sand under a tree pouring steaming hot tea into tall glasses.

How can they drink hot liquid on a day like today?

Nearly home from school, I'm wondering if the rubber on my shoes is going to melt before I get there. If it's 120 degrees Fahrenheit in the sun, the sand must be at least 150 degrees Fahrenheit.

How do my students walk ten miles home wearing only flip-flops? Since being here, I haven't heard anyone from Guidiguis complain of the heat. They merely say whether the sun *is* or *is a lot*.

"*Suzannedee!*" Saidou, the merchant, yells. He's sprawled out on his rug rocking his prayer beads. His companions chat as they generously drop sugar cubes into their tea.

Saidou says, "*Ah donne nah, Suzannedee?*"

I don't understand what he's asking, so I shake my head.

"*Nangay donne nah?*" The sun is, isn't it? he asks.

"*Oho, sobajo am, nangay donne, nangay donne doodee.*" I say, yes, my friend, the sun is; the sun is a lot.

"*Oho, nangay donne doodee! Ah eedee tee nah?*" Yes, the sun is a lot! Don't you need some hot tea? I know Saidou's not offering tea since men and women don't drink or eat together. But he's asking me if I know that I need to drink tea in heat like this.

"*Kigh! Kigh!*" I shake my head. Why on earth would I drink anything hot? It's the last thing I need. Saidou switches to French to explain what I can't understand in Fulfulde. He says drinking hot tea will cool me down. He asks if I will try it. I say yes.

When I get home, I rip off my clothes as if they're on fire. In the kitchen, I gulp down cold water, letting it spill out of my mouth and roll down my neck, chest, and stomach. I tilt my head backward and pour cold water over my head. It falls down my hair and lower back. Then I take the wet sheet out of the bucket of cold water from the refrigerator. I run with it into the living room, lie down, and cover my body with it. Ahhhhh. Heaven. There are tiny delights hidden within each moment. If I look hard enough, I discover joy in being alive and in Cameroon. Some days, I have to look harder than others.

I close my eyes and feel the succulence of the sheet's coolness over my body. But it's so hot that the moisture quickly evaporates, and I'm left even hotter than before.

Is Saidou right? If I sweat, will I cool off?

I throw on some shorts, a T-shirt, and running shoes. I haven't run in Guidiguis in the daylight, preferring to hide uncovered legs and shoulders in the concealing darkness of early morning. The villagers will disapprove of shorts and a tank top while I'm running, but I certainly won't wear a sweat suit in over 100-degree heat.

I hear the students passing outside my window, going home.

I walk out the door and stretch. I tell myself that I have the courage to go out there and run in the daylight and in front of my students. I leave my house and begin by running easily down the sandy road and past a compound of mud huts. The villagers working in their fields stop and stare. As I pass the women and children at the well, I can hear a hushed shock ripple through them. They whisper, What does the white woman think she's doing running half-naked through the village?

I pass Foulbe men sitting like African masks under the shade of the tree. Do they only lie around, groom each other, and nap while their wives do the cooking, cleaning, washing, planting, harvesting, child care, shopping, and water pumping? Maybe that's why some men marry more than one woman; the more wives you have, the less work to survive.

Saidou shouts again, "*Ah donne nah?*"

What does that mean!

I wave and continue running along the tree-lined street. I wish there were miles and miles of trees to run beneath. When I finally catch up to students walking home, I'm hurt to hear them laughing at me. The girls don't say anything, and I have a feeling they've never seen a woman running before. Are girls not allowed to run? I hear the boys speaking Tapouri, and they laugh, talk, and then laugh again.

Now I feel naked, running only in shorts and a tank top. Will they disrespect me for not covering myself with sweats?

I want to get as far away from the boys as I can, so I pick up the pace. To my surprise, Abbo, a sweet, helpful boy and one of my brightest students, takes off his straw hat and starts running next to me. His eyes are serious but gentle. Abbo smiles easily, even at the moment of choosing not to stick with the pack and be different; it's as if showing courage were the simplest and most natural thing.

"Hello, Teacher!" Abbo exclaims.

"Hello, Abbo!" I say happily.

"I want to run with you," he says.

"Thank you. I'd like for you to run with me," I say, and secretly thank Abbo for saving me from the pain of his friends' laughter.

Abbo runs with grace and speed. He's not even breathing hard while I'm gasping for breath at this pace and trying to keep up. Some students laugh and mimic the two of us running together, but then others join in and start running.

The younger children are getting out of the grammar school a mile from my house. Each one carries a mini-chalkboard. They aren't in uniform and instead wear traditional clothes. Foulbe boys wear long *bu-bus,* and girls wear sarongs and tailored blouses. Students from kindergarten through fifth grade stop when they see me running with my students toward the paved road. The younger boys join in, and we slow down so they can run with us. They giggle as if running tickles their toes.

When I look back, I'm surprised to see nearly twenty boys behind me. Some are serious, concentrating on form and breathing, but other boys are having fun and just can't stop laughing. As the sun lands on the earth and slowly disappears into a red pool, the children and I run together without conversation, hearing only the rhythm of our feet on the pavement, and our collective breathing is one solid breath. Our communication is the blinking of eyes, our smiles, and a bouncy pace. A breeze moves through the acres of millet fields, and it reaches out to caress our hot cheeks.

Abbo sticks with me whether I move to the front of the crowd or slow down. He looks down at me and smiles, then begins singing a Tapouri song. The boys leap in when Abbo sings the chorus and sing without inhibition. I only listen, letting the melody flow through me and through the desert's living creatures.

"Teacher, would you like to hear a song in English?" Abbo asks, only a heartbeat after finishing his tribal song. I nod, and off he goes.

"One, two, three!" Abbo shouts.

Everyone sings, "Wonderful!"

"A boy, a girl, a man, a woman!" Abbo calls out.

Everyone sings, "Wonderful!"

"A tree, a stone, a cloud, a sky!"

"Wonderful!"

"A donkey, a field, a sun, a moon!"

"Wonderful!"

"My sister, my brother, my mother, my father!"

"Wonderful!"

"My teacher, my teacher, my teacher, my teacher," Abbo sings and smiles at me.

"Wonderful!"

We run along the road, picking up the pace with the joy of our song, and Abbo continues to point out everything we see before us, and we respond by shouting out, "Wonderful!"

I can feel spirit singing in my belly, and I wonder if that's where my soul lives. The rhythm of the song dances in my veins and rushes like an ocean wave into my heart. I feel I belong. Not to somebody or even to the village, but now I belong to myself. I've been waiting for this.

While I sing "Wonderful," I think that I've never gone through my daily routine being thankful for everything my eyes can see. Now my thoughts are only of what I'm presently blessed with.

I feel so good, I can't help myself. I sing out "Wonderful" at the wrong time, repeating it again and again and again. The boys laugh and shout "Wonderful" with me even though I'm totally out of sync. We sing loudly and gloriously as if we're dedicating our hearts to seeing everything on Earth as wonderful.

I'm singing "Wonderful" to life: I have lived another day. I sing to the sky, the sun, the wind brushing through my hair and dancing in millet fields. I whisper a declaration to myself that I want to dedicate my life to people and stop chasing after things. And it's clear that my companions' singing is the water that's quickly filling the void in the dry well within me.

Sweat falls like rain from every pore and drips down my back, arms, legs, and neck. When the sweat cools the body down, it's not as hot. Maybe Saidou was right. When temperatures go soaring, the best thing is to get hotter.

As we approach the trees of Touloum, five miles from Guidiguis, we encounter several Tapouri women walking home from the market. They are drunk from millet wine called *bil-bil*. But they carry huge sacks of millet and water jugs on their heads, chickens and ducks under their arms; and even though they can't walk a straight line, they have no problem balancing items on their heads. They tease one another, daring each other to run with the white woman and her students.

Their feet shuffle jokingly with us as they begin to run, laughing in a drunken frenzy. The women playfully slap each other's hands, running with me in a Makosa dance step. They shake their hips, the sacks on their heads not even teetering—though the chickens squawk when they're squeezed tightly from their owners' laughter. I laugh so hard that I get a side-stitch under my rib and slow down in order to breathe.

Running has lifted my spirits beyond the boundaries of Earth and sky. Miracles come when I live my dreams, no matter how small or insignificant they may seem. I'm filling empty moments with my own laughter.

As the women become breathless, they stop. Abbo and I pass, listening to their talk about the run. As the boys turn off the paved road one by one and head home, I turn back toward Guidiguis. Abbo's village is farther ahead, but he's concerned about my safety. He tells me he'll escort me back to Guidiguis and then turn back. I try to reassure him that I'll be fine, but he disregards my protests.

We run in silent meditation, our eyes fixed on the trees in the distance. We pick up the pace and glide along under the setting sun. Abbo tells me that sometimes singing is all he can do to alleviate his sadness. Singing can't take the pain away, but it can uplift a spirit when all else fails.

When we return to Guidiguis, the children walking home from Koran school scream, chase us down the road, and take my hands. There are nearly half a dozen kids on each side of me. Most of them drop out after a hundred yards, but a few boys continue down the dirt road with us.

Saidou is still sitting under his tree. There is a patch of sand stuck on his forehead indicating he's said his prayers. Saidou shouts once again, "*Ah donne nah, Suzannedee?*"

"Abbo, do you know what that means?" I ask.

"He's asking, 'Are you'?"

"Am I what?" I ask, not getting it.

"You are?" Abbo asks.

"You are" is like Lydie saying "I am being!"

"I am!" I say excitedly. I get what Saidou's asking.

"Tell him you are, and then ask him if he is."

"How do I say *I am?*"

"Say, *Me donne.*"

"*Me donne,*" I say. "*Ah donne nah?*"

"*Oho, Suzannedee!*" Saidou says, and claps! "*Oho, me donne!*"

I really am!

"I am. *Me donne.*" I say to Abbo.

Abbo nods, and when my house is in sight, he says good-bye, then turns and heads back.

"I am," I say to the wind. "I am," I say to the women at the well, to the children following. "I am," and then I sing out, "Wonderful!"

I can always hear Doc before I see him.

As I'm ending a run and racing toward the entrance to my compound, Doc's singing weaves through the air like the sweet scent of freshly baked chocolate chip cookies. I stop and listen a moment. When I finally catch my breath, I feel the notes fill my heart with music, and I walk through the gate.

"Hello, Suzanne! I'm happy you're home," Doc says.

"What's up, Doc?" I ask.

Doc leans his head all the way back. He looks up at the stars in the sky. He turns his head to the east, then to the west, and finally looks at me confused.

"No sign of anything. You expecting rain?" he asks innocently.

"Ever heard of Bugs Bunny?"

"Bugs who?"

"Bugs Bunny, the rabbit."

"A what?"

"A rabbit. You see, there's this hunter named Elmer Fudd, and he's trying to catch Bugs Bunny so he can eat him."

"Are you hungry?" Doc asks.

I shake my head.

"Whenever Bugs Bunny outsmarts Elmer Fudd, he says, 'What's up, Doc?' "

"Fudd is a doctor?"

"No, Elmer Fudd is a hunter. Bugs Bunny always says, 'What's up, Doc?' Then he laughs and runs away."

"I don't really understand the question," Doc says. He reaches into his blue sweat suit pocket and takes out a package wrapped in a paper bag. He offers it to me with a shy smile.

"I brought you a present," Doc says.

"Thanks, Doc." I enthusiastically take the small package and rip it open.

Meat chunks. Barbecued.

I stare at it. What am I supposed to do with it?

"Goat chunks," he says. He takes a chunk from the bag and pops it in his mouth. He waits for me to do the same.

Why do Cameroonian men think goat meat is so romantic?

I take a goat chunk and place it in my mouth. I chew and chew and chew, but the meat is so tough that my teeth can't break it up enough to swallow. When Doc's not looking, I spit it out. I'm sure I'll become a vegetarian when I return to the States.

"I packed a picnic," Doc says. "Would you like to drive into the desert and have dinner with me?"

I can stay home and stare at the walls, write another letter home by flashlight under the mosquito net, go to sleep at eight o'clock—or . . . have a beautiful moonlit evening with the hand-some doctor.

"I need to wash up, and then we can go," I say nervously. I wonder what I'm going to wear.

Doc nods and sits down on my wooden stick chair.

As I take a bucket of water to the back of my house to wash, I hear Doc sing "Tonight's the Night," by Rod Stewart. Funny how he knows all the words to a Rod Stewart hit but has never heard of Bugs Bunny. Who decides what music and TV shows come to Africa from the States?

As we get into Doc's car, I ask myself if I know what I'm doing. Doc drives past the high school, to the bald area of land where Lydie learned how to ride a bike. He stops the car and turns on the radio, then pushes in a cassette of Rod Stewart's greatest hits. He comes around and opens my door.

"Would you like to dance, Suzanne?" Doc asks in a husky voice and then bows to me as if we're at a grand ball.

"I'd love to," I say.

Doc offers his hand. I take it, and he leads me out to the sandy dance floor.

I put my hand on his shoulder, and he squeezes the other hand lovingly. Doc pulls me in close and holds me tightly. He presses his cheek against mine as he guides me in rhythm with the music, his body relaxed and confident. His hand strokes my lower back, coaxing me to relax. We dance slowly to a soft love song. He whispers the words in my ear and the heat of his breath lights each match inside me. The moonlight sparkles on our clothing as we become one body gliding through the radiant night.

Doc pulls his cheek away from mine and looks into my eyes. I shift my gaze to the moon. There are feelings that I haven't meant for him to see. He smiles and puts his cheek on mine again. My heart flutters like a baby bird wanting to learn to fly.

"Suzanne, do you have the feeling we were sent to Guidiguis to meet?"

I nod and close my eyes. I hold on tighter, afraid I'm going to fall.

"It's as if I've been waiting for you to come back to me," he says.

"I don't know what to say, Doc."

Doc pulls his head back to look at me. He holds my face in both of his hands.

"You don't have to say anything."

Doc moves his hand across my cheek, and his fingers hold my chin. He tilts my head up to meet his lips. He kisses me softly at first, scared I'll run away. His lips brush mine, and his hands run down the back of my neck. His kiss gets stronger and deeper. His arms hold me tighter. I become frightened by the force of his kiss and push him back. His lips stop moving over mine, and he pulls back.

"What is it?" The tenderness of his voice makes my heart shudder.

"I'm afraid," I say, and my eyes turn away from his.

"There's no reason to be," he whispers.

"I feel too much. It's just too much, that's all."

Doc's hands cup my chin and he tilts my head so that I'm looking into his eyes glowing with the moon inside them. He smiles warmly as he runs his fingertips across my cheek and then gently and slowly over my trembling lips. He kisses me and pulls me closer to him and holds me there.

"And I feel too much. Love what we have together."

"It's not going to go anywhere. We can't start this."

"It's not our decision when to start or stop," Doc says convincingly.

"We'd only hurt each other, Doc, but we can stop it here and now . . ."

Doc interrupts and grips my shoulders tightly, shaking them as if needing to wake me from a bad dream.

"I love you."

"You can't say that! It's too soon and you're going too fast and you don't even know me."

I pull away from him and feel a tidal wave of panic coming straight toward me. There's nowhere to run and hide this time. What can I do?

"Doc, will you take me home?"

Doc picks up the basket and opens my door. As he moves around to the driver's seat, I sit inside and stare at the moon, which constantly watches—but says nothing.

It's the rainy season, and it's raining everywhere except in Guidiguis. We've only had one rain, but other villages are getting drenched. It seems the rain stops just before the sign that says in French "Welcome to Guidiguis" and then continues at the end of the village boundaries.

No one has been able to explain why it's happening.

Until now.

Yesterday, a Foulbe man, Moussa, and his sons dug deep into a dry riverbed for water and made a small pool out of mud. They lifted buckets of water from the well and poured it into the pools for their cows to drink. This morning, they returned with their herd of cattle to the well in the dry riverbed. But when the father and sons got to the riverbed, they discovered a family of elephants stealing their water. Without this water, their cattle will die. Without the cattle, the family will have nothing to sell at the market. Their survival depends on beef. Moussa ordered his sons to stay behind while he chased the elephants away.

The elephants, now desperately in search of water, migrate in the extreme north along the river from north to south. Guidiguis happens to be in the middle of this yearly migration, and usually, the villagers are prepared for the elephants and scare them away with a mob carrying torches. But since Guidiguis has only had one rainfall, this herd of elephants was completely unexpected.

When Moussa ran toward the animals shouting for them to leave the water alone, the elephant got angry. It charged and trampled Moussa, killing him instantly. The boys ran back to the village and told the story.

The story spread like wildfire. And since the Foulbe couldn't find and slaughter the elephant that murdered their brother, they found someone they could hold responsible, a Tapouri merchant, Boubakari.

Boubakari doesn't sell his bags of millet to the Foulbe because he knows they turn around and sell it for a higher price at the market. He sells it himself for a slightly lower price. Boubakari sells more bags of millet using this strategy, but the Foulbe don't want to lower their prices. Instead, they'd like to run Boubakari out of the market.

Last year, Boubakari became very ill. He found it impossible to continue working in his fields or at the market. Boubakari lived off what he had saved and guarded his bags of millet for the following year. But now that we're suffering a horrible drought, millet has become scarce. The Foulbe don't have much millet to sell, and at this time, the price for a bag of millet is soaring. Boubakari is profiting, as he still has last year's bags of millet, which he can now sell at a very steep price. He's making more money than he ever imagined. A curse turned out to be a blessing.

The Foulbe and the Tapouri are not enemies. But they're not friends, either.

Moussa's family, torn by grief, desperately needs to explain his death. And they've found someone they can hold responsible—Boubakari. The Foulbe are saying that he's a sorcerer and that he's responsible for the drought. They say he used black magic to keep the rain out of Guidiguis so he could sell his bags of millet for a high price. The Foulbe also say he's a lion who changes back and forth into a human being. As a lion, they say, Boubakari led the elephants into the riverbed and up to Moussa's well. Once Moussa got there, Boubakari killed him.

The part I don't understand in hearing the story—first from Valentine, then from Calixte, and then from Clotilde—is what the Foulbe think Boubakari's motivation was for killing Moussa. I understand that they want to explain the drought somehow, and I can see why they're jealous of Boubakari's good fortune, but why use him to explain Moussa's death?

As I walk to the center of the village in search of a tailor who can make a new dress for me, I stop and listen to different villagers telling their side of the story. I ask if there will be a tribal war, and they look in my eyes and ask if the sun is 'a lot.'

As I pass Moussa's compound, I hear the women wailing behind the walls. This stops me. Tears well up in my eyes, and I feel terrible for their loss. The sound of their crying tells me that Moussa was a beloved husband and father. This is a tragedy for both Moussa and Boubakari.

I wish I could say something to the women in Moussa's compound to let them know I acknowledge their pain, but I know I'm not allowed behind the entrance to their home. The Foulbe have strong traditions and don't allow the modern world to penetrate. I bow my head to the fifty Foulbe men who are showing their grief by sitting in front of the family's compound on mats and carpets spread over the sand. There is no talking, praying, or tears among the men. They sit together in silence to show their support to Moussa's survivors.

Saidou, sitting with his brothers, hisses to catch my attention. I approach the men, who turn to stare at us talking. Saidou greets me in his usual friendly manner, and I'm shocked that his greeting is so jovial. Shouldn't he show more respect to those in mourning? And won't the villagers think we're an item?

"*Suzannedee, ah eedee diddlee deeboh Moussa.*" Saidou points inside the mud-hut compound, but I look at him and shake my head. I can't go into a Foulbe compound without being invited. Saidou tries to convince me, but I'm shy and frightened. Saidou gets up and sighs. He takes me by the wrist and leads me behind the mud walls of the compound. Then he leaves me alone without explaining the custom.

Moussa's mother, wife, and daughters are in the nearest hut wailing, crying, and screaming. They shake, beating a rug with a broom; they hug and rock, getting up now and then to pace back and forth in front of the hut.

The women don't stop what they're doing when I arrive, and that puts me at ease. Nearly twenty women are preparing food: grinding millet, stirring porridge, shelling or grinding peanuts, smashing onions and garlic, or slaughtering, skinning, or cutting up chickens. The young girls are filling the barrels with water, then journeying back outside to the well for more.

I approach the girls emptying their buckets and ask where I should go. Six girls take me by both hands to the wailing women.

At first, I'm scared to interrupt their wailing, but then a young girl pushes me to go ahead and greet the women.

When I approach, Moussa's mother stops wailing, as though she's been acting it out all along. Moussa's wife and daughters continue screaming, but they watch my interaction with their mother. Moussa's wife doesn't look more than thirteen years old. His daughters look a few years older than she.

I greet the mother, who nods her head and rocks back and forth, and says "*Botum*," meaning "Good," to everything I say. I shake her hand good-bye, and the women, still wailing, nod and smile at me as I turn to leave.

I lift both hands, palms facing out, and thank everyone as I leave the compound. Everyone sings good-bye to me in Fulfulde.

Then a woman asks me, "*Jam bah doo nah, Suzannedee?*"

"*Jam core doo may,*" I say. Yes, I'm alive—still here.

I wonder if the reason I see their attitude toward death as casual is that they know that the difference between life and death is only your spirit's being in your skin or not.

Perhaps they know that death is only the soul's finding freedom.

23. LIZARD SPEAKS

I hear the Earth sigh
And feel her tremble
From the rush of tears
Spilling into her oceans
And the weight of footsteps
Carving into her soil.

I have watched the people,
Tried to speak with them,
To answer their prayers whispered and sung.
But they cannot hear my voice
Over the clamor of the noise they make
With their angry shouting and blaming
And waving clenched fists.

I watch over this land
As the dead
Walk across my back
While others tear the Earth apart.

It's elephant season again. The villagers on the outskirts of Gui-diguis say that the elephants are stealing their wine.

I am in an overcrowded bush taxi talking to Ahmadou, a local man from the Foulbe tribe. His new royal blue *bu-bu* robe stands out in sharp contrast to the colorful but threadbare garments of my fellow passengers. After attempting to respond in Fulfulde, I switch to French, answering his puzzled question about why an American woman would teach for free for two years in the Peace Corps. He nods seriously, then seems to feel an obligation to warn this *nasara* about the danger of traveling to the capital during this time of year.

The problem, says Ahmadou, is with the elephants and sweet millet wine.

"It began years ago, when lions were numerous in the desert bush country near Chad." Ahmadou shifts in his seat and gazes out the window at the vast dry land racing by. "In those days, lions were just beginning to discover black magic and would experiment by changing riverbed potholes of water into calabashes of wine. The lions used the wine to celebrate at big feasts and seasonal dances. In this part of the bush, all species rejoice during full moons, since they often bring cooling breezes during the hot, dry season. The lions were never able to resist a moon celebration and often made more wine than they could possibly consume. When it came to the end of the season and the elephants began their migration, they found hundreds of potholes of good millet wine in the riverbeds. Of course, the elephants eagerly drank the wine and, in time, grew to like it even better than water."

Ahmadou's story is so captivating, I don't even mind the woman next to me falling asleep on my shoulder or the chorus of irritated chickens and goats in the back of the van.

"As lions mastered black magic," he continues, "they learned to transform themselves into human beings. And after having experienced the joy of being human, most could never go back to the way things were. Therefore, the feasts became rare as the lions progressively become extinct."

Now it all makes sense. Lately, the elephants have been randomly tearing up entire villages, peeling off pointed straw roofs over mud huts and tossing them into the air with a flick of their mighty trunks, all in search of calabashes of wine. The villagers have been complaining that, after the elephants drink a village dry, they never leave a franc to pay for the excellent wine they've polished off. Furious with the elephants, the villagers have torched their fields in order to frighten the ponderous creatures away.

Ahmadou asks if I've ever seen elephants in these parts. I want to tell him that the only time I'd seen elephants was while walking home after trying more than a few calabashes of millet wine myself, on the request of the Lamedoh. Those elephants were the color of sweet, ripe mangoes, and they were dancing to jazz that they were playing in the cornfields at sunset. They repeatedly lifted and lowered their trunks like golden saxophones. I don't know the words for golden saxophones in French or Fulfulde, so I tell Ahmadou that I've never seen any elephants.

Suddenly, the bush taxi comes to a screeching halt. We are at the end of a two-mile traffic jam in both directions.

A traffic jam in the middle of the desert?

Three dozen teenagers wearing rags over their bloated bellies storm past us, snarling. In their patois, they shout in unison, raising their plows, machetes, and handmade knives high, then even higher. Ahmadou explains that the elephants have struck again. One very young boy wearing a Burger King uniform stops in front of my window and yells at me.

I don't understand his words, but I know why he's yelling. I'm white. I come from the richest country in the world, and I could probably gather enough money to help him rebuild his mud-hut compound.

I fumble with my French and limited Fulfulde, not quite conveying my feelings, but Ahmadou seems to understand.

"*Oho, oho,*" he says, nodding.

Can I really understand his loss, not only of his parents but his crops, his cows, his entire village?

Ahmadou interrupts my thoughts and says, "The boy is telling you that he has nothing left. He has nothing. He says that you have everything, *nasara*."

As the Burger King boy turns away, I can see his exposed buttocks through worn holes in his trousers. They are covered with sores, oozing with puss.

A pack of angry children gather around the Burger King boy, and he raises his machete and screams, urging his young army forward. As they follow the boy past bush taxis and private cars stacked up like cars on the Los Angeles freeways at rush hour, Ahmadou tells me that this is the fourth time the elephants have destroyed their village. All the wine has been consumed, the millet fields and cornfields have been flattened, and the compound of mud huts has been completely leveled.

And until now, nothing has been done about the elephants.

Each time the elephants strike, the villagers simply suffer their incredible bad luck, slowly rebuild, and replant. Alcohol production and consumption increase during these hard times, so the elephants, smelling the tantalizing aroma from afar, return each year for the delicious sweet wine.

This time, the villagers have become angry enough to take action and so have decided to block the only paved road connecting the north of Cameroon to the south. Adult farmers barricade the bridge, machetes and plows in hand, ready to attack. They vow not to let a single car, truck, bush taxi, bike, or person across until both the king of the provincial capital and the mayor arrive and order the extermination of all wild elephants in the extreme north of Cameroon. They also demand a large donation by the government to help the village get back on its feet.

By now, sweat is dripping down my neck. As I move the head of a small sleeping boy carefully off my lap, his mother wakes, rolls her head off my shoulder, yawns, and takes the child into her arms. I lick my salty, chapped lips. I need a drink of cool water and to get away from other sweaty bodies.

Nearly everyone in the car follows me out, even the chickens, and a few of us crouch in the sparse, angel-shaped shadow of a naked tree. My ears ring, and what I imagine are bells in celebration of a new pair of wings is only the sound of silver coins in pockets of the Muslim men spreading their sacred carpets and mats for prayer. All the Muslims open their water jugs. They vigorously scrub their hands, feet, ears, and faces, then start chanting to Allah. I take a drink from my canteen and am surprised to suddenly be out of water.

I am worried.

I stand up and start pacing. We could be stuck here for hours—maybe a day or two. Who knows where the hell the king and the mayor are? And I seriously doubt their interest in a tiny village ransacked by elephants. My mouth falls open as the men languorously pour water over their delicate bodies. Their wives sit with the children, breast-feeding, bathing infants, and gulping water as if it would flow endlessly from a faucet.

What are my traveling companions thinking? Don't they know that we could die out here in the middle of nowhere? We have no water and no food.

I double-check my backpack in case all that praying five times today has suddenly turned stones into bread. Inside, I find a couple mushy guavas and a few kola nuts. The red kola nut, bitter and heavily caffeinated, is used for a specific custom: when given, it's a sign of friendship. The neighborhood women presented me with a few the morning I'd bought my daily peanuts from their stand on the way to school. I hadn't eaten the kola nuts yet because they became precious to me. It was as if a magic spell had been cast on them. Every time I reached into the tiny cloth bag of kola nuts, they transformed into sparkling rubies in the palm of my hand.

I yawn and plop down next to the woman and her child who had borrowed me for a pillow. I feel an unspoken tenderness between us. Small moments of beauty make language unnecessary. She smiles at me as she lifts the child to her breast. I smile back and dust the dry salt from my forehead.

I am parched. What if I die out here?

Will I ever see my mother again? Will I taste sweet, cold, delicious Chunky Monkey ice cream one more time? Or watch the sun set over the Pacific? My life in the States seems so distant, so rich and full of friends and family, running water, and Safeway. I hunger for all of it.

I'm not ready to die.

Several hours later, my vision blurs, and I begin to rock back and forth. The woman lowers her child to her lap and pulls an orange from her basket. She peels it quickly and offers it to me. I try to accept, but my arms won't obey. They just hang limply at my sides. I can't keep my eyes open or sit up straight. The woman moves close enough to put an arm around me just as I feel ready to fall face forward into the sand. She pops a slice of orange into my mouth. I eat it slowly, and she gives me two more. Then she pushes the hair back out of my face, and my vision comes back into focus. I look up into her warm black eyes. There is something achingly familiar between us. She nods and puts the orange into my hand. She pats my back as she picks up her canteen and hands it to me. I sip from it, then eat another slice of orange.

Ahmadou returns from prayer with a few others, and they sit next to us. Each offers a little of what they have. A cup of water is filled and passed without a word said. These people know something I have yet to learn: many jugs of water put together make a cup for everyone.

Ahmadou offers me boiled peanuts. The Foulbe bush taxi driver shares his deep-fried roots in a pepper sauce. Another shares locusts. A few aren't cooked too well, and the insides splatter in my mouth. Another man has boiled potatoes. I'm excited because this is food I recognize, so I savor every bite. I try spicy fried termites for the first time and actually enjoy them. Surprisingly, my stomach remains calm; nothing even thinks about coming back up. Another woman sits beside me and offers the juiciest slice of papaya I have ever tasted. I close my eyes, lingering in heaven. We devour the papaya together and coo like pigeons in love.

I thank my traveling companions for the food and water. They thank me for thanking them, saying *"Oh say ko, oh say ko jour."* Bellies full and thirst quenched, we feel a new energy moving within us. Another day of life has been granted. We sit for a long moment of silent gratitude to one another and to the Earth. By now, the sun has tilted, and we watch the threads being sewn between our souls. A delicate sigh escapes the wind's lips and moves us all to smile.

Suddenly, I remember I have the kola nuts. I pull out each sparkling ruby nut and everyone accepts with two open hands and bowed heads. I'm grateful their definition of friendship is an unspoken custom.

Our silent prayer is suddenly broken by loud cheering from the army of children.

We stand up to look. Maroua's king and mayor are driving up in identical black Mercedes. The king is dressed in fancy peach-colored traditional Muslim robes, with a flaming red cap on his head. He's supposed to have been in the village awaiting the birth of his hundredth child. He's a giant man, tall and wide. His rings sparkle in the sun as he climbs out of the air-conditioned car, wiping the sweat off his fat forehead and second chin. He smiles at the sight of the mayor, dressed in a European-tailored black suit and shiny shoes. He's been with the president of Cameroon, discussing emergency aid to help the extreme north get through the upcoming famine.

We all watch the villagers talk with the king and the mayor. The king often jumps up and down in boyish anger. The mayor only paces and scratches his head. The villagers, especially the children, don't allow either man to bully them into a quick fix. The kids aren't afraid of the big, fancy men; they have nothing to lose. They raise their plows and machetes, shouting and demanding that they haven't been clearly understood. The political leaders don't want to hunt down the elephants because they're afraid that if they do, America and other countries might cut off financial aid. They offer other solutions, such as more money and more livestock. But the kids roar angrily, pushing their aunts and uncles and other adults aside. They scream so loudly that I'm convinced the elephants can hear their death sentence.

In the distant trees, I can hear the elephants singing. Their song is a sad lament, nothing like the jazz I'd heard them play the night the millet wine went to my head. I want to tell them to run, to never come back, to cross the borders into Chad or Nigeria. Go anywhere, but leave this place now.

The villagers don't budge off the bridge for three more hours, not until the documents are signed and stamped. The elephants will be hunted and killed for their crimes, and a large sum of money will be given to the villagers to rebuild again.

The children are wild with joy. They sing and shout and run through the crowd raising their plows and machetes even higher. The Burger King boy takes off his straw hat and wipes his forehead. He sits in the middle of the paved road and lowers his head into his hands. Perhaps he's weeping because he has lost so much and because he is not accustomed to winning. And maybe because his life is a struggle just to survive.

I want to sit down and take him gently in my arms and cry with him.

The woman next to me must sense this because she turns to me and puts her son into my arms. I hug the child, being careful not to let my tears spill onto his forehead.

People climb back into their cars. The goats and chickens are loaded into the bush taxi. We pack into the vehicle and speed off. The radio is playing some high-beat Cameroonian music, but all I can really hear is the spirit of the victorious children singing in my heart. I hold the little boy on my lap, and he plays with my hair.

Again, the bush taxi comes to a screeching halt. A huge snake lies in the middle of the road. The driver plunges forward and runs over it, then reverses and runs it over again. He does this several times until someone shouts in French, "It's dead. Let's go!"

We continue along the road. Twenty minutes later, a tire explodes. The boy on my lap holds my face in his hands and gives me slobbery kisses. As long as I feel loved, little problems don't really bother me. And anyhow, it's only a flat tire.

Once again, we climb out of the bush taxi.

All I had wanted to do that day was reach the provincial capital and get to the bank before it closed. By now, it's 5:30 in the afternoon. The Muslims begin to wash and pray again. I think about home and about my ATM card and try to remember my PIN code. I want to explain that, in the States, there are money machines on every corner. You put your card in, press a few numbers, and out comes cash. I don't have the words. And even if I had them, it would be a lot more fun to try first to explain a Burger King drive-through. Or maybe a roller coaster. Or ice skating.

I kiss the boy in my arms. He smiles as he pees on me. It doesn't matter. I hug him and laugh. I can't help it. The Foulbe men, the women, the driver, and the rest of my traveling companions laugh, too. And it seems that even the animals are laughing with us. By the way our toes tingle at the movement of the earth, we can feel the elephants tramping across peanut fields in the distance. The sun sets, and already we can see the full moon rising.

I hope the lions will come out. They say that lions can't resist a moon celebration, and I definitely wouldn't be able to resist a calabash of sweet millet wine tonight.

As I hear Doc's car pull up outside my house, I turn off the flashlight and close my journal. I lie underneath the mosquito net and push the light on my watch; it's almost midnight. What is Doc doing here so late?

Knock! Knock! Knock!

I don't move, and I don't say anything.

"I know you're in there! Open the door! I want to talk with you!" Doc shouts.

Knock! Knock! Knock! Silence.

I hear him lean his body against my door. His voice is softer now. "Suzanne. Please. It's me, Doc. I don't understand why you doubt me when I believe in you."

I sit up, throw off the mosquito net and get out of bed. I tiptoe to the door.

"I know I frightened you the other night, but now you're scaring me. I feel you'll run away as fast as you came into my life. I don't want you to go away. I won't let you go."

Doc leans his head against the door. I step back, not wanting him to hear my breathing or my heart pounding its fists on the window of my mind and telling me to open up and let Doc in.

"Suzanne. I'm sorry. Please let me see you."

I want to open the door, but I'm too frightened by how he makes me feel.

"I need you, and I think you need me, too," says Doc.

I want to cry on his shoulder as he consoles me with his sweet songs of love.

"Let's have some problems and solve them," Doc says, and I smile.

I'm still a moment, then I reach down to turn the key. As I open the door, Doc peeks around it smiling, as if he knew all along that I would.

"Choose us, choose us," Doc says and steps into my house and sweeps me up in his arms. He kisses my forehead, my eyelids, my cheeks, and finally my lips. His kiss lingers and plays tenderly until my hands reach up to his neck. I wrap my arms around him and squeeze him tight. I return his kisses, and he chuckles and hums a song. I laugh with joy at the music he makes, then run my hands through his hair. Doc picks me up in his arms and closes the door behind us.

"Please give us work, Miss," Egré says. "We'll do anything you need us to do." François nods his head eagerly and shifts the stick from under one arm to the other. He looks at Egré and then at me. They both plead with their eyes.

François taps Egré on the shoulder and says something to Egré in Tapouri. I wait for the translation, but there seems to be a conflict. Egré throws me a look and then turns his back to me. He whispers to François as if he's afraid I'll be able to decipher what he's saying.

Egré turns to me. I have the kind of feeling you get when a street hawker is about to open a long black coat and sell you a watch. He tells me what François said, but I'm not paying attention to the words; I'm trying to figure him out. He's nice-looking, neatly dressed, very charming—and something tells me that he's done this song and dance with other whites before.

"Miss, François has only one leg. His family has given up on him. He'll never be able to make a decent living because no one wants a crippled worker. François saw you at the market, and you were kind to him. He left home to prove his value to his family. If you can give him work, then François can gain back his integrity. It's up to you."

"I really don't have any work for you both," I say, and feel terrible for not hiring them.

"You need water from the well," Egré says.

"Yes, but—" I stop because I don't know how to explain that I don't feel comfortable having servants. I would feel like a white slave owner. What would the villagers think of me? How could I tell the folks back home? I'd be ashamed to admit it.

"I'll do François's work. I'll be his other leg. He can take the money for it," Egré pleads.

I raise my eyebrows. Egré's too good to be true.

"I can also go to the market and bargain for reasonable prices," Egré says.

"She paid a hundred francs for a tin of peanuts," François says. How did he know that?

"And she paid triple the price for a pile of onions," François adds.

"Miss, it's terrible the way you were treated at the market. If you hire us, we can make sure you'll never again be cheated."

"You boys have a good point," I say, "but I'm not quite sure if I want to have people working for me. I don't feel right having servants."

"We need work, Miss. You would be helping by hiring us," Egré adds, and François smiles sweetly at me. "François and I need to find a way to pay for our schooling, and you need protection when you sleep. When you leave for Maroua, someone needs to guard your house from thieves. If you adopt us as your sons, we could take care of you and you could take care of us. We could be a little family. In Cameroon, everyone is family."

He has me, and he knows it. Is it written all over my face that I feel alone and sometimes unable to take care of my needs?

François gives me another dashing smile. "We need to work, Miss. I want to bring money to my family and show that I am able to contribute."

"We can wash your clothes and your floors. We can kill and clean your chickens and prepare traditional meals for you."

"I'm just not sure I want anyone working for me. I thank you for your offer, but I'll have to think about it. Come back and ask me next month. I'll have an answer."

Egré nods. François hangs his head, and I feel guilty for turning them down. Egré picks François up in his arms and walks slowly out of my compound.

The daily trips to the well, the haggling at the market, the walk to the post office, and the search for food connect me to the village. Cleaning my house and washing clothes by hand ground me and give me a sense of accomplishment when teaching frustrates me and makes me feel that my work here is useless.

But I would like to help Egré and François earn some money. I smile and think of having two adopted sons around the house. In Africa, everyone is a part of an extended family. Even I am becoming a part of that circle of relatives.

It made me warm inside to hear Egré suggest that I "adopt"

them. I could help pay for their schooling, and they could in turn help me survive out here. The pain of loneliness is getting less and less as I learn to cope, but I wouldn't mind having some company during the week when Doc is too busy to leave the hospital. Two adopted sons living with me would be a little adventure to have.

And anyway, who would really be adopting whom here? I'd feel as if they were taking me in as their "mom." I'm sure they have more to teach me about survival in the desert than I have to teach them about anything.

When they come back next month, I won't resist their charming smiles. I'll say yes, we can be a family.

27. FABRIC OF MY FAMILY

As I'm being measured for a dress I've designed, the tailor's five daughters, sitting on the straw mat at the corner of the mud hut, giggle and cover their mouths. The tailor is on his knees, biting on a couple of pins, his eyes focused at my waist on the material he'll make into a skirt. Every so often, he calls to the girls and tells them to be quiet. But he has no idea that I'm making faces at them, which causes them to laugh louder after he reprimands them.

Sali is so serious as he moves around me, his eyebrows pinched tightly together and the pins grinding against his teeth. Sali pushes the pin into the material, then sighs when he leans back. He leans forward, peering at the cloth up close, and then readjusts the pin by taking it out and moving it only a centimeter. He finally steps back, making sure that each pin is in the perfect spot. Then Sali circles me, walking around me several times, getting a look from far away and then up close. He sighs, gets on his knees again to take the pins out and start over.

I've never had a dress custom-made before and had no idea that it was this much work. I designed a simple suit for a royal blue fabric I bought while shopping with Vann during training. At first, Sali said no, he couldn't possibly sew a suit from the design I drew. Then he said he couldn't give me the quality I wanted since he only has a manual sewing machine. I assured him that his pedal-powered machine was fine. Then he said he only does traditional women's clothes. I pleaded with Sali to give it a try since the only other choice I have in tailors is in Maroua. I told Sali I'd pay whatever price he asked, and he finally agreed but gave me an extremely low price. He said if I liked the dress, then he'd charge me the going rate for the next one I asked him to do. I was pleased with Sali's honesty and because he takes pride in his work.

The girls in the corner are from three to ten years old and are exquisitely dressed in beautifully colored sarongs and blouses their father made. Sakinatou, the oldest daughter, walks through the entrance carrying a large bucket of water on her head. Her hair is covered by a cape that falls from her head to her ankles and wraps around her lovely face so that only her eyes are showing. She walks gracefully past us, dropping the face covering and smiling at me as she enters.

The girls are happy that their older sister has returned, and they move onto their knees and bounce excitedly. I imitate them by laughing, then covering my mouth. They squeal with delight. Sakinatou sits on the mat with her sisters. With their arms wrapped around each other, they huddle together and whisper about me. When they turn to me, they cover their eyes and begin a new game of peeking at me through their fingers. I do the same. When we peek at each other at the same time, we laugh, then hide our eyes behind our hands again. When we catch each other peeking at the same time, we laugh together. Sali, on his knees and peering closely at the pin on my left side, shouts at the girls to calm down, then says my name with a whiny tone to get me to be still.

His voice makes me laugh so hard that I move and Sali accidentally sticks me with a pin. I yell out in pain, but Sali has fallen back on his heels and laughs at me. I throw my shirt up and take the pin out. I press on the tiny puncture to stop the bleeding. Sakinatou leads the five girls out of the corner, and they tackle their father. He falls on his side and then rolls to his back. Sali wrestles with them, but once his hat gets knocked off, he stops playing and stands up. He dusts himself off and smiles, saying something in Fulfulde about my being a big kid. As I nod in agreement, Sali unpins the material from my waist, then sits at his sewing machine to get started.

The girls turn to me and take my hands, each holding onto a finger as they twirl me around, singing my name, *"Suzannedee! Suzannedee! Suzannedee!"*

I pick Sakinatou up in my arms and spin her around. Sakinatou's eyes bulge out because she's scared of the sensation; then she lets out a tiny giggle. When I set her down, we're both dizzy, and we stumble around the room as if we're intoxicated. Everyone laughs until we plop down on the straw mat. Then the girls tackle me, shouting for me to pick them up.

"Hokeeam, Suzannedee! Hokeeam!"

I pick up the next oldest girl and twirl her by a wrist and an ankle like an airplane. Sakinatou imitates me and picks up the youngest girl. Sali, working, tilts his head and smiles as he catches glimpses of us. The girls are laughing and screaming so loudly that it disturbs and frightens Sali's ancient mother, who comes rushing to the front of the compound to see what's going on.

She stops at the doorway with a six-year-old boy. She tells him, Ahmadou, to stay behind while she finds out what's happening. Like a shadow, he follows her into the room. So do three goats, a couple of chickens, and a duck.

Ahmadou doesn't take his eyes off me, telling me that he longs to be spun around, too. He holds his hands together and smiles at me as if praying for an airplane ride, but as soon as the old woman enters the room, her eyes tell me to stop playing. I set the girl down, and she pulls on my hand. I point in the direction of the old woman, and the girl's hand falls from mine.

The girls and I are quiet now, and even Sali stops working. I have a feeling the old woman thinks I've done something terribly wrong. The girls look to their grandmother and then to me. But how do you explain to an adult what it feels like to fly? Adults don't play with children in Guidiguis, and the kids are hungry for games and affection. The girls call her *Dada*, meaning "Mother." They explain that I'm a teacher living here for two years and Sali is making me a dress for school. The old woman turns to Sali, saying something that makes him resume his work. His foot pushes the pedal of the sewing machine, but I'm too much in shock to make mine move an inch.

But the old woman stares at me until I back away from her and toward the entrance of the compound. Her eyes order me to leave. Suddenly, she turns and walks away, and the animals follow her.

Stunned, I quickly cross the street and turn down a sandy path that will lead me home the short way. I think of the old woman's eyes, which speak without saying a word of her language or mine. There's a place inside me that yearns to be a part of someone's family, and yet the villagers wouldn't think of adopting me into theirs. Most are friendly now, but there is a well-defined boundary built to protect themselves and those they love from foreigners. They call each other brother and sister, and even strangers are family, but I am still *nasara* and will always remain so, I believe.

I came to Africa searching for a people I could belong to and a family I could call my own. But my white skin prevents me from getting closer. And back home, my Spanish and Native American roots don't make anything grow or blossom. For me, they are only names with no meaning. I have been searching the world for traditions of my people and identity, for someone to tell me where I came from and where I'm going. But still I have no answers. Just more questions and more feelings of being all alone in the world.

I hear a child shouting. I stop, and when I turn around, I see little Ahmadou racing after me and calling my name. He quickly catches up, pulling at my skirt and rubbing his face in my hands like a purring kitten. I hug him and then try to send him back home. I continue walking, afraid of seeing those eyes the old woman used on me.

He takes my hand and says, "*Hokee am, Suzannedee! Hokee am!*"

I look down and see a smile so wide that I can't resist his request. I pick him up around the ankle and wrist, then spin him around like an airplane.

Ahmadou's eyes get big and scared. His eyebrows are pinched together as if he's holding back a giant scream.

"Eeeeeeee!" he finally yells out. I'm sure he's going to get me in trouble with his grandma, so I slow down and set him on his feet.

He smiles up at me and hugs my legs tight. I bend down and hug him, then say good-bye.

"*Hokee am, Suzannedee!*" Ahmadou says again.

I shake my head and walk on.

Ahmadou says good-bye but continues to follow me.

I stop and say good-bye in Fulfulde again, he says good-bye, but then he still continues to follow me.

We cross the bridge, and I say good-bye for the last time.

But Ahmadou doesn't say good-bye. He runs across the bridge and leaps into my arms.

"*Hokee am! Hokee am!*"

I give in and swing him around like an airplane again. He laughs and screams and laughs and screams some more.

When I finally set him down, he's so dizzy he can't even walk.

I squat in order to hold his shoulders and keep him from falling over. He copies me by putting his hands on my shoulders and looking into my eyes.

"*Me eedee ma,*" Ahmadou says.

"*Me eedee ma,*" I say.

This time, I know exactly what those words mean.

I leave the door open after coming home from school at noon because there's an unusual cool breeze blowing through the village. It's time for everyone's daily *siesta*. I like how the French and Spanish call a nap a *siesta*—sounds like *fiesta*, a party in your dreams.

I do my usual routine of taking the bucket out of the refrigerator and wringing the sheet and placing it over my entire body in order to get cool so I can quickly fall asleep.

I wake up from a dream at the sound of something moving through the door. It comes quickly across the floor, faster than I can open my eyes and focus. I'm sure it's the lizard running into the house, so I close my eyes again. But then I hear it hit against a bucket of water. I bolt up and see its tail slithering into my bedroom.

A snake!

"Snake," I say, but no one can hear me, and it takes a moment for it to settle in that I have to face the snake on my own.

What do you do when a snake slides into your bedroom? Did the Peace Corps manual say anything about how to kill one? Of course not, so what can I do?

Run!

It's the only thing that makes any sense. I just need to run across the living room and through the door to my neighbor's house without getting the snake's attention. But where's the snake?

I stand up on the bed and listen for snake movement. No sound. I step down to the floor and take a breath. Still no sound. As I run across the living room, I hear the snake darting across the floor in my bedroom and then see it shooting into the kitchen. It's long and brown. Could be poisonous. Deadly even.

"Ahhhhhhhhhhhhhhhh!" I scream as I run out of the house at full speed. *"Il y a un serpent dans ma chambre!"*

I throw my sandals on the sand, stuff my feet into them, and then run like mad. But my neighbor's house is closed for *siesta*. I do like how everything shuts down from noon until three o'clock. That's what's wrong with America: we need to take more naps. But

I don't like when an emergency occurs in broad daylight and no one's around.

I can hear Yves snoring in the living room. Alex is whispering between his sobs to Clotilde, who soothes him with her soft singing while dipping her washcloth in a bucket of water and cooling her son down with the wet towel. The temperature must be over 120 degrees Fahrenheit.

Clap! Clap! Clap!

No answer.

Finally, a naked Alex comes to the door and pushes it open with one hand while rubbing the tears from his eyes with the other.

"*Bonjour!*" Alex says.

"*Bonjour. Yves est là?*"

"*Il dors maintenant.*"

I know he's sleeping, Alex. Wake him up, will you?

Clotilde comes to the door, tying her sarong and looking at me as if I must be crazy to be walking around at high noon.

"*Ça va, Suzanne?*"

No, it's not going well, I think to myself. How do I say that there's an enormous snake in my bedroom, and it wants to eat me alive?

I simply say "snake" in French and her eyes pop open.

"*Un serpent? Je vais chercher Yves!*"

"*Merci bien, mon amie,*" I say, relieved that the mention of snakes gets people's attention.

While Clotilde wakes her husband, I imagine snakes in my latrine in the middle of the night when I have to go to the bathroom, snakes slithering across the floor in my classroom, snakes in the road when I'm running in the early morning darkness, snakes in my shoes while I'm sleeping outside. I hate snakes.

Yves pops out of the house, holding one of Clotilde's sarongs around his waist, dragging his sandaled feet across the porch floor. Clotilde hands him a towel, and he wipes the sweat from his face, neck, chest, and arms.

"*Il fait tellement chaud ici.*" Yves says, as he looks up at the clear sky. No clouds, no rain coming. Only more heat.

Clotilde tells him that there's a snake in my bedroom and

calmly asks if they can help. Don't they know that this is an emergency?

"Un serpent? Bien sûr on va t'aider!" Yves says, and I feel reassured that I'm not alone in Africa to fend for myself.

Yves goes inside and comes out quickly, wearing a pair of pants and closed shoes. He holds three machetes. He can't possibly be expecting me to actually use one of those.

Clotilde, now dressed in another sarong wrapped very tightly around her waist, locks the house and sits down and ties the shoelaces of a pair of tennis shoes.

"You don't have closed shoes?" Yves asks.

"They're in my bedroom," I say, and imagine the snake jumping out of the house and its fangs going straight for my big toe.

Clotilde kisses Alex and sits him on the bench. Alex starts screaming that he wants to come, and she tells him that where we're going is no place for babies. "Let's go, Suzanne," Clotilde says, and stands, waiting for me to stand up.

I'm only feeling a little hesitant. I tell her that I don't know how to use a machete. "Nonsense," she says, and takes me by the hand as if I was born knowing how to use the thing.

She drags me to my house while Alex stays behind howling like a wolf.

"I'm sorry for disturbing you both and causing you trouble," I say, and wipe the sweat off the front and back of my neck.

"It's nothing," Yves says. "We're neighbors."

As we approach the house, Yves explains our strategy. He'll go inside and chase the snake out. As the snake comes out, we'll all try to hit it with the machete.

"I'm not sure I'll be able to do a thing once I see him," I say.

Yves chuckles and pats me on the shoulder. "You'll do fine." He understands that I may be too frightened to move at all. Clotilde looks surprisingly calm and unaffected by the snake or by Alex's tantrum.

Yves marches into my house as if facing a snake were nothing. Clotilde and I stand outside the door, she on one side and I on the other. The machetes are raised, and we are ready to strike. We hear tin dishes crashing, silverware spilling on the floor, a couple of glasses shattering. Then we hear Yves hollering at the snake. He simply tells the snake to leave.

Yves comes out of my bedroom yelling, "Ahhhhhhhhhhhhhhh-hhhhh!"

The snake comes skittering out the front door. Whoosh! Clotilde hits its tail. Whoosh! I hit its head. Yves comes running out of the house and smiles when he sees that the snake is dead.

Only I don't believe it's dead. I swing the machete again. Then again. Then one more time, until Yves puts his hand on my shoulder to stop me from hitting it again.

"It's dead, Suzanne," Yves insists.

"Oh," I say, as if I really didn't know.

The snake is cut into six pieces and is bleeding on my front porch. Yves and Clotilde look at me strangely. I set down the machete. Clotilde gently eases it out of my hand. "That's not a poisonous snake," Yves says.

I wish he hadn't said that.

"The Tapouri say when that snake visits you, it's good luck," Clotilde says.

"Good luck? Out here? What kind of luck can a snake bring me out here?" I ask, feeling irritated that God made snakes at all. Killing snakes with machetes is not what I had in mind when I signed up for Africa.

I dreamed of banana leaves, palm trees, coconuts, pineapples, and exotic flowers. Not the desert and certainly not snakes.

"This is something to write home about," Yves says.

He's right.

Dear Mom,

You won't believe it. Call me Towanda, the Amazon. I killed my first snake! I would have saved the skin and kept it like a trophy, but some students came for it and took it home for dinner. They say it tastes like chicken. I don't really believe it. They asked me if I'd like to try it, but I'm not ready for that experience.

I tried fried termites for the first time, and they weren't so bad. They were bite-sized and crunchy like Doritos. They tasted like the peanut oil they were cooked in, with something like jalapeño juice squeezed all over them. What I didn't really care for were the fried locusts. Granted, they had honey on top, and I thought they were going to be sweet like Cheerios, but someone didn't quite cook the locusts all the way, and their insides exploded in between my teeth. I had to swallow so I wouldn't offend the cook.

I sure miss your *chili verde, chili rellenos*, Spanish rice, and beans.

I can hear you already—telling the family and your friends that your daughter is wrestling snakes, eating raw insects, and whipping around a machete. You know, if I can kill a snake, then I can do anything. You'd be proud, Mom. Your daughter is growing into a wild woman. Like mother, like daughter, they say.

Can you find out what the distance of a marathon is? I'm thinking of training for one. As you said, "Shoot for the moon. Even if you miss, you land among the stars."

My camera was stolen, so the only pictures I can send you are my drawings. The one included in this letter is of little Adèle, who lives across the sandy street. She's discovered that I have candy and comes over every day. A little bit of sugar can be the highlight of the day. Please send more Kool-Aid. All is well in the desert of Africa.

Maybe when I get back I'll get a snake tattooed around my belly button.

Love,
Suz

P.S. I was just kidding about the tattoo.

"There's no way I'm sleeping outside," Doc protests as he watches me set up the wooden stick-bed at the side of my house.

"Listen, Doc, you're more than welcome to suffocate inside the house where it's 120 degrees, but I'm sleeping outside where it's cool."

I fluff the pillows and tuck in the sheets.

"But there are scorpions and snakes out here," Doc whines like he's five and afraid of monsters under his bed.

"They won't bother you, Doc. The Foulbe knew what they were doing when they designed this bed. It's just not termite-proof," I say. I take off my shoes and place them on the sand. "But I guess they make more money that way. Kind of like nylons that run."

"What are nylons?" Doc asks, and sits on the bed.

"An extra skin women put on their legs to wear under their dress."

"From what you've told me about skinny American women who wear extra skins, I'm surprised I like you so much."

I pick up a pillow and whack Doc across the head. He picks up the other, swings, and gets even. But I quickly change tactics, tackling and mercilessly tickling him until he begs me to stop.

"You're lucky I'm letting you off the hook so easily. Next time I won't be so kind, Doctor."

"You should be good to your doctor. You never know when you might need my services."

"Actually, Doc, I'm feeling a pain right here." I point to my lips, and Doc gives me a kiss.

"Will you look at that, everybody! Amazing! I'm cured!" I say sarcastically.

Doc whacks me in the head with the pillow.

"Do you sleep out here every night?"

"Yes, I'm not scared," I lie, and puff my chest out and flex my muscles. "They'd better not mess with Towanda, the Amazon!"

"I'm being serious, Suz. When are those boys coming back? I like the idea of you adopting them; they can protect you when

I can't be around. I don't feel comfortable with you outside by yourself."

"Then sleep out here, you big chicken, and I'll protect *you*."

"When did you get so brave?"

"Since I killed my first snake," I say proudly as I get into bed, putting my hands under my head and staring out at the stars. I take a deep breath in and sigh. "You never get to see stars like this in the States. I'm beginning to fall in love with the desert sky."

Doc leans over and kisses me, then takes off his shoes and stretches out beside me.

"Do you ever think of staying here with me?"

"Doc, please, you know we shouldn't talk like that."

"But not everywhere in Cameroon is like it is in the extreme north," Doc says. "The only reason I'm here is that someone up above sent me to meet you. I'm looking forward to going back to my village, starting my practice, and having a family."

I sit up and say, "Doc, please don't. You know I can't stay and you can't leave."

"You could come with me to my village, meet my family, and see it for yourself. You might fall in love with it and never want to leave."

"Doc, it's a war zone down south. We're lucky to be where politics don't touch us."

Doc turns over on his side and runs his hand through my hair and down my neck. He stops at my shoulder and caresses the skin all the way down to my fingers. He holds my hand and squeezes it tight.

"I dreamed last night that I married you," Doc says in a husky voice.

I start to cry and Doc kisses away my tears as he holds my face in his hands.

"Please don't give me an answer now, but think about looking up at the African stars with me forever."

A letter arrives summoning Clotilde and me to help with Sunday dinner at the mayor's house. Three other mayors from surrounding villages are coming to discuss solutions to the upcoming famine and the possibility of a nationwide strike. The teachers have also been invited, so Clotilde tells me to bring my bike—since her husband will take her home on his motorcycle.

"I didn't know that Yves has a motorcycle, Clotilde. I've never seen him ride it," I say, as we begin our walk to the mayor's house.

"Petrol is expensive," Clotilde says. She looks worried and swallows hard. "Yves wants to save as much money as he can in case the government doesn't pay during the strike."

"Do you think there will be a national strike?" I ask.

"I don't know how there won't be," she says.

"Peace Corps might get evacuated if Cameroon goes on strike."

"I'll cry if you go," she says.

"Me, too."

Clotilde takes my right hand off the handlebar and holds it as we cross through the old market field and toward the Lamedoh's compound.

"The Lamedoh is waving at you, Suzanne," Clotilde says.

When I look toward his compound, he smiles and motions for us to come.

"Must we visit him?" I ask.

"Have you met with the Lamedoh?" Clotilde asks.

"Yes. He gave me a goat's head, then asked me to marry him."

"Oh? We better say hello, Suzanne. You don't want the Lamedoh as your enemy. He can cause a lot of pain."

Suddenly, Marlon Brando as the Godfather appears to me, and I imagine getting the Lamedoh angry and returning home to find a dead goat in my bed.

"You're right," I say.

The Lamedoh sits in the shade in front of his enormous compound on a throne finely crafted from wooden sticks and strings of leather. The surrounding mud wall of his African castle is over twenty feet tall. I imagine fifty or more mud huts behind these walls occupied by wives and children. No one knows how many of each, since his women aren't allowed to leave the compound. At the Lamedoh's feet are his servants, who sit on rich burgundy carpets. A barber is trimming the Lamedoh's driver's mustache. Other Foulbe men are cutting each others' fingernails, shaving each others' faces, or just lying lazily in the shade.

I think of the women on the other side of the Lamedoh's walls, who are at this very moment washing clothes, cooking, working in the fields, carrying water to the compound, pounding millet, or taking care of the children. How can these men sit here grooming each other while the women work for everyone's survival?

"*Jam bah doo nah, Suzannedee?*" the Lamedoh asks.

"*Jam core doo may! Ah donne nah?*" I ask.

"*Me donne!*" the Lamedoh says, and chuckles.

Clotilde turns her head and stares at me, surprised. She remarks on the Fulfulde I've learned.

The Lamedoh greets Clotilde but shows no interest. He offers his hand to me. I don't want to shake it, but I can't insult the Lamedoh in front of everyone.

I step forward, and he gives me a seductive look. "*Me eedee ma.*"

As I shake his hand, he tickles my palm with something that feels like paper.

I step back. A 10,000-CFA note is in my hand. It's worth about $40 U.S., but here its value is more than $100.

"*Me eedee ma. Me hokkee ma cheday ah didlee saray am.*"

It takes a moment to understand the real meaning of his words. The Lamedoh has suggested I take the money and come back to his house tonight.

I take the money, crumple it up, and throw it in his face. King or no king, I will not be insulted like that. The Lamedoh's eyes flash. I step backward, shaking, but stare just as angrily while holding my ground. The Lamedoh stands, his eyes never leaving mine. He shouts something cruel at me in Fulfulde, spins around, and stomps toward his compound.

"Suzanne!" Clotilde says.

I step back until I'm next to Clotilde. The servants are standing and yelling at me in Fulfulde. They roll their mats, collect their water jugs, throwing insult after insult at me.

The Lamedoh stops at the entrance to his compound and turns to look at me.

The driver picks up the 10,000 CFAs and walks toward me.

"Who do you think you are? That wasn't wise! You'll pay for this!" the driver says in a hostile tone in French.

"You're in trouble now, Suzanne," Clotilde says.

The driver returns to the king, who stares as if wishing a death curse on me. "Let's get out of here, Clotilde."

I jump on the bike and point for her to jump on the handlebars. She hesitates, thinking—I'm sure—of what the disapproving villagers might do, and then hops on. I pedal madly and we speed away. We can hear the Lamedoh's servants yelling after us for a good mile.

I'm steering wildly as we race down a small hill. Clotilde screams for me to slow down because we're going to crash into a tree.

"Hold on, Clotilde!"

"I'm holding!" she says.

"Hold tighter!" I say, and we both laugh as I manage to gain control of the bike and save us from crashing.

"Oh, Suzanne, you did a terrible thing to the Lamedoh!"

"I know. I can't believe that I did it!" I say, and laugh.

"I'm so glad you did!" she says, and laughs too.

I want to call attention to Clotilde's bravery and defiance of social codes by mentioning her sitting on the handlebars, but I have the feeling that our nervous laughter says it all.

When we finally get up the hill at the *carrefour,* I have to stop the bike to catch my breath. Clotilde jumps off, and every time we try to stop laughing, one of us starts—and then we laugh all over again.

"I've got to walk away from you in order to stop," Clotilde says, as she walks toward where Saidou is selling guavas. I follow her, trying to catch my breath and wondering what I'm in for with the Lamedoh.

Saidou sees Clotilde and me approaching. He stands to greet me. *"Ah whadee nah, Suzannedee?"*

"Oho, me wahdee sobajo am. Jam bah doo nah?"

Saidou is asking me if I've arrived. I answer, "Yes, I've arrived."

He asks me again and again and again until I want to shout, "Yes, I've arrived, damn it! I'm standing right in front of you, aren't I?"

But I simply smile and go through the procedure of greeting and asking how his family is, how the goats are, and the chickens and the sun and the moon and everything else under God.

Clotilde pokes me in the side with her elbow.

"Ow!" I yell out.

"Him, too?" she says, and laughs again. As I try to communicate, I speak Fulfulde through my giggles, trying to say that I want to buy the pile of ripe guavas.

Saidou looks at me, then over at Clotilde. His smile slowly fades, and he waits for us to get ahold of ourselves.

Clotilde hits me to get serious, and I hit her back. It starts all over again, and we can't stop laughing.

Saidou sits back down, frustrated that he doesn't know what we're laughing about. When we calm down, Saidou doesn't want to have anything to do with us. I finally ask him how much for a pile of guavas, and he gives me a very steep price.

"Come on, *sobajo am. Hokee am un bon prix,*" I say.

Saidou puts the pile of guavas in a black plastic bag and hands them to me. I offer him money, but he shakes his head and motions with his hands for us to go.

I hop on the bike, and Clotilde hops on the handlebars. We push off, zigzagging all over the paved road, laughing hysterically. Nearby, a group of Foulbe men's mouths fall open, and I feel a sting of guilt for not being culturally sensitive. I know that women aren't supposed to ride bikes and *two* women making a scene on a bike is a disgraceful display.

Clotilde takes a guava out of the bag, rubs it on her skirt, and takes a bite. She holds the guava up to my mouth, and I bite. Juice runs down my chin, and I lick it with my tongue. Scornful looks continue as we pass other Foulbe men reclining on their mats. It only makes us feel more outrageous, and we purposely get louder.

"I feel like a little girl in school again, Suzanne."

"Me, too!"

Now I'm pedaling as fast as I can. Clotilde gets frightened and yells for me to slow down. I speed up to tease her. When Clotilde bribes me with another bite of a guava, I slow down. Fruit is so rare that I savor every drop of the succulent juice.

"I feel like singing," Clotilde says, and begins a lovely song in her patois—while drumming on her lap to provide the rhythm.

I turn down the path leading to the mayor's house and notice that I'm smiling. I hum the chorus, she repeats, and my head dances in circles to her music. Clotilde continues her song with a more passionate drumming on her thighs.

"It's a song my mother would sing when she put me to bed," Clotilde says, almost yelling it out to the trees and sun above us.

"It's beautiful—"

"I feel I've been sleeping for a long time," says Clotilde.

"I know the feeling—" I say.

"Now I'm awake!" Clotilde says, stretching toward the sky, arching her back and embracing the new awareness she has in her body.

Like Clotilde, I'm not sleeping.

Every cell in my body is awake and alert, prepared to give anyone who insults or attacks a good fight. I will never again allow someone to intimidate or hurt me or get away with sexual bullying. Looking at Clotilde before me dancing to the ending of her mother's song, I make a promise to myself to stand up for me, no matter what the consequences. Dignity is more important than sparing someone's feelings.

I'm coming true. Today I found out that I can be my own heroine.

When I have a victory, I will celebrate by honoring the spirit of women. I will make a ceremony for those who've taught us how to step on the path toward our future, making it different from the one our mothers suffered. It will be different, I tell myself.

And then an old Navaho chief inside me, who tells me that his name is Windchanting, has just pronounced me a warrior. I've wrestled the serpent, and I've won.

This time I've won.

I open the small bottle of my favorite shampoo that I just received in the mail from Mom, and I'm paralyzed for a moment. I have no choice but to remain still, letting the perfume permeate the air and tickle my nose. Slowly I inhale, and my lungs are drenched with memories of home, where there are hot showers and bubble baths and moments of sweet luxury. Although I'm happier now than I ever have been, I can't see myself living in Cameroon long-term. I get too homesick for the life I once knew. If only Doc would think about leaving Cameroon.

Don't go there, I tell myself. Just be in the moment.

I sigh. In Africa, if you want a little extravagance, you simply have to create it for yourself.

Recently in Maroua I bought a huge bucket to store water in, but now that it's empty, it looks like a good place to attempt a bath. It's been so long since I actually sat down and soaked in the tub that, while making three trips to the well, I begin to fantasize about what it will be like. The women greet me and invite me to join them, but I can only think of resting my head, closing my eyes, and basking in the vanilla-scented bubble bath and the tangy fragrance of the shampoo.

I bring three buckets into my bedroom and then drag the heavy bucket in from the kitchen. I pour in the bubble bath and then fill the huge bucket with water while creating a delightful number of bubbles. I tear off my wet and sticky clothes and hop into the tub. I hold my breath, go under, and wet my hair as water overflows onto the floor. I massage a tiny amount of shampoo onto my scalp, wanting to make it last as long as possible. I smile upon hearing the Muslims chanting prayers and the cows mooing down the road.

I really am happy here. I lean my head back and close my eyes and drift to sleep.

When I wake up, I see Doc pulling a wooden stick-chair into my bedroom. He smiles warmly, and I sit up. He leans over and gives me a strong hug and a long kiss hello.

"All day I was thinking of leaving the hospital and coming over to visit you."

"I'm glad you did," I say, and wipe the shampoo off my forehead.

"May I?" Doc asks as he reaches for the little bottle of shampoo. He pours the entire contents of the bottle on top of my head without waiting for a response. I think of the first time he brushed my hair, the day we met.

Doc sits down on the chair and works a good lather up, massaging my neck and kissing and tickling my ears every so often. I move my hands up around his legs and rest my hands on his strong thighs. Then I pinch him above his knees and he innocently laughs, as if he didn't know that he could be tickled.

He runs his fingers through the tangles, so gentle and careful not to hurt me in any way. I tilt my head back to look up at his eyes upside down. He laughs; I see all the love he has for me shining in his dark African eyes.

I could really love this man, I think to myself. And I think he could love me, too.

Something tells me that this is what life is all about—the tiny moments of awareness of love. That's the miracle, when your soul's infectious bliss and joy races through your human veins and fills your heart with awe.

I close my eyes as Doc continues to massage my scalp, tenderly pulling and twisting and scrubbing my hair. I find my heart singing a song in celebration and realize that I am again praying with the Muslims as they chant through the village at their regular hour. I'm doing my own rendition of prayer to Allah on the inside.

I listen to my breathing and how it changes whenever Doc is around. My hands fall from his knees down to his ankles. My fingertips run up and down the muscles in his legs as he begins to sing a sweet Cameroonian tune.

"How will I ever let you go and return to the States?"

"Shhh, Doc. Be here with me, just here right now, your hands in my hair and your songs in my ears."

"I love you, Suz."

"What?" I ask. I heard him, but I just want to hear it again.

Doc stands up and then instantly sits fully clothed on my lap in the tiny bucket as most of the water spills out onto the floor.

"You heard me, you big chicken!" says Doc, smiling, know-
ingly using my American vocabulary against me.

I scream and laugh and don't know what to do about this crazy
African man. Doc laughs too and gives me a long, tender kiss that
says everything we don't know how to say.

Dear Mom,

I've learned how to cook Cameroonian food. Calixte, the mayor's wife, has taken me under her wing. She says I'm too skinny and need to fatten up. I've been to her house for several cooking lessons, but, Mom, they go on forever. I miss cooking authentic Mexican food—enchiladas, *tamales, chili verde, and* homemade corn tortillas. There's no place like home. I tap the heels of my shoes together: click, click. I guess it only works for Dorothy in Oz.

First of all, Mom, to start lunch, I have to be there at seven in the morning on a Saturday since it takes up to six hours to prepare a meal. In the States, we take it for granted how easy it is to put a meal together. For instance, when you buy a chicken at Safeway, it's already dead. You know it's been defeathered, gutted, and cleaned. All you have to do is open the plastic wrap, rinse it, and put it in the oven. Here, you've got to chase the chicken through the field in 100-degree heat. Let me tell you, chickens are no dummies. That chicken knows it's his *head* when you start coming after him. Killing them is the hard part. I couldn't do it. I'm just not ready to kill my dinner yet. It feels so primal. The six women at the mayor's house working on stools in a circle laughed at me for taking so long to catch the chicken. And then tears filled my eyes when they told me I had to kill it. I said I couldn't possibly take the chicken's life. The mayor's wife laughed at me, then grabbed the chicken with one hand and a machete in the other. She placed her feet on its wings and its claws, and then, in one slice, she cut the chicken's neck. She let it bleed to death, and then, like a tornado, she defeathered, gutted, and cleaned it.

After that, Calixte told us we had to dig up the peanuts in the fields and then shell them. She was also out of firewood to heat their huge metal cooking pots, so Clotilde and I took two machetes and went into the bush to cut some trees. We cut down two small ones with the machetes and dragged them back to the mayor's wife. Mom, I'm getting the swing of this machete business.

After boiling the peanuts, we smashed them with rocks for the sauce. This took hours. I can see why Planters and Jiffy make so much money. It's a lot of work for a little peanut, and who wants to do it?

Then, like gold miners, we sifted through our bowls of rice soaking in water to get the dirt, rocks, and sticks out. Whenever I said my bowl was done, Calixte would plunge her hands into it and find another small rock or stick. She'd lift it up to show everyone.

"Americans don't know how to clean anything!" Calixte said, and the women laughed. Everyone except Clotilde, who gave me encouraging smiles as she cut leaves and sorted out the flowers and threw them aside.

"In the States, we buy our rice in a clean bag, and all the rocks and sticks are already taken out. All you have to do is put it in a pot of water," I said, cracking another peanut shell open and throwing the nuts into a bucket. Everyone gasped at the concept.

Wait until I tell them how we buy our chickens!

"Your country is rich if you can pay for someone to clean your rice," Calixte said. She stirred the pot that was sitting on the rocks and then pushed in the tree branches to keep the fire going.

The women nodded, agreeing that I'm rich. A woman took Clotilde's bucket of sorted leaves and sliced them into tiny pieces. Another woman started peeling the skins off the roots.

"You buy your peanuts already shelled and cooked?" asked Calixte.

I nodded, and Calixte threw her hands up in the air, then slapped them on her thigh. "What did I tell you? She's rich!"

"Animals?" Calixte asked.

"Already dead, cut in pieces, and wrapped in plastic."

"Ça! Comment!" the mayor's wife was in spasms.

They agreed that it's no wonder I don't know how to do anything in the kitchen.

"I bet someone washes your dishes for you," Calixte asked.

"Some people have machines that do it for you," I replied.

That really did it. Now Calixte really got upset. How could life be so unfair?

"You can't cook, and you can't do dishes!"

Another woman jumped in and said, "No wonder you're not married."

The women laughed at me again.

"That's not true," I said, too afraid of what they might say if I revealed that I had been married. "I know how to cook different dishes in the kitchen."

The women looked up at me from their buckets as if I were joking.

"What do you know how to cook?" asked Calixte. She stirred the pot again and then wiped the sweat from her forehead.

"It's true," said Clotilde, coming to my defense, "she can cook."

"I can cook Italian, Chinese, French, Mexican, and Japanese," I said proudly.

Mom, there's no way that I'm going to let them insult your daughter like that. I learned to cook from you, and you learned from Grandma, and she learned from her mom, and so on and so forth.

"Well, then," said Calixte, "you must cook Italian for the mayor and me."

"I'd like to, but I can't." I pushed my peanut bucket aside and helped Clotilde take the leaves off the branches.

"And why not?" she asked, standing up to move her stool away from the smoke of the fire.

"The ingredients for Italian food are very expensive. I'm not paid enough to buy those kinds of foods. The idea of the Peace Corps is to live at the level of the teachers I work with and to be paid accordingly."

The teachers' wives quickly agreed that I don't have enough money to cook Italian food.

"You didn't bring any money with you from America?" asked Calixte, as if that were the craziest thing she's ever heard.

"The Peace Corps told us not to bring any money. They'd like to get rid of the 'rich American' idea that everyone has in mind."

"But all Americans are rich," said Calixte. She scooted her stool near another woman and helped her peel potatoes.

"We have homeless people in America," I said.

"Homeless?" Calixte asks. "What does that mean, *homeless*?"

Everyone stopped cleaning, cutting, slicing, rinsing, and peeling.

"Some Americans don't have family or friends. Maybe they lost their job and then their house and they're on the streets trying to live in a cardboard box."

"That would never happen in Cameroon! Why doesn't anyone take them into their home? Get them on their feet?" Calixte asks, as if there were a simple solution.

"There are too many to help," I said.

The women shook their heads, not understanding how we could have clean rice, shelled peanuts, dead and cleaned chickens, but also homeless people on the streets. Then they went back to work.

"I think your country shouldn't kill chickens for people until the homeless have a home."

"And no one should have a machine that washes dishes until everyone has a place to sleep," said Clotilde.

"I agree," said I, wondering how America is ever going to achieve better results if we keep on doing what we're doing.

There is a long pause in the conversation as the women continue working; then Calixte says, "If the mayor gives you the money, can you make Italian food for us? I want a taste of America."

Love,
Suz

Clap! Clap! Pause. Clap! Clap! Clap!

I look up from the letter I'm writing, and my heart leaps. I recognize the pattern of the clapping. Lydie is back!

I jump out of my seat and run out the door.

"Lydie!" I say, grabbing her and squeezing her tight.

"Good to see you, Miss," Lydie says. She greets me with a laugh and a French-style peck on each cheek. Her eyelashes tickle my face like butterfly kisses.

"Miss, guavas have come to Guidiguis!" Lydie says, and hands me a bag of ripe guavas with a juicy smile.

"Lydie! Please come in!"

I push the mosquito net aside, and Lydie walks through, lighting up the room with her smile. I take a guava out of the bag and sink my teeth into its sweetness.

"You need to wash them first, Miss, or you'll get sick."

In all the excitement of seeing Lydie again and having fresh fruit, I've forgotten about getting amoebic dysentery. I spit out my next bite in the palm of my hand but worry it's too late. I imagine critters already growing in my belly.

Lydie follows me into the kitchen, where she takes my guava and pours water over it from a plastic teakettle. She scrubs the yellow skin with her nails and then examines it closely.

"Now you can eat it," Lydie says, and hands it to me.

"Where have you been?" I ask, wondering how much of the truth I'll hear.

Lydie doesn't answer. She plops down on the mat and picks up a pillow, holding it against her chest. Her eyes focus on an ant struggling to carry a large crumb above his body.

"I've missed you at school," I say.

"I visited my big sister in Kaele," Lydie says, and leans forward to get a better look at the ant, which is determined to get the crumb home.

"I haven't seen you since the morning you learned to ride a bike," I say. She settles back on her pillow and looks into my eyes for the first time. But something's missing. Where has the fire gone?

"Yes, Miss," she says, and lowers her eyes. "You see, my brother didn't ask what happened to me, why my legs were bleeding. He assumed I'd been on my knees in the bushes with a village boy. He threw me out of the house."

"Lydie, why didn't you tell me?"

"Miss, I didn't want to involve you in this thing."

"But you're my friend. If you need something, I'm here to help."

"Miss, you help me."

"Why didn't you tell your brother what really happened?"

"I knew it would make him even angrier," she says, and turns her gaze to the little ant. It stops and walks over its crumb several times.

"Then how did he find out?" I ask, my mind racing in different directions.

"My big sister knew I couldn't have done such a thing. She asked for the truth and then wrote my brother a letter. Soon after, he spoke with you. Miss, I know he said many things that hurt."

I nod, remembering my confusion after speaking with Mr. Mfoumba.

The ant picks up its crumb and carries it above its body again.

"He's jealous that you are free to live your life the way you choose," Lydie says.

We are silent for a moment, she in her thoughts, I in mine.

I am free.

I forget that I'm free until someone points it out. A definition of real freedom has only begun to take shape and form since my arrival. I'm only beginning to understand how much I have; Lydie is beginning to see how much she doesn't.

"I'm sorry, Lydie. I didn't realize the price you'd pay for daring to learn how to—"

"Miss," Lydie interrupts, "the price is nothing. Do you think he can take away what you put inside? You are here only once in my life. I want to learn a different way from you. I want to be strong enough to be myself."

"Lydie, I think you're showing me what strength is."

Out of the corner of our eyes, we see the ant making a fuss. It climbs over the crumb and stands on top of it as if telling it to behave. Then the ant climbs down off it and resumes its work with new fervor. It never gives up.

"Lydie, what do you want to do?" I ask, and lean back against the wall next to her. We both look out the window, our eyes chasing our dreams.

"To go to school. I want to be a teacher. I know that I can be, instead of only *wanting* to be."

"I know the feeling," I say.

"Do you think our lives are any different from the little ant over there? We carry our wishes on our backs and climb the long road home. We stop every now and then and get angry that it isn't any easier. But the bigger our dreams, the heavier the load. Because there are those who will laugh and tell us that our crumbs are too big to carry."

"Yes," I say. Her wisdom makes me smile.

Truth is powerful enough that one needs only to speak it simply and softly.

I close my eyes and imagine Lydie flying her dreams like a kite and chasing them along a beach in the sun.

35. LIZARD SPEAKS

She sleeps underneath a sea of stars
While night's stowaways tresspass in her dreams.

I journey across inner tempests
To navigate her through,
To free her from ghosts storming her peace.

I discovered her soul crouched in darkness
Taking refuge in the cave of lost children.
I saw her crying and tearing at her skin,
Scratching at thorns embedded deep in flesh,
Blood and pus oozing out of infected wounds.

I reach out to her, and she turns away,
Knowing I am here to retrieve her
Spirit, breath, and song.

Too frightened to return to her body,
She runs from me as if I am
The stranger
Who grabbed her on the beach
And crumpled her up,
Who threw her in the car like
Paper in a wastebasket,
Who forced himself inside her,
Ripping and tearing the tiny opening
Of her seven-year-old body.

Her only resistance was for her soul
To scramble and fly away,
To watch her child's testimony
Before a judge from a great distance.
Her existence became numbness and darkness,
A hiding from bearing witness to the sun.

With a shaman's ceremony of drums
I will bring her home,
Removing the haunting from her flesh,
Opening inner eyes to truth
And leading her out to the light.
I will hold a mirror up
So that she may recognize her radiance.

I wake up to see Doc's eyes wide open and staring at me.

"I can't sleep," he says. "It's too hot. This is hell, isn't it?"

"At least we're together," I say dryly. Then I turn over and put the pillow over my head, hoping he'll get the hint.

"That didn't help. I still can't sleep," he cries.

"Well, I can, so shhh!"

Hastily, I turn over, fluff my pillow, and sigh. If I have to spend one more night without sleep and listen to his paranoia all night long . . .

Doc settles down, and just when I'm drifting off to sleep, he asks, "Suz, are you awake?"

"No, I'm not!" I say, turning onto my back and flinging my eyes open to stare at the stars and wonder if love is really worth all this trouble.

It's too hot to sleep inside, but in being outside, Doc wakes up at every little noise. He often bolts up, turns on the flashlight, points it around the compound, and asks, "What's that? Did you hear that? Is someone trying to break in? Are those scorpions? A spider crawling? Is that a snake I see over there? Shouldn't we go inside?"

I haven't gotten a good night's sleep in a week.

I guess sometimes that's the way it goes—the one you love is the sole person who can irritate you beyond reason. Didn't someone say somewhere that love brings up everything unlike itself? At the moment, I'm experiencing raw annoyance and strong feelings of dislike, and the poor guy really didn't do anything. I guess I've always believed in living happily ever after. But then is this what love is all about—loving through the moments of being fed up, annoyed, and wanting out?

Doc turns over and stares at the stars with me.

"Ever wonder if the wishes you make upon stars will really come true? Or if we do write our fates in the café in the clouds as you suggested?"

"Doc, I'm trying to sleep, and you're being philosophical."

"Well, if I can't sleep, I'm certainly not going to let you!"

Doc moves to the end of the bed and tickles my feet. I never should have taught him that trick. It's backfired on me a number of times.

"OK, I'm awake, now stop!" I say, but he's learned how to be stubborn. I don't think I've been a good influence.

"Shhh. You'll wake the neighbors!" I hiss, annoyed that his laughter and playfulness are always so uninhibited even though I've expressed my desire to keep from flaunting our relationship to everyone.

"I had a terrible dream."

"Again?" I ask.

"It must be your cooking." Doc says. "It's giving me bad gas."

I strike him with a pillow.

"It's true," and he laughs, even though he knows I'm sensitive about my cooking. How the heck am I supposed to cook decent food when they have none of the ingredients that I'm used to here? Locusts, goat meat, powdered couscous, leaves, onions, and peanut butter don't exactly spell gourmet food to me.

"Well, maybe you should cook more often!" I say angrily.

He woke me up for this? A good night's sleep in the desert is hard to get, and I get woken up for our first fight.

"That's all right by me, but that really is a woman's duty. You should learn how to stay in your place."

"What? My place?! A woman has her place? Thank God I was born American and not African! I'd hate to have to slave over you for the rest of my life!" I sit up in bed and wonder why I ever thought that a relationship with someone of a completely different culture would work.

"Look, you're sleeping here more and more often, and I really think I could use some space now and then. I don't need your protection. I survived my first months here just fine before you came along. And I used to actually get some decent sleep without you waking me up every time the wind blows."

"I'm sorry I have been such a nuisance to you. I can leave."

Doc bangs his shoes on the side of the bed and gets dressed.

"You know, I have an important job—a job that I love. It's not a matter of life and death, but I need to get enough rest so I can give my students a decent lesson. I'd appreciate it if you'd respect that."

"I'm sorry I awoke you. I only wanted to tell you how much I don't want you to return to the States."

"You see, that's my point. You're so romantic, you can't even see straight! It's not even a matter of you considering leaving and coming with me to America. Since I'm the woman, it should be me who sacrifices. I'm telling you, Doc, I am not going to stay in Cameroon. I couldn't spend the rest of my life serving you and making your babies."

Doc puts on his shoes and gets the car keys out of his pocket. I didn't really want him to go, but I don't know how to ask him to stay at this point in the argument.

"Doc, sometimes I don't know what's going on inside me."

"I know what's going on inside of you, but when will I ever hear you say 'I love you'?"

"Perhaps I don't!" I say, and I don't know why I said that. He knows I'm lying, but he storms off.

I wish I could take those words back.

Why did I want to hurt him? Although I'm angry that he thinks he knows me better than I know myself, it's more about the fact that he won't even consider coming with me to the States.

But why should it be me who stays?

I have dreams of being a teacher of a class smaller than 100 students, with carpets and recess and a desk not being eaten by termites.

I bang the shoes on the bed, move to the latrine, and pour a bucket of water over my head. It's as if there's a fire outside and a fire raging inside me, too.

Sali is sewing on the buttons to my new blue suit when I walk into his compound. The suit looks just as I described it, and I'm excited to have something comfortable and beautiful to wear to school. Sali has sand on his forehead since he's just come back from praying at the mosque. My hand wants to wipe it off, but I know he's as proud of the sand as Christians are of the crosses they wear.

Sali greets me in Fulfulde, declaring that God is great and God is good.

"*Ah hum didlee aye!*" Sali says.

I raise my hands, saying, "Yes, indeed, God is great and very, very good."

Sakinatou sees me as she's returning from the well. "*Suzanne-dee!*" she shouts.

The children inside the compound hear my name and come to greet me. They run full force into my arms and hug my legs, singing out my name while jumping up and down. They ask me to pick them up because they want to fly.

God is great and God is good: I'm thankful for friends I've made and for Sali's family embracing me when I'm suffering from loneliness. But I haven't seen or heard from Doc in a week. I didn't realize I'd miss him so much.

Sali yells at the children to sit and be quiet. They do so without hesitation. His eyebrows are pinched tightly together.

Something's wrong. What is it? What can I do to help?

Sali says something about his mother's being very *eeowdou*.

I ask in French, "*Qu'est-ce-que c'est 'eeowdou'?*"

Sali demonstrates by bending over holding his stomach and moaning.

How do I say *help* in Fulfulde? I try in French.

"*Je voudrais vous aider,*" I say, and point inside the compound. Sali doesn't understand, but Sakinatou translates for her father. After he replies, Sakinatou sets her bucket down, takes me by the hand, and leads me into their compound.

Inside, I discover Sali's mother, Dada, flat on her back, moaning. There's no one with her; she's alone under a straw ceiling held up by tree branches in the center of the compound. Her eyes are closed, and I'm afraid of her opening them and being upset to find me.

Sali's wife is sifting millet powder outside a round mud hut. Sakinatou says that the woman bent over scrubbing the family's clothing in a large metal bucket is Sali's older sister. The other woman, chopping wood with a machete, is Sali's youngest sister. A two-year-old boy toddles around the compound, looking like the king of the castle. He marches to his mother, leans over her clothes, pulls on the breast swinging back and forth, and sticks it in his mouth. He suckles, then discards it when done.

The women look at me and nod, too busy with their work to greet me formally. Maybe they don't like my being here. It's hard to tell since they seem so indifferent. I almost regret offering to help.

Sakinatou tells me in French that her grandmother has been sick for two days.

"Will she see a doctor?" I ask.

Sakinatou frowns and shakes her head. "Women don't go to doctors," she says. I knew that—didn't I? I think of Aïssatou and close my eyes. I see her face and her family, who treated her no differently than this.

"It may be serious, and there's a good doctor in Guidiguis," I say, insisting on making this time different, and at the same time hoping for an excuse to go see Doc.

"No, Dada has never left the compound."

Oh. I see.

"Do men go to the doctor?"

"Sometimes," she says.

We approach Dada, who opens her eyes and looks at me for awhile. She closes them and moans in pain. Doc needs to see her.

I kneel on the edge of the mat and wonder what I can possibly do to help. When I put my hand on her forehead, her eyes pop open. She looks into my eyes, but this time, her gaze is gentle and sweet, so I don't move my hand. There's no temperature, a good sign. I smile to reassure her that I'm going to take care of her.

The old woman's ancient eyes melt into a pool of black fire that sweeps across the space between us. A flame ignites inside me, and for a moment our souls communicate in a language that only spirit speaks. She extends her hand, and I take it. Tears spill out of my eyes in celebration of the trust she's put in me. I pledge to myself that I won't let her down.

"*Me oudou. Me oudou jour,*" she says.

"*Ah eedee dofta, nah?*" I ask.

She waves her hand—no she doesn't need a doctor—but she squeezes tighter.

"*Me oudou, Suzannedee.*"

She puts my hand on her extremely bloated stomach. I gently push the sarong down her waist to examine it more closely. Her belly is hard, as if something's alive inside. She won't go to the doctor, but maybe he can come here. I'm sure he sees these symptoms all the time and knows exactly what to do. As I stand up, Dada holds my hand tighter. I ask Sakinatou to explain that I'll return with something to help her.

Dada looks in my eyes and squeezes her eyes shut and then opens them; it's as if she's winking at me with both eyes.

I repeat what Sakinatou tells Dada. She pats my hand and then lets it go. She closes her eyes, and I can feel her faith swelling up inside my heart. As I'm walking out of their compound, a million questions fill my head. Were they going to just let her lie there in pain until she died? Was her fate to be the same as Aïssatou's? Is that why Dada's eyes reached out to me? Am I her only hope of getting better?

I feel responsible for Dada as a daughter would feel about her mother. Although I'm worried about Dada, I smile at the realization that I've become a part of Sali's family.

38. THE HOSPITAL

I'm riding my bicycle into the hospital grounds, completely un-prepared for what I see. The hospital consists of two white cement buildings about 200 feet apart with broken windows and very old paint. A limp Cameroonian flag hangs from a pole between the buildings where sick people rest and wait. Tapouri men and women are camped out in front, lying on plastic mats and wrapped in sarongs. Over twenty crying children, their bellies swollen and aching, are being soothed by their mothers. I hear a woman screaming from inside the hospital, and I stop my bike.

How can I ask Doc to make a house call? If he's the only doctor in Guidiguis, how does he cope with over 100 patients desperately needing care? How does he ever manage to get away from the hospital?

As I walk through the entrance, I see floors covered with people moaning, crying, and yelling for the doctor. Those near the door see me, and one pulls at my ankles, pleading with me to help him. He asks for medicine, and I can only shake my head. The smell is overwhelming. It's as if someone had died and had gone unnoticed for quite some time among the sick crowded together on the floor.

I cover my nose and run outside. I lean against the building and wait for the sky above me to stop spinning.

I see Doc rushing to the main building, speaking angrily to a male nurse. Doc sees me but passes as if I don't exist. "Doc?"

No response.

"Doc?"

Doc spins around and charges toward me like an angry bull.

"What do you think you're doing here?" he demands.

"I need your help," I say, my voice shaking

"You shouldn't have come! You know there are lepers here, AIDS patients, and others with illnesses you could easily catch. Go home immediately! I don't ever want to see you here again!"

"Doc, please, listen. I think Dada, I mean, my Foulbe mother, has worms. She's in pain but can't come to the hospital. Women from Foulbe families don't get treatment and—"

"Suzanne," Doc interrupts, "people are dying as we are speaking, and you want me to save your friend a little discomfort? Don't you hear the woman screaming? She and her baby will die if I don't go now. Your friend will live. Believe me."

Doc turns and leaves.

Tears are falling down my cheeks, making it difficult to see the road ahead as I ride through the village. I can't return to Dada empty-handed; I need to come through for her.

At the *carrefour*, the Foulbe merchants holler and wave when they see me riding. Saidou, seated in front of his piles of guavas, waves for me to stop. I continue riding, not wanting anyone to see me crying. Saidou stands up suddenly and comes running into the street.

I stop the bike and quickly wipe away the tears.

"Jam bah doo nah, Suzannedee?"

I shake my head.

Saidou asks what's ailing me, and it all comes out. Sali's mother is sick with worms, I don't have any medication to help her, the doctor is too busy to help me because there are so many sick people in Guidiguis. People are dying. A woman is screaming.

Saidou puts his hand up for me to stop; he understands. He borrows a bicycle from another merchant and tells me to follow him home.

When we arrive Saidou shows me a modern cement house, which he and his family don't live in. He uses it for storing merchandise he sells at the market. He takes me to the back of his house, where his family lives traditionally. Six mud huts make a circle, and three women are working on the noon meal. Saidou's eight children are eating out of one bowl on a mat near their mothers. They stick their right hands into a bowl, tearing off a piece of the thick porridge. They shape it into a ball and dip it in an oil sauce, then they put it into their mouths. No wonder so many in Guidiguis are sick.

Saidou calls his mother to come out of a mud hut. She greets me as if we're long-lost friends. Saidou says something in Fulfulde that I can't make out, but I'm sure she thinks I'm going to be her next daughter-in-law. She excitedly shakes my hand, repeating my name over and over again.

Saidou leads me back to his storage house. As I enter, I discover a gold mine. There are boxes and boxes of toilet paper. He urges me to buy what I need. I grab a couple of rolls and look around for other things: batteries, matches, a kerosene lamp, a cheap flashlight, peanut oil, powdered milk, and detergent.

Meanwhile, Saidou is rummaging through his treasures. Finally, he locates a Nigerian bottle of tablets to treat worms. I thank him for all his trouble but am concerned about two things: will anything made in Nigeria really work, and what do I have to do in return?

Knowing how desperate I am to help Dada, Saidou is not going to budge. He reminds me how easy it is to buy the things from him that I need within the village. He'll continue to be convenient if I pay the right price.

If the medicine doesn't work, at least I've shown Dada that I care enough to help. I'm sure she'll appreciate the medicine, and I pray that it works.

As I'm walking home I realize that I need to find a way to apologize to Doc and ask him to forgive me.

I need to tell Doc that I love him.

I'm sleeping outside when I'm awakened by the sound of a motorcycle speeding down the street. I hear the usual bats screeching inside the roof of my house, but they no longer keep me awake, so I quickly fall back to sleep. But then I bolt up in bed; I hear a woman running through the village and screaming.

Lanterns are lit throughout the neighborhood. I hear Clotilde's footsteps and Alex's sobbing as they come over by flashlight. Clotilde claps twice and enters my compound. She shakes my hand as she sits on my bed and rocks Alex back to sleep. I light a lantern, wondering what has happened.

"It's something horrible," she says. "Yves is getting dressed and riding to the *carrefour*. We'll wait together until he comes back."

"Someone is dead?" I ask, and Clotilde nods.

Another clap at the entrance, and we welcome Valentine and her twins; they all come in and sit on my bed. The boys give me big kisses.

"What's going on?" Valentine asks.

"A mother's son has died," Clotilde says.

Clap! Clap!

Adele comes in and climbs on the bed, sucking her thumb. She hugs me and sits on my lap.

Clap! Clap! Pause. Clap! Clap! Clap!

"It's me, Miss. It's Lydie."

"Come in!" We yell in French at the same time and laugh. Lydie enters and also sits next to me.

Clap! Clap! Clap! Clap!

A woman I've never met comes into the compound and shakes my hand. She's Pauline, Adele's mother. Her baby boy is strapped to her back; she unties her sarong and moves him into her arms, then sits and shakes everyone's hand.

"Would anyone like something to drink?" I ask.

Everyone says yes. I go into the house and turn on the lights.

"Need any help?" Lydie asks.

"Sure," I say.

We see a rat scurry across the floor. I scream at the surprise.

"I hate rats," I say.

"Me, too," Lydie says. "They're dirty."

"Are you both OK in there?" Valentine sings out, and laughs.

"A rat scared me, that's all," I say.

"If you tell a student, they'll catch it for you and eat it," Lydie says.

"They eat them?" I ask, stunned.

"In the desert, they eat anything they can," Lydie says, and opens the fridge.

I wonder to myself if I've eaten a rat, cat, or dog at someone's house? Thinking it impolite, I never asked what it was I was eating.

"I don't have enough cups for everyone," I say, taking out four plastic cups. I grab two bottles of water and one bottle of cherry Kool-Aid.

"We'll share, Miss," Lydie says. I offer her the first drink, but she shakes her head. "I'll wait." We bring the cups and bottles out. Lydie fills the cup and offers everyone their choice of water or Kool-Aid.

Clap! Clap!

Egré and Abbo call out their names as they enter the compound. At first, I'm surprised to see Abbo because his family lives in a faraway village, but then I remember that he's been staying with Egré during the school week and only going to his village on weekends.

Egré sits on the bed with us, but Abbo only shakes everyone's hand, then sits against the wall of my house.

"There have been too many disturbances tonight," Egré says. "It's not safe in Guidiguis."

Abbo explains that a Tapouri woman's son was killed. Thank goodness something woke us up because a group of Chadians were stealing everything in sight while we were sleeping.

Since all of us gathered here are foreigners to the desert, we asked for a little more in-depth explanation about the Chadians.

"Chadians are worse off than Cameroonians," Egré says. "They'll even eat fish eyes. During the dry season, people sleep outside, and they sleep very deeply. The Chadians walk across the borders and set up camp in the bush, only a few miles away from a nearby village. While we were sleeping, they were walking through Guidiguis stealing everything in sight: animals, clothes, dishes, bags of corn and millet, machetes, buckets, and anything else they could get their hands on."

Everyone looks at each other in surprise. We thought it was safe to sleep outside in Guidiguis; the locals do, and they've never said anything about Chadians.

"Are you serious?" Valentine asks Egré.

"Yes, the Chadians are a problem. You should lock your door and set a trap."

Abbo stands and steps into the lantern light. "Miss," Abbo says softly, "I'm worried for your safety. How wise is it for a white woman to sleep outside on her own?"

The women nod and verbally agree with Abbo.

"The Chadians could enter your compound," Egré says, "take the key from around your neck, open the door to your house, and take your stereo, cassettes, and all your valuables."

I couldn't live without music. They have a point: I shouldn't sleep outside alone.

"Stealing would be the least of their crimes, Miss," Abbo says.

The women talk about how terrible it is to live in fear. The southerners are appalled at the Chadians and reminisce about how safe it is back home. The women hate the extreme north of Cameroon and can't wait until their husbands get appointed elsewhere.

"Miss, why did you ask to be sent to Guidiguis?" Pauline asks.

"I didn't ask. The Peace Corps sent me here. I was hoping for the beach."

They laugh at my misfortune.

"Miss, please," Abbo says seriously, "let Egré and me guard you."

"We are scared for you, Miss," Egré says. "You need to adopt us as your sons."

The women encourage me to take Abbo and Egré up on their offer. They think I'm crazy for having slept outside on my own. I'm lucky, they say. Something could have happened.

"OK, Abbo, Egré, your job starts tomorrow night. Be here by nine o'clock."

They sit down against the front door.

"We start right now," Abbo says. "We will protect you as we would our own mother."

Two motorcycles speed up to my house. Yves, the other English teacher, Benito, and Valentine's husband, the gendarme, turn their motorcycles off. They walk through the entrance without clapping.

"A Tapouri boy by the name of François and a young Foulbe motorcycle driver have been killed," Yves says.

"Their murderer has not been found," Benito adds.

"François? François with one leg?" I ask, covering my mouth to stifle a cry. I'd begun to think of him as my future adopted son.

"Yes. François was coming home from selling at the market on the back of a motorcycle. A truck with no headlights ran them over," Benito says.

Tears well up in my eyes. In Africa, life is here and then gone so quickly.

"They brought the boys' brains to their mothers and pieces of their bodies they scraped off the road in plastic bags," Valentine's husband says. He picks up both of the twins in his arms and kisses their cheeks. Yves takes Alex from Clotilde's arms and holds him while he sleeps. Benito excuses himself and drives home to his family.

"We caught the Chadians," the gendarme says.

We cheer and promise each other to be more careful.

Abbo puts a hand on my shoulder. "*Asha*, Miss. I know you're sad for François."

I look at Abbo, confused.

"*Asha* means I'm sorry for your pain," Abbo explains.

The women, husbands, boys, and children sit with me in the darkness for what seems like hours.

When they leave, they wish me a safe journey through my sleep. I say a prayer that we will all live through another night. I thank God for my friends. I am blessed.

It's 125 degrees Fahrenheit. I'm teaching my students about nouns. There are only seventy-five sixth graders in this class, and I'm grateful for not having thirty more bodies. The crayons just might have melted. I hand out a crayon to each student; they've never seen one before, especially not these scented crayons my mother sent. One student figures out that his yellow crayon smells like a banana and puts it in his mouth to take a bite.

When I notice, I call everyone to attention and hold a paper up so they can see my example of an orange tree. I pass it around and ask the students to smell the drawing. They smell their crayons and then draw pictures of nouns we've learned. When they hold their noses up to the paper to smell the scent, they laugh and share it with their neighbors.

We draw everything we can see and name: trees, cows, donkeys, the sun, sand, a hand, a foot, a face, a school, a Cameroonian flag, a boy, a girl, an American teacher, a boy riding a motorcycle, a mud hut, a clear sky, a passenger on the back of the motorcycle, a uniform, Lydie clapping at my door—just arriving.

I instruct the class to continue drawing everything they see as I go to the door. Lydie's eyes are wide, and her hands are shaking.

"Miss, there's an emergency," Lydie says, trying to catch her breath.

"What is it, Lydie? Are you all right?" I ask.

Lydie shakes her head. "I was in science class when Yves was called out by a motorcycle driver. His wife is in the hospital. Clotilde has lost her unborn baby."

"No, not the baby. No. Clotilde."

"Miss, you must come now," Lydie says.

"But my class, Lydie. I can't leave without permission. The principal isn't here."

"She may die, Miss, she's bleeding," Lydie's voice cracks, and she holds back the tears.

I take the key from around my neck and give it to Lydie.

"Go to my house and get my bike. Ride it to the *carrefour*. Tell a driver to come collect me. Tell them it's an emergency. I'll see you at the hospital."

In fifteen minutes, a motorcycle comes for me. If the principal asks where I went, I'll tell him my presence was requested and I couldn't argue. I dismiss the class early for lunch, and they're overjoyed since the smells of the crayons have made them hungry.

While holding onto the speeding Foulbe motorcycle driver's waist for dear life, I wonder if Doc will yell at me for returning to the hospital. I'm sure he's cooled off by now and is missing sleeping outside and making wishes upon falling stars.

When I arrive at the hospital, Lydie is waiting outside. A little six-year-old Foulbe boy stands in front of my bike, guarding it with his life. Lydie introduces me, and he shakes my hand, then asks me to pick him up and twirl him around like an airplane. News travels fast. I promise him that when I return, I'll pick him up.

Lydie leads me by the hand into the hospital. Yves, Valentine, Pauline, and Calixte are sitting on a blanket outside the operating room. I raise my hands up to greet everyone, but there are no smiles and no news of how Clotilde is doing.

Lydie and I sit on the blanket. When I start to cry, she puts her hand on mine.

"These times are hard," Valentine says to me while breast-feeding one of the twins, "but we've got to be strong for those who need us." Yves stands up and paces in the few feet of space we have between us and the patients lying on the floor.

"She's too skinny to hold a baby in her belly," says Calixte. "She needs some fat covering those bones in order to feed the baby while it grows in her."

"This is the third baby she's lost!" Yves shouts, then begins pacing again.

"Whose fault is that?" Calixte says. "She walks through the village looking like a skeleton. You spend money on things instead of your own family."

Valentine stands up and waves her finger at Yves and Calixte. "Shhh. Clotilde's spirit can hear us. She just might want to leave if she hears us arguing. We've got to be strong if we want to keep her here."

Yves walks away and out the door. I'm not sure whom he's angry at the most. "Clotilde won't go anywhere. She's got Alex to make into a man," says Lydie.

"A better man than that husband of hers," Calixte says. She takes a brush out of her purse and starts brushing my hair.

"Calixte, stay out of their business," says Valentine. "You don't need enemies in your village, certainly not the husband of your best friend."

When Calixte finishes with my hair, I leap up and start pacing. The women fall into silence and wait. These women are used to waiting.

I hate waiting.

I can't stand the wretched smell of the hospital and how death knocks on everybody's door. Life isn't precious here. You're alive today and gone tomorrow. Will I make it through my time left in Guidiguis? How do I know that the African desert won't kill me? That's the problem: you live your life as if you have time, but you never know when death will take your soul away.

What follows death? Why don't we know? I'd do anything to find out where we go and what we do there. Maybe we come back again. How else can I explain why there's so much between Doc and me? From our first meeting, I've felt as if I've known him all my life. Who knows? With all this time on my hands, it's interesting to daydream about how life might be if . . .

Doc's assistant cracks open the door and looks at us. My heart skips a beat, and I hold my breath for word about Clotilde's status. The assistant steps out of the room and looks both ways for Yves. The women stand up to receive the news, but he only turns back inside to Doc to say that her husband is not there. I peek through the crack and see the other assistant taking off Doc's gloves. I can't see Clotilde, nor can I read Doc's face. The assistant closes the door, and we settle in for more waiting. Lydie sits back down, then suddenly leaps up and heads out to find Yves.

Doc opens the door, and I rush to him, tears flowing down my cheeks. He puts his hand on my shoulder and smiles. He waits for the other women to gather around. As he starts to speak, Lydie and Yves walk through the door.

"There was a lot of internal bleeding that was difficult to stop, but she's fine." We breathe more easily.

"She's going to need rest and help in the kitchen. I won't release her from the hospital for three days. We'll see how she recovers. Yves, she'll need some medication you can purchase at the front desk."

Yves nods his head and asks, "When can I see her?"

"Come tomorrow morning. She'll be sleeping all afternoon and night."

"Thank you, Doc," I say. "You saved her life."

I long to be held in Doc's arms again and tell him what I've been hiding in my heart.

Doc squeezes my shoulder again, and I smile. I'm glad he's not angry with me for returning to the hospital.

As if reading my mind, he says, "I still don't think you should be here. Your immune system is not strong enough to take the impact of the diseases in the hospital."

"Thank you for letting me stay," I say, realizing how much I've missed him.

"How is your Foulbe mother doing?" Doc asks.

"OK. I bought Nigerian medicine. Saidou says it works."

"Maybe. Maybe not. I'll bring some medicine when I come see you," he says. With those words, I light up like the sun bursting through the darkness.

"And something for amoebas," I say glumly. I know it's my fault I'm sick.

"Who else are you trying to cure?" Doc asks with a smile.

"Me. I ate a guava without washing it. Two, that is. I ate two guavas," I confess.

"Be careful. I don't want anything more to happen to you while you're here. Remember my promise to your mother?"

Doc squeezes my hand, and I try not to look so happy during this emergency.

"Go home. I'll send word of her condition if I can't come to see you myself."

I join the women outside, and they follow Yves with angry eyes as he speeds off on a motorcycle.

"What is it?" I ask Lydie.

"Yves won't pay the 10,000 francs for the medication Clotilde needs."

"He really doesn't care if she lives or dies," Calixte says.

"He's stubborn with his money, that's all. He's worried about the future. Maybe suffering a little pain now will help them not to suffer so much later," Valentine says.

"Yves knows he can depend on other people's good hearts to help his wife. He stands back knowing full well we'll come up with the money."

"I'll pay it," I say. "I don't want Clotilde to suffer a moment longer."

"It's not your responsibility," Calixte interrupts. "That man needs to learn how to take care of his family. I won't let you pay."

"Clotilde has been my friend since the first night I arrived. She never let me suffer as long as she could help it. I'm going to pay for all of us. We'll ask Doc not to tell her anything so she'll be able to believe her husband paid it."

"It's not right," Calixte says. "You'll regret this."

"Maybe so. We'll see."

Calixte arrives as she promised, with all the ingredients to make a pizza. I tell her to send the car back at seven o'clock, and I'll come with the meal. Calixte asks if I'd like her to invite the doctor, and I say yes. Although I've never expressed my feelings for him to anyone, it must be written all over my face.

I'm disappointed that Doc hasn't come to visit in two days. It seems as if he doesn't care if I'm sick or not or how worried I've been about Clotilde. It's OK, I tell myself; he must be busy at the hospital. And anyway, I'm leaving in nine months. Funny, I think to myself, time enough to birth a child before I return home. During these last months in Cameroon, it is I who is getting ready to be born.

I feel a clarity, an understanding that continuing with Doc would not only be painful when I leave, but it would probably prevent this chrysalis phase that I've been going through to finally reach a point of maturation. I need to go through this journey on my own in order to learn the lessons necessary to grow. Maybe this caterpillar really is becoming a butterfly.

As Calixte gets into the car, I run back to her and knock on her window.

"Don't invite the doctor, Calixte. He's very busy."

Calixte smiles and rolls the window back up as her driver speeds her away.

I walk over to Lydie's house and invite her to help me, since Abbo and Egré don't seem to like my cooking. They've only moved in three days ago, and they're already complaining behind my back. They say it's too spicy (Chinese food) and too difficult to eat (Mexican food). Tonight they've both decided to eat with their families, saying they've been taking advantage of my generous nature for far too long.

But I'm not sure they're being honest. The other day, I heard Abbo and Egré speaking a mixture of French and Tapouri while washing dishes and clothes on the front porch.

Egré said something about seeing me run scared out of the latrine.

"Yeah," Abbo said, "she still had her skirt pulled up around her hips, screaming at the top of her lungs, just because she saw a tiny scorpion."

"Listen to this," Egré said, "before she smashed a cricket with her tennis shoe, she said 'Sorry, Mr. Cricket,' but he was making too much noise singing some love song, and she couldn't sleep."

"I've seen her talk to lizards, too!" said Abbo. "Don't tell anyone!"

"I won't," Egré said. "The villagers already think that she's—"

"She won't even kill a lizard."

"I know. She persuades them to 'kindly get out of her house,' " Egré said.

"Do they?" Abbo asked.

"They do," Egré said.

"Did you have stomach pains last night?" Abbo asked.

"Yes. Did you see how she smashed the beans and then cooked them again? Do you think we should tell her she shouldn't do that? I know that's why I had terrible bubbles all night."

"I don't know. You know how women are about their cooking. Miss might be insulted by our advice," said Abbo.

I'm not insulted. But Cameroonian teenagers are a lot harder to parent than I thought. I didn't like the fried locusts they prepared for dinner that much either, so I'll call it even. I do plan on saving them a slice of pizza. Who in the world doesn't like pizza?

Lydie and I pour the flour and roll the dough to make pizza crust. I've never actually made pizza crust from scratch, but Vann passed on a Peace Corps cookbook with a recipe for pizza. She said it was just like making tortillas, only bigger and thicker.

As we roll the dough for two pizzas with a beer bottle, Lydie and I have a terrible time keeping the sweat from dripping off our noses into the dough.

"Miss, any word about Clotilde?"

"No, I haven't heard anything from Yves or the doctor."

"That must mean good news," Lydie says, and I agree.

We slap and roll the dough in silence, discovering that pounding it as hard as we can seems to be enjoyable.

"What is Italy like?" Lydie asks.

I describe the Italian history I know: the influence of Catholicism on the art, the great painters, the opera, the landscape, the wine, and the food.

"Oh, Miss, whenever you tell me about another way of life, my heart hurts. Everywhere else is better than here."

"That's because you only ask to know the good things about other places. I can tell you the problems if that would make you feel better."

"Yes, please tell me the problems."

We chop onions and cry together as I describe drug addicts, mass murderers, terrorists, the homeless, and world war until Lydie tells me to stop or we'll spoil the pizza sauce. Lydie says that what you talk about while cooking dinner has a lot to do with the way the meal turns out.

We finish cutting the cheese into tiny pieces and spread it over the tomato sauce. We finally put the pizza in the oven when the boys come home. The first thing they say when they walk through the door is that something smells delicious.

I puff my chest out and tell them they are about to have the most divine eating experience of their lives. They try not to laugh because I said that about the meal when I cooked Chinese and Mexican.

When the pizza is done cooking, I bring it proudly to the table and cut them each a slice. Egré takes a bite and burns his tongue. I tell them to blow on it, and they look at me strangely. I demonstrate by blowing on their pizza, and Abbo asks why I would give them food that is too hot to eat. Good point.

I take both pieces back, blow on them, then hand them back to them.

Abbo and Egré give me the American thumbs-up on the pizza. They learned this from being in my English classes. They ask for another piece, and Lydie and I have our second slices with them. Pizza is a hit. Onions and cheese fall down our chins, and our tongues rush to catch every morsel. Pizza has never tasted so good. Egré asks what the white stuff on the pizza is, and I explain that it's cheese. The kids have never heard of cheese, so I tell them how they make it from cow's milk. Abbo and Egré think it's strange to drink another animal's milk, but they agree that it tastes good.

Just as we're finishing, the mayor's car arrives to take me to his house for dinner.

"You cooked for us like a mother," Abbo says.

"We'll call you 'Mom' at home and 'Miss' at school," Egré says.

"It's OK by me," I say to the boys.

Lydie smiles, for she knows that she and I have a different relationship. Most of the time, I feel that Lydie's older, as if her soul has been deeply carved by the life she's lived. It's different with the boys: although they are both older than Lydie, I feel as if they could be my sons. At first it feels funny to be called Mom, but I'm happy to become a part of the extended Cameroonian family.

What exactly am I getting myself into by adopting two Cameroonian sons?

But perhaps even before formalizing it, we'd already become a family. They're my soul family. And who said family had to be related by blood?

We've already planted a garden under the kitchen window, built a new fence around the latrine, cleaned the house of termites and ants, burned a wasps' nest, made each other's traditional recipes, and brushed our teeth side by side under the full moon before going to bed.

I like having Abbo and Egré as part of my family. I feel as if I'm home. I kind of like the idea of having already-made, growing-up sons, each one over six feet tall.

But they certainly don't look a thing like their mother.

42. LIZARD SPEAKS

Hold your wick high
To the place where
The wind does not blow.
I will light the flame.

When you are bitter weary,
Look and you will see
To the place beyond
Human understanding.
I will sing so that you might hear
And awaken from your deep sleep.

And you will sing so that others may hear.
Be still and listen closely.
Across desert fields,
The wind whistles a tune
That beckons your soul.

Hold your wick high
So that I may light the flame.

Clap! Clap!

I look up from the bucket of laundry I'm sweating over on my porch, but I don't see anyone.

"*Oui? Qui est là?*" I say.

Clap! Clap!

"*Oui? Je suis ici. Venez!*" I say, inviting my guests to approach.

One of Valentine's sons pokes his head out from behind the straw wall, checking if it's safe to enter. I smile and wave him forward. The boy puts a toe out, testing unknown waters, and when he steps forward, he pulls his twin brother from behind the wall. The twins ease their way around the straw as if they're winding around a theater curtain and onto the center of a stage.

I wave them forward again, but the twins hesitate, then slowly tiptoe toward me. When they get close enough, they just stand with their arms wrapped around each other. They watch as I continue to wash my underwear.

Today is hotter than usual, maybe over 125 degrees Fahrenheit. Every task feels like a prison sentence. My back is screaming from leaning over the bucket and scrubbing. I've tried washing the desert and sweat out of my clothes, towels, and sheets. But it's not coming out, even with a scrub brush. Sweat drips down my nose into the bucket of clothes.

"*Bon-bon*, Miss," the first boy says, as he approaches me now, half naked, twirling the outie of his belly button and pulling the hand of his twin brother forward. His eyes are shy and dart around like corn popping in hot oil. The other twin squirms in the grip of his brother; his eyebrows are pinched together in hope that the answer is yes.

I'm surprised how resistant I am to giving up my last two pieces of candy. Caramel is one of the few moments of joy I have left to anticipate. Since being here, I've developed a terrible sweet tooth. But it's for the children, I tell myself—two very cute twins who need some sugar more than I do.

"*Oui, mes amis, il y en a.*"

When I enter the house and grab the last two pieces of caramel,

I sigh. The children will never know just how difficult it is to make this sacrifice.

When I appear in front of them like the Tooth Fairy waving her wand, the boys bounce up and down. They hold out two hands cupped into a small bowl to graciously accept the gift. They put the caramel in their mouths and close their eyes at the first taste of sugar. They slowly drift down onto the sand in front of me, and I imagine birds chirping in circles around their heads.

I wish there were just one more caramel left so I could join them in their small piece of heaven.

Since there isn't, I plump back down on my stool, plunge my hands into the bucket, and begin singing "Old MacDonald Had a Farm."

The twins crack up every time I do a "moo-moo here" or an "oink-oink there." I can't help but giggle with them as they roll their bodies over and over on the ground laughing hysterically, the sand sticking to their sweaty foreheads and making their faces nearly as white as mine.

I look up as their older sister is walking by. She drops her water bucket and joins us on the sand in a "baa-baa here" and a "baa-baa there." She continually covers her mouth, as if enjoying herself were a crime. Then she falls backward, rolling back and forth, holding her tummy because laughing that hard hurts.

"And on his farm, he had a cat, E-I-E-I-O. With a meow-meow here and a meow-meow there, here a meow, there a meow, everywhere a meow-meow. Old MacDonald had a farm, E-I-E-I-O."

The kids meow with me and then laugh at the sensation of a meow tickling like a feather in back of their throats. I am still laughing with them when I stand up and start chasing them. They screech in delight as we run around to the front of my house.

Suddenly, the sky becomes very dark.

The children come to a dead stop. They look as if they're going to explode. I catch up to one of the boys and pick him up in my arms. He screams. I quickly put him down, and he runs out of my compound and around the straw fence.

Oh no, not again.

Hey, come back! I was only playing!

The other twin looks up at the sky, and terror runs through his body like an electric shock. It's not me they're afraid of; it's the sudden darkness.

Can it be locusts approaching our village?

The sister handcuffs her brother with a forefinger and thumb and leads him quickly out of my compound.

The wind blows lightly through my hair, and I wipe the sweat off the front of my neck. The breeze grows stronger, and I lift my hair and feel it caress my skin. I hear the shutters bang hard against the outside wall. Is there someone there? I turn and look. A thick black wall is heading straight toward us. I hear the screams and running of the women and children en route back home from the well.

Then I smell it.

I've forgotten how sweet the rain's fragrance is. The water is ripe in the air, like guavas ready to fall from the tree and juicy with the richness the earth craves.

The temperature drops twenty degrees within seconds.

Oh, yes!

The rain, the rain, the rain is coming!

That black and orange lizard comes crawling across the yard. He seems to be in a big hurry. What is it that I don't know?

A fierce desert storm slams into us at full speed. The sky is black as night now, and the wind rattles dishes drying in its path. One leg at a time, I move from the side of my house to the front, fighting the wind that wants to knock me down. I close the windows and shutters, and as I'm closing the front door, the lizard sneaks inside.

What sounds like a violent tornado is only a wind lapping the house. I'm frightened by the storm. I sit on a chair and hug my legs, hoping it will end soon.

The rains come, and the wind subsides. The lizard comes out from hiding and moves quickly across the living room. I stand up, following him like a curious cat. He stops at the door. I open it and see the rain for the first time in months.

The rains have come!

I feel like singing!

The rains have come!
I feel like laughing!
The rains have come!
The children are singing!
The rains have come!
The children are laughing!

I leap outside after the lizard and stop on my front porch, watching the orchestrated dance of falling water move like a ballet through the village. The lizard darts through the door and rushes out to get wet. I, too, am aching to be out in the rain, to have it caress my body.

I move around to the side of the house, the most private part of my yard. I lift my hands high in the air and twirl around, laughing and dancing in circles. The rain drenches my clothes. I rip off my shirt and sarong and toss them aside. I linger for a moment, debating, then off come my bra and underwear. I stand completely naked in the rain and feel as if I'm being baptized by a universal mother.

I arch my head back, closing my eyes, opening my mouth to taste the cool water on my tongue. I swallow and allow the rain's soul to fill me. I become connected to an inner part of myself that pulses in my blood. I feel my heart beating in my belly. I open my arms wider and embrace the rain falling over me like a shower of rose petals.

I push the wet hair back from my face and smile at the lizard, who led me out to this succulent moment. The rain washes away the old, baptizing me so that I may start anew.

Morning

The call for prayer wakes me from my sleeping beneath the stars. If women were allowed in the mosque, I'd journey through the morning darkness to pray with the Foulbe. I'd like to begin the day with a ritual of chanting, prostrations, and prayer at the sacred temple. Why are women forced to pray at home? Why are they forbidden to enter the holy place?

The chanting inspires me to get out of bed, as if the call were a magnet and I were the metal object. Instinctively, I do one full prostration on the sand. I chant only the name of Allah again and again but am aware of its powerful vibration resonating from my throat and lungs out to my fingertips and toes. As I look up at the stars before I kneel, an electrical sensation rushes through my veins telling me that I'm home. I've just found the key to the door.

When I walk through, I discover that the people of Guidiguis have moved into the vacancy within my heart. I wake when they wake, I pray when they pray, I mourn death when they mourn, I work when they work, I rest when they rest, I eat when they eat. And when they greet me and recognize spirit living within all of us, I, too, recognize spirit living within myself and everyone. All of their ways, their language, their daily routine have become a part of me.

As I do my last prostration, I remember that today is Vann's birthday! Since I promised her I'd be there to celebrate, I'd better get moving. Even though it's market day and there should be plenty of cars coming in and going out, everyone travels in the morning, and my best chance to get out of Guidiguis is to start by 6:00 AM.

"Gumbo! Quiet!" I say to the new puppy that Vann gave me when she came for her last visit. I try to keep him from frightening the Foulbe cow herders walking past our house by holding him and stroking his head. Cameroonians are terrified of dogs since many have had experiences with rabid animals. Gumbo lies back down and moans. "You're too good of a watch dog," I say.

I head toward the latrine, and Gumbo follows me into it. He

watches me bathe, then follows me into my bedroom, where I get dressed and packed. As I head out the door, Gumbo begins wailing and barking so loudly that I melt. I untie his leash, and he follows, all the while jumping on me and licking my hand.

When I get to the market, I see several bush taxis unloading people, animals, and merchandise. Knowing there'll be a long wait for the fifteen-passenger car to fill up, I sit on a rock and play with Gumbo. The driver smiles at me, and I recognize him from being stuck in the desert waiting for a solution to thieving elephants. This man had offered me his fried roots in sauce when I had nothing to eat and nothing to offer in return.

The driver hops on top of the bush taxi to unload baggage and goods to eager passengers wanting to hurry to the market and make some money. I stand up on my tiptoes and stretch my hand to the top of the car in order to reach him. I greet him by putting my left hand under my right wrist, a Cameroonian custom to show great respect.

"Any more run-ins with elephants?" I ask.

"No," the driver says, and laughs. He throws a bundle of clothing tied with ripped cloth to the ground. "Have you acquired a taste for insects?"

"No," I say, and laugh, too. "My adopted students have made them a few times, but I didn't like them as much as that day when we were all starving."

A woman getting out of the van stops and tells me something in a language I've never heard before. She pokes my puppy's tummy, then laughs. Gumbo barks at her, but she continues laughing at him while walking away.

Noticing my confusion, the driver translates. "She said your dog is good and fat and will be delicious in soup."

"My puppy is not to eat," I say, offended by the idea.

"You'd better watch your puppy closely. He might disappear in the night."

"No! No one is going to eat my dog!" I say, and pull Gumbo into my arms. He licks my face and wags his tail. The thought of anyone eating my dog nauseates me.

"Times are hard, Miss," he says. "People are hungry. Didn't you hear this morning's news? The president announced that everyone's salary must be cut." The driver hops down from the top of the car, dusts his hands off, and wipes his forehead with a handkerchief.

"Cut?" I ask, surprised that the president would do such a thing when the people are already angry, complaining that he has rigged the elections.

"Men are afraid they won't be able to feed their families. Soon, your dog will look delicious," the driver says, as he opens a bottle of water and sits down on the sand to begin washing for prayer.

"No one in Guidiguis will eat Gumbo," I say, terrified that he's right.

"Then the Chadians will. Times are even harder there, and it's exactly why bandits have started pulling over bush taxis, taking everything they can."

"I haven't heard that," I say, surprised.

"They pulled me over yesterday. They took my gas, passengers' belongings, their animals, and money."

"That's terrible. *Asha.*"

"It'll get worse. You're not taking anything on your trip you can't afford to lose?" I shake my head but recall that I do have a lot of money in my purse so that Vann and I can celebrate her birthday. Maybe I shouldn't bring as much. I put Gumbo down and take a sip from my canteen. It's going to be a hot one today.

"Be careful. People are poor now, and they'll get even hungrier. A man will do anything to put something in his belly. Watch yourself."

"But the villagers should be OK."

"They depend on selling their crops to government employees: teachers, doctors, nurses, and government officials. If workers are no longer bringing money into the small villages, people will starve."

"Will there be a national strike?" I ask, worried that I'll be sent home.

The driver sighs and looks away from me. I follow his gaze, looking over the land he loves: the fields, the children chasing a new soccer ball in the paved road, the people of different tribes working together to set up the market, and the morning sun rising in the sky. The driver continues to look out across the land as if he were taking a picture and placing it in an album in his heart.

"This will change when the strike begins."

"How will it change?"

He turns to me, shaking his head. His anguish and loss of hope for his country soften my eyes. I want to console him; instead, I fold my arms across my chest.

"The salary of the military was doubled while other government workers had theirs cut. It's a bribe. The military will kill anyone who strikes. They've been sent to new posts. It's easier to kill another tribe; they don't look like your mother or brother."

"Won't Cameroon unite?" I ask.

"Too many languages in Cameroon and not one to unite us. For some villagers, their only resistance is their tongue. If we had one common language, perhaps Cameroon could make a decision to unite, no matter the tribe or the differences."

"I'm worried for Cameroon."

"In times of crisis, all we can do is pray."

I nod in agreement. Funny how I hadn't thought of doing that. Praying is doing something. Perhaps I'll ask God to help me find a way to Kaele. Now I'm being silly. I'll just pray for peace instead.

"Do you think you'll fill up this morning? It's already 10:30 AM, and I'm the only one."

"The news today will keep everyone's money in their pockets. I'm afraid no one will be traveling to Kaele today."

"Thank you."

"No need to thank me."

"For everything," I say.

We shake hands, and I return home.

I need to see Vann. I need a hug and someone to tell me it'll be all right.

Midmorning

A woman waves to me, and I cross the street to say hello. It's Saidou's mother pushing a cart of chickens to the market. She asks me how the sun is treating me. "This sun is too much today," I say.

She agrees with me and claps—but when she sees Gumbo, she shakes her head. In a flash she unties a chicken and gives it to me.

She points to my belly, but I don't understand. I think she wants me to eat chicken rather than dog. I attempt to pay her, but she won't take my money. She waves me off as she continues her journey to the market.

I stand holding a chicken by its feet.

Gumbo barks at the chicken. The chicken squawks at Gumbo. I yell at them both.

Vann will be upset. She'll wait all day for me to show up. What I wouldn't do to get a single telephone installed in Guidiguis.

When I reach home, I open the door and notice my bicycle.

There *is* a way to get to Kaele! My own two legs! I can bike to Vann's house! Although the Peace Corps bicycle only has one speed and it's not easy, Kaele is only twenty miles away and should only take three hours.

But the heat . . .

By the time I get everything loaded, it'll be almost noon. It's already 110 degrees Fahrenheit. The temperature could rise dangerously high on the road, where there isn't any shade. I'll have to take plenty of water to avoid dehydration. I take a bottle of cold Kool-Aid out of the fridge and a frozen Kool-Aid canteen out of the tiny freezer.

After loading everything, I tie the chicken and Gumbo down on my front porch. I'll ask Lydie to come and feed them. I put the backpack on my shoulders and climb on the bike. Gumbo is barking and gets the chicken worked up. It jumps in a feeble attempt to fly away. Gumbo turns on the chicken, then aggressively chases it to the end of his leash. This isn't going to work. I'll have to take them both.

On the right side of the handlebars, I tie the chicken by its feet, upside down.

Then I take some clothes and toiletries out of the box tied onto the back and put Gumbo in it.

I say a prayer that we'll make it safely to Kaele.

Noon

The villagers at the *carrefour* yell when I pass. They shout my name and wave for me to stop, but I just keep on riding. I'm sure they think I'm nuts to attempt a journey in this temperature.

Pedaling is difficult in this heat. I can't get enough oxygen from the burning hot air in my lungs to move the bike faster than a slow ride. At this rate, it'll take me four hours. I look out at the endless desert, at the golden fields of dry weeds, trees stretched out in the distance without a single leaf, and the long paved road before me. Vultures circle high above, waiting for me, the dog, and the chicken to surrender. I imagine scorpions and snakes slithering through the high weeds and the sun ready to fall on my head. The desert feels like an enemy I have to conquer.

After only thirty minutes, I have to stop for water. My clothes are completely soaked with sweat. As I take a drink, I look back at the trees of Guidiguis. I could still turn around and go home.

My mother was right. I have a stubborn, Taurus, bullheaded frame of mind when it comes to certain things. I can't turn back because the villagers will laugh at my failure. As I drink more water, I feel more determined. I pour water in my hand, and Gumbo drinks it. I sit the chicken up and give it water, too. Then I hop on the bike, and away I go.

The wind is no relief, as it blows only heat. I begin to play a game of saying "Wonderful" to everything I see, especially the things that bring me discomfort. Even though the sun is merciless, I say "Wonderful." I say "Wonderful" to the road that turns so that now I'm riding against the wind. I sing out "Wonderful" to the many miles ahead. In this height of the dry season, the desert looks like a sea of raging yellow fire. It's so hot and dry by 1:30 PM that I no longer sweat. The sweat instantly evaporates, leaving behind only salt on my forehead, neck, and back. I feel that I'll burst into flames at any moment.

I see a snake in the road and swerve to the other side, nearly crashing. I pedal faster, my heart beating wildly, then look back and see that it's not moving at all. It's only a rope. I'm relieved, but when I look ahead, I'm at the very edge of the road. It's too late to recover, and the bike heads swiftly down a hill. I steer past desert bushes and thorny trees but crash into a termite mound. Gumbo falls out and barks. The chicken hollers. The termites rush out to assess and repair the damage. I pick Gumbo up as he catches a termite with his tongue. As I walk the bike back up to the road, a bush taxi seems to appear out of nowhere; it zooms by, honking its horn several times and making my hair stand on end. I'd be on that vehicle right now if only I'd waited.

"Meant to be," I say out loud to Gumbo. "Anyway, we're having ourselves an adventure, right?"

I open a bottle of Kool-Aid and am surprised that it's still cool. I gulp it down, then close the top, and just as I'm putting it away, I see the big black and orange lizard running toward me. I close my eyes, but when I open them, he's not there. Great. The snake and now the lizard. I'm hallucinating.

As I get on the bike, I see the lizard again. When I blink, he disappears.

I've got to get off this malaria prophylaxis I'm on. Hallucinations are said to be a side effect of mefloquine. The drug hasn't been seriously tested over any length of time in the United States, but Peace Corps volunteers are to take it weekly for two years and three months. What other side effects will I be experiencing? Hallucinations are scary. I'd rather take my chances with malaria.

I get on the bike again, determined to be more careful, and aware my eyes may try to deceive me. I try to pedal harder, desperate to get to Kaele.

The desert silence is broken by motorcycles speeding up behind me. The motorcycles slow down and follow. I turn my head and see three *gendarmes*. Are they going to pull me over for riding a bike? They're speaking in their patois and holding steady behind me. Gumbo barks at them, but they can't hear him over the loud buzzing of their motors. I can't slow down; I can't bike off the road; they have me pinned in front of them. What do they want with me?

When they finally pass, they look over and laugh. As they speed away, I stop. I'm shaking all over. I take a drink of water, but my hand shakes so badly that the water spills. When I've calmed down, I get back on the bike. I thank God they didn't harm me. I ride for nearly an hour, denying my thirst as I'm too anxious to get to Kaele to stop again. As I pass a tiny village, the villagers wave at me and shout, "*Suzannedee!*" How do they know my name this far out?

When I look ahead, I see that the three *gendarmes* have blocked off the road with large rocks and sit under an old straw roof. They're guzzling beer and sitting back in their chairs, talking and having a good time.

I reach the barricade and stop.

The three policemen come over with guns in one hand and beers in the other.

"Do you have an identification card?" the big fat one asks.

"Yes, but it's at home," I say. I could kick myself for forgetting it. I know better than to travel without it. If they make me turn back to Guidiguis when I'm nearly in Kaele already, I'll go ballistic.

"Do you have a receipt for your bicycle?" the skinny one with sunglasses asks, as he circles me and the bike.

"No, I don't," I say. This is absurd!

"You'll have to wait over here, Miss," the serious one says. He hits his baton against his hand and chugs the rest of his beer.

"But I'm a Peace Corps volunteer. I'm riding to Kaele to see my sister."

"Are you a spy?" the fat one asks. He puts his face in mine, and I want to hit him.

"No, I'm not a spy. I'm a teacher. I work in Guidiguis," I say.

"Do you belong to the opposition party?"

"No," I say, irritated that he doesn't know what the Peace Corps is. "I am a volunteer. I don't belong to any party."

"I know who you are!" the serious one says, putting his hands on my handlebars. "You're working as a spy to bring down our government!"

"Believe me, Sir, I have no interest in your government. I am here for your children. I teach them."

"You'll have to wait here," the sunglasses man says, and points to the straw hut.

"But I really can't wait, you see. I'm expected in Kaele."

As I take my backpack off my shoulders, he takes it from me.

"Get off the bike and sit down over there, Miss!" the serious one says.

Shaken, I get off the bike. I'm scared. The driver was right. In times of crisis, the only thing we can do is pray. Dear God, please don't let anything happen to us.

"She's an American spy!" the serious one says to the sunglasses man.

The fat man puts his hand in the box, and Gumbo bites it. He barks at the two other policemen, who are looking at the fat man's hand with great concern.

"What's this?" the sunglasses man asks.

"My dog."

"I hate dogs," the fat man says.

"*Moi aussi*. Take him out of the box!"

The serious one grabs Gumbo by his neck, and Gumbo barks at him. The sunglasses man pulls out his gun.

"No!" I say. "Please! Gumbo is my friend. Please don't—" I start to cry and shake.

Gumbo bites the serious one's forearm, and he drops Gumbo and kicks him hard. I run to Gumbo and pick him up, holding him tightly in my arms and soothing him.

The fat man pokes the chicken. "And what's this?" he asks.

"Dinner," I say.

"Sit down!" the serious one yells at me, and I go inside the hut and wait.

They walk off a few steps together, and I pet Gumbo and tell him not to bite anymore. It'll only get us in more trouble. Please help me get out of this mess. Make sure I get home safely to my mother. Hear my prayer.

Afternoon

The *gendarmes* make me wait for over two hours—without access to water and without any further directions or information. I don't know why they're holding me prisoner. A few times, I start to nod off to sleep, but Gumbo licks my nose every time he sees my eyes shut, and I wake up.

The commander of Kaele drives up in a jeep. He's a short, bald man who walks tall and proud. He looks at me while talking to the *gendarmes* and gets their story. He nods at what they're telling him, then walks toward me before they're finished. He hitches up his belt and clears his throat.

"Miss?"

"Yes, Sir," I say, and then clear my scratchy, dry throat.

"My officers tell me that you don't have an identification card."

"I forgot it at home, but I can assure you that I'm a teacher in Guidiguis who is trying to get to Kaele to see my sister."

"Who is she?"

"Evangeline Rivers."

"Yes, she's a teacher at the high school. I know her."

"We're Peace Corps volunteers. Teachers. We work without pay."

"Yes, Miss, I know what the Peace Corps is. You may go now. Miss, it isn't wise for a woman to travel by bike on her own. There are now Chadian bandits in the extreme north. I'd be more prudent."

I thank the commander and get moving right away. I don't stop for water until I'm far out of sight. I pull to the side of the road and gulp down the ice, now melted into cold water in my canteen. But I drink too much too quickly and am forced to bend over and vomit. As I try to stand, my head gets light and dizzy. The world is spinning, making me more nauseous. Slowly, I sink to my hands and feet, then throw up the guavas I ate for breakfast. I'm hallucinating again, for I see that black and orange lizard running across my fingertips. I move to a kneeling position, looking to the sky.

"Dear God, please help me make it to Kaele."

Ask me anything. You only need to whisper.

"Oh."

Next time, don't wait so long.

I rub my eyes and feel very strange to be talking to my mefloquine hallucination. The Peace Corps warned us about the side effects. I had no idea that they would go this far. "I've got to make a trip to Yaounde and change my malaria prophylaxis. It's pushing me over the edge. I know it."

In the stillness of the desert, you hear your voice.

For some strange reason, I see an image of Moses on the mountain talking to a reptile instead of to a burning bush, and I laugh at myself. Am I comparing my delusional mind to the conversation God had with Moses? I sigh. I'm ending this right here and now. I climb on my bike and start pedaling again—trying to run away from the voice.

Is it so hard to believe God is in your skin? I am alive!

This isn't funny. I'm hearing voices in my head, and it's scaring me. I stop the bike again and look up at the sky.

When you're still and silent, the answers are within.

I close my eyes. With a deep breath, I feel a pulsing, vibrant energy living within me. Spirit moves through my body like an electrical current. I've walked steps on a spiritual path, but nothing has ever gotten me this close to experiencing the Divine inside myself.

"But how do I relate to you? What do I need to do to experience you?"

"Ah donne nah?"

"Oho, me donne."

I am with you even before you call. I am there even when you don't.

I whisper softly, "Dear God, please help me get to Kaele."

Wonderful.

Late Afternoon

I made it! I ride through the Kaele village feeling like a champion. I can't wait to tell Vann about my experience in the desert. She might think I'm nuts, but I'm sure she's guessed already.

When I finally pull up to Vann's house, I'm disappointed that the windows and doors are closed. Vann's neighbors are crushing millet in large wooden bowls, and they wave to me, saluting me in the local language, Moondong. I wave back and nod. When I get off the bike and walk to the house, I see a note that says, "Suzi-Monster—Went surfing. Be back soon." I laugh aloud at her joke.

I'll wait here. I tie the chicken and Gumbo to the tree on Vann's porch and slowly drink the water in my canteen and share it with the animals. Sitting on the steps of Vann's house, I hold my head in my hands. After fifteen minutes, I unfold a sarong and lie down under the shade on the front porch.

Gumbo falls asleep, and the chicken paces back and forth across the porch. I close my eyes and touch my belly, remembering the glow. Could it really be that we only need to whisper? I fall asleep and dream about flying over the desert, but without a plane or wings. In my dream, I hear Gumbo bark, and I wake up to see a Cameroonian man running toward me.

"Suzanne! Suzanne!"

"Yes?"

"My name is Ousmanou. I'm a colleague of your sister. She sent me to you."

"Where is she?"

"The Kaele police called her to their prison."

"Is she in trouble?"

"I don't know what's happening to her."

"Will you take me there?"

"Yes, come."

I wrap the sarong around my shorts and slip on my sandals. Ousmanou takes me by the hand, and we run a mile to the police station.

Eight children sit with a big woman nursing a newborn on the steps of the police station. They stare at me when Ousmanou and I walk up the stairs. Three children are crying for their mother. She tells them to wait their turn.

We walk into the police station, and I see Vann sitting on a chair in front of a large desk, where a policeman sits writing notes.

"Start over again and tell me exactly what happened," the policeman says.

"But I've told you the story three times," Vann says, but stops when she hears us. "Suzi! You made it!"

Vann stands up and gives me a hug.

"Are you OK?" I ask.

"Yes, although I've been stuck here for two hours."

Another policeman walks through the door, pushing his prisoner, who wears ripped and dirty clothes, his hands cuffed behind his back. One eye is swollen shut, and his lip is bleeding. He sits on the floor against the wall only ten feet from Vann.

The prisoner snarls at Vann when he sees her, and Vann turns to the policeman behind the desk.

"Is this really necessary?" Vann asks.

"I'd like to hear both sides of the story."

The other policeman brings me a chair. I pull it close to Vann and squeeze her hand before she begins her story. She takes a breath and looks at the prisoner.

"I took my refrigerator to this man here to have it repaired. The price was negotiated, and we settled on 38,000 CFAs. When Ahmadou returned it, it didn't work."

Ahmadou kneels and spits at the floor.

"It did work! When I returned it, it did work!" Ahmadou says.

"For one day!" Vann says, her face getting red. "Now I'm out 38,000 francs, and my refrigerator still doesn't work."

Ahmadou cocks his head to the side and mimics Vann, "Now I'm out 38,000 CFAs, and my refrigerator still doesn't work."

"Let's stop playing games here!" Vann says, and stands up, ready to leave.

The policeman leans forward, yelling, "I'm in charge here, Miss; sit down."

Vann sits, and I notice that my right hand is clenched in a fist.

"Now do you want your refrigerator fixed or 38,000 CFAs?" the policeman asks.

"If it's this guy repairing my refrigerator, no thank you. I want my money."

Ahmadou spits at her feet.

"We'll try to get the money from his family outside. Until then, Ahmadou remains in prison. Thank you, you're free to go."

"I'm free?" Vann asks.

The policeman nods, and Vann laughs sarcastically, turns, takes my hand, and leads me out the door. As we walk down the steps, we see Ahmadou's family. His wife is breast-feeding another baby and looks up at us with tears in her eyes. An older child picks up a two-year-old baby and rocks him. Vann turns her head away and looks out at the village. As we pass the family, they look at us, their eyes begging for mercy. I take Vann's hand in mine, and her eyes fill with tears.

Vann picks up the pace, and I have to jog a few steps to catch her. I put my hand on her shoulder, and when we turn the corner, Vann turns into my arms and cries.

"Damn him! How can I go through with this when his family desperately needs the money!"

"Vann, what he did was wrong."

"His family shouldn't pay for his crime! The children are sick and hungry."

As we walk back to Vann's house, we hear someone yelling behind us. It's the policeman calling Vann back.

"Oh, no," I say. "What could he possibly want now?"

"I can't do this. I have to drop the charges."

"Miss! Wait!" the policeman shouts.

We stop, and Vann squeezes my hand.

"Miss, listen, we'll help you this time, but if you get into another pickle like this again, don't come crying to us. Unless, of course, you'd like me to come visit you."

"That won't be necessary!" Vann says, and turns away. "Suzi, I'm not going to make it. Every damn day I want to go home. I just hang on until tomorrow. If you hadn't come, I might have thrown in the towel."

"I'm sorry, Vann. I wish I could do something."

We pass a cement house and hear the TV blaring inside. A man with a big belly, dressed only in a sarong, brushes his teeth on his front porch. He spits, then looks up and sees us. I hear the theme song to *Dallas*. Funny how I can remember it after all these years.

"He's seen us. It's my colleague, Henri. We must say hello."

"Hello, Miss! I see your sister has come!" Henri says.

He shakes our hands as if we're family, but then I remember that everyone is a brother or sister in Cameroon. Vann introduces me, and he welcomes us into his compound, calling out for his family to set the table.

"Yes, she's come to celebrate my birthday," says Vann.

"Miss! You didn't tell us it was your birthday! We would have made a feast!"

"Thank you, but my sister is here, and we have so much to talk about."

"Yes, but I will have big sister come with a plate."

"Thank you, but it's really not necessary," says Vann. I think about Gumbo and the chicken on her porch and hope they're OK.

"It's not a problem. Come in and watch TV with us. *Dallas* is coming on now."

"I can hear the music," I say.

"Yes, we love American TV. Everyone in America is so rich."

"Not everyone," Vann says.

"Oh, but yes! Every street is paved in America. So many beautiful houses, and everyone owns a car. There is so much food, and everyone is fat."

Henri smiles and rubs his tummy. "Time to eat. Please join us."

"I'm sorry, but we have to go," Vann says.

An older man walks out of the house and greets us.

"Old man! Come and meet our guests," says Henri.

"Fat man, your wife has prepared some food. Come."

The old man waves at us and smiles. Then he waves to all of us to come in. He disappears inside the house, and Henri quickly finishes brushing his teeth and rinses.

"Funny how they use adjectives. I wonder how they describe me," Vann says.

"Pointy-nosed, small-breasted, skinny-assed, tight-lipped white woman," I say.

"Thanks a lot!" Vann says, and hits me on the shoulder.

"It's true. I heard them," I say, and wink.

"Come in, come in!" Henri says.

Vann looks at me and we both nod, then follow him into his house. Except for the light of the TV, it's dark inside. Children gather at the door of the house to watch from a distance, heads stacked one over the other, five feet high. They look at us and then at the TV, as if we look like the actresses from the show. Now and again, they laugh at us, something Vann and I are both getting used to. We sit down on an old beat-up couch and watch *Dallas* while our host disappears behind a door of beads. The walls are painted bright aqua but are darkened where children have played and imprinted dirty hands two and three feet from the floor.

Henri's wife enters carrying a silver tray with two big bowls covered with cloth tops. She smiles lovingly at us, and I feel undeserving of such graciousness. She offers us a warm water bowl to wash our hands. Vann washes first while the old man comes to greet us. We offer our hand to shake, but he refuses since we just washed them.

"What would you like to drink?" Henri's wife asks us.

"Water would be fine."

"No, please, we're offering you."

Her eight-year-old son walks through the back entrance carrying four large bottles of beer and an opener under his arm. He sets the beers down and opens them. We turn to each other and raise our eyebrows; we're being treated like royalty.

Henri returns dressed in an ironed, button-down cotton shirt and blue jeans.

"Thank you for joining us. I hope you'll like what my wife prepared."

Henri's wife smiles as she takes the tops off our two bowls. It's gumbo and *fou-fou* corn. We move closer to the coffee table to eat this meal with our hands. This is going to be very messy since gumbo is very slimy, the okra crushed until it's goo.

In English, Vann says, "I'll make you some real Cajun gumbo for your birthday."

"You speak good English," Henri says in English, and his wife laughs. "I want to speak good English, too. Will you teach me, teacher?" Henri asks Vann.

"Sure, you can come to my classroom every day from nine to ten."

He laughs and then says in French, "I want to be rich like an American. To be rich in this world, you need to learn the language of business, English. That's why I watch *Dallas*. It teaches me more English."

Henri eats the gumbo by scooping it up easily in his hands with a small ball of *fou-fou* corn. I try to imitate him, but the gumbo spills down my arm, and Vann laughs at how messy I'm getting. She tries to scoop up the gumbo sauce and gets it into her hand with a ball of *fou-fou* corn but then spills it on her shirt. I laugh, and she mimics me.

The TV shows the Ewing house, and Henri sighs. "Americans are so rich."

"Not all Americans are rich," Vann says.

"Oh, yes, Americans are so rich. Look at this house. They have so much land, but they don't grow any corn or beans. They buy everything in a supermarket."

"My family is poor," Vann says, and Henri laughs at her.

"You are American! You have money!"

"No, my family is Cajun. They live in the south of the United States. They've been discriminated against for hundreds of years. They have no land but have been pushed from Canada to Louisiana, then forced to live in the swamps."

Henri laughs and then turns to me. "You, too, your family is poor?"

"Yes. My family is Spanish and Native American. The Navaho tribe has suffered a lot at the hands of the white man. Many brown-skinned families have never had a chance to break out of poverty. I'm the first to continue with my studies and go to college in my family. They've never had the money to go to the university."

"Education is the way many Americans became wealthy, but when a people is oppressed by another, it becomes nearly impossible to break out of it," adds Vann.

"But America is the land of the free! You can say what you want and do what you want, and you want to tell me about oppression?" Henri laughs hard.

I'm not eating anymore. Vann washes her hands.

"Henri, there are different situations in America. There are many types of people who come from all over the world. Some come to America poor, and they remain poor. Their children may or may not break the cycle."

"But America is the land of milk and honey. Work is everywhere! You work, then you retire and live off the fat."

"That's not the way it's been for me or my family," Vann says.

"Nor mine," I say. "I've worked hard and have attained little. I'm working for the Peace Corps, so I'm working for free."

"You're not working for free! Why would anyone work for free?" Henri says. "I know you get paid well."

"Well?" I ask, now completely offended. "I disagree, Sir; I get paid in order to live, but I don't get a salary."

"Of course, you get a salary! No American works just to survive!" Henri exclaims.

Vann and I look at each other and know it's time to go.

Vann looks to Henri's wife, who sits cracking peanuts at the back of the room.

"Thank you for the wonderful meal," says Vann, standing up to leave.

I wash my hand and follow Vann.

"No! You can't go! *Dallas* isn't over yet. Then there's *Dynasty* in the next hour."

"Thank you so much," I say, "but I haven't seen my sister in a long time, and we need some time to visit with one another. Thank you."

Henri gives us an angry glare for leaving so abruptly. He was enjoying the debate, unaware of the suffering that people of color have inherited from past generations. It hits me that in each little corner of the world, people are struggling to be free and understood. If we could only walk in someone else's skin . . .

Vann and I wave good-bye to the children watching us. She puts her arm around me, and I put my head on her shoulder.

Evening

Vann and I are lost in our thoughts, reliving parts of our lives that we struggled through. We don't say a word until we get into Vann's compound.

"I get tired of the stereotypes of Americans! Why is *Dallas* shown on TV?"

"Good question," I say, as we approach Vann's door.

"Suzi, you biked here in this heat! And with your puppy?"

"Yeah, well, it was that or break a promise."

Vann gives me a hug. She opens her door as I untie Gumbo. When he sees his brother, Miff, he goes crazy. They wrestle and play-bite each other.

While Vann opens the windows, I chase the chicken.

"Come here, you flock of feathers, you. Vann is going to—" I bring my fingers across my throat and leap after the chicken. I catch it by its feet and bring it into the house.

When I enter the kitchen, Vann has her back to me. "Happy birthday, Vann."

She turns around and screams when she sees the chicken. Definitely the worst reaction I've ever gotten from any birthday present I've given.

I hand the chicken to her. She takes it by the feet and holds it out at arm's length.

"What am I supposed to do with it?" she asks.

"Well, you're supposed to eat it, Vann," I say.

"But it's alive!" she says.

"Yes, well, they come that way."

"Can't you make it look like it came from Safeway?" she asks as she hands the chicken back to me.

"Me? I thought you knew how. You're Cajun."

"And you're an Indian warrior," she says.

"But I don't know anything about being Indian."

"Yes. Well, then . . . then it's . . . then it's my birthday, so you have to do the dirty work!"

"Talk about ruffling feathers," I say, and take the chicken back. I walk outside, mumbling to the chicken that this is not going to be too pleasant since I've never killed one before.

The chicken squawks and flaps its wings as it tries to get away. I'm not sure I can go through with this.

"Vann, bring me a knife, will you?"

Vann runs out of the house without a knife. "What do you need?"

"A knife. I need a knife."

"Oh," she says, and runs back into the house.

When cooking with Calixte, I saw her put a foot on the chicken's feet and wings. When I do it, the chicken really squawks, and I lose my nerve. I step off the chicken, and it doesn't fly away. I must have broken its wings. Tears fill my eyes. I step back on the chicken and lose my appetite. I'm not sure I can take the life of another to feed myself. It feels like a horrible thing to do to an animal, and yet back in the States I've eaten chicken hundreds of times.

Vann comes running out of the house again and hands me a knife.

"Boiled water, ripped sheets," she says.

"We're having chicken *fajitas,* not a baby!"

"Are you really going to kill it?" Vann asks.

"Yes," I say.

"How could you?" she asks.

"Vann, I've already broken its wings. Do you want to go out and eat some more slimy sauce and cement *fou-fou?*"

"God, no, I hardly ate a thing at Henri's house. I'm starved."

"Well, then, could I get a little support here?" I ask, irritated by the guilt I feel for taking the life of another. Eating meat has never felt wrong before.

"What are you going to do?" Vann asks innocently.

"I slice its head off," I say, trying to remember exactly what the mayor's wife did. That's kind of hard since I was covering my eyes and trying to keep from throwing up while she was butchering the chicken.

"No, I think you just slice across its neck. Just slice. It's like slicing bread. OK?"

"Just slice," I say.

"Or chop. But not the whole head. Just chop so it bleeds to death. Then hold it."

"Well, if you know so much about killing chickens, why don't you do it?" I ask.

"I can't kill a living animal," Vann says.

"It's a chicken!" I say.

"It's alive, you know."

"But you can eat it once it's dead," I say.

"Well in the store, someone has killed it anyway, so we might as well—" she says.

"Indulge ourselves. You know, the Native Americans only ate to survive. When they would eat, they would ask each animal to sacrifice itself. Then they would take the animal's life and then offer its spirit thanks for another day of life granted to them."

"I don't remember your asking the chicken's permission," Vann says.

"No, I didn't, and that's what feels wrong," I say.

"Do you need a moment alone with the chicken, Suz?"

"Yes, I do."

Vann leaves, and I kneel down to the chicken, holding its wings in my hands.

"I'm sorry for nearly taking your life without asking permission. Please forgive me for not showing compassion. It's difficult to practice it in daily living. Please, if you will, give up your life to us so that we may continue to live on the earth."

The chicken stops struggling and stares at me without blinking. I stand once again on it. I bring the knife across its neck and then hold it in my hands as the warm blood spills out.

As I wait for her to die, I thank her. I can feel a change inside, for all of a sudden, the chicken has become a "she" instead of an "it."

Vann comes out with a bucket, and I gently place the chicken's body inside.

"I've never killed before. I watched the life drain out as I looked in her eyes."

"She's in chicken heaven now."

"What do you think happens when we die?" I ask.

"I don't know. Part of me thinks that this is all there is," Vann says.

Vann pours boiling water from a teapot over the chicken.

"I have a hard time living without believing that there's more

than this. I'd like to think that we reincarnate until we reach en-
lightenment."

We sit down on the steps and pluck the feathers from her body.
The chicken's dirty, and Vann winces at the smell.

"Do you believe even animals and insects reincarnate?"

"Zen Buddhists won't even kill a bug; they have reverence for
all living beings. Plus, it may be Grandpa Joe or Great-Grandma
Helen."

"Do you think you knew this chicken before?" Vann asks.

"Absolutely. In our next life, we'll be the chicken, and she'll eat
us. Karma. What goes around comes around."

"I don't like the thought of that. Will I really come back as a
chicken?" Vann puts her hand around her throat.

"I'm only joking."

"I wouldn't mind being a bird or a dolphin," Vann says.

"I'd like this to be my last life," I say.

"Do you believe in reincarnation?" Vann asks.

"I grew up in and out of Zen Buddhist monasteries, so I haven't
really questioned it much. Perhaps I do believe."

"You're full of secrets. The Buddhist monastery is the first
mention of your past. Mostly, you've only mentioned Catholic
theology."

"I've lived several lifetimes just in this one," I say.

"How's that?"

"It's a long story—a book, really."

"Do you think you'll write it?"

"Perhaps. Once I've healed," I say. "I'm on my way to the heart
of it."

"I had a feeling that you've suffered a great deal in your life.
You always understand me when I tell you about my past. Maybe
writing will be the healing."

I look at Vann and then down at the feathers. I couldn't be like
this animal, stark naked in front of someone. I'm afraid to show
the tears in my eyes. I don't want to answer any questions or explain the events I've survived.

And yet somewhere inside myself I do.

Because what if I die in Africa? What if no one ever knows my story? I want to tell someone what I've lived through. Will anyone ever know me?

"Do you practice a religion now?" Vann asks. I wipe tears away with my sleeve.

"I just practice being."

Night

Vann holds one end of the wooden stick bed and I hold the other as we move it outside into her backyard, where Vann has built a straw fence and a roof in order to hang a mosquito net over the bed. She's run an extension cord from the house and has plugged a fan in and placed it underneath the net. This will be the first comfortable sleep I've had this hot season.

"Next time, I'll make Cajun food," Vann says.

"No chicken."

"The *fajitas* were delicious. Thank you for being the butcher."

"Happy birthday, Vann. I wonder what the next year holds for us."

"Me, too."

We settle into bed, and I ask Vann to tell me more about her family history. She tells me about the Cajuns, how they came from France to Canada. How their race was once called the Arcadians and how they were forced to move south to Louisiana. She says that most people think Cajun is a spice or a recipe and not real people. She explains how the Cajuns lost their land and now live in the swamps. As we drift to sleep, the fan blows on us, and we feel safe in each other's company.

We're awakened soon after by someone yelling bloody murder, "*Ginaroo! Ginaroo! Ginaroo!*" Vann sits up and pokes me.

"Are you awake?" Vann asks. I can feel her trembling.

"Of course, I'm awake! It sounds as if someone's being murdered!"

"What do we do?" Vann asks.

"We stay still. The villagers know what to do."

Vann lies back down and holds my hand.

"This would be scary if I were alone," Vann says softly.

"*Ginaroo! Ginaroo! Ginaroo!*" the man's voice yells out again.

"The voice is coming closer," Vann says.

"You're right. Do you think he's being chased by someone?" I ask.

Vann sits up again. "Where's the flashlight?"

"Right here." I hand her the flashlight, and she slips underneath the net.

"You're not leaving me here alone!" I say, getting up, too.

"*Ginaroo! Ginaroo! Ginaroo!*" a man is screaming, and it sounds as if he's close to our house.

"What's that?" Vann asks.

"He's pounding on your door," I say.

"What do I do?"

"Let him in!"

"What if he kills us?" Vann asks.

"It sounds like something is trying to kill *him*."

With me following behind, Vann unlocks the back door. We move to the front door, where a man is shouting that it's the "*Ginaroo*" and to please open the door.

"It sounds like Ousmanou," Vann says.

"Open the door, Vann."

"What if what he's running from comes in?"

The man is crying "please" and pounding harder on the door, as if something horrible is coming closer.

Vann turns the key and opens the door. Ousmanou comes in wide-eyed and sweating. He closes the door quickly behind him and tries to catch his breath.

Vann moves to turn on the lights, but he screams, "No! Don't do that! He'll know we're here!"

"Who, Ousmanou? Are you in some sort of trouble?" Vann asks.

Ousmanou nods and moves away from the door. "The *Ginaroo* came for me."

"What is the *Ginaroo?*" I ask.

"An evil spirit. A monster. The *Ginaroo* eats your soul alive."

"He's a ghost?" Vann asks.

"Yes, worse than a ghost. He's flesh and blood when he wants to be and spirit when he wants to be."

"What does he want with you?"

"I was walking home, and he saw me. It's nearly funeral season. He's waiting for spirits to be released by their families. The *Ginaroo* is out, and he's hungry. He'll eat anything that walks across his path."

"Will he follow you in here?" Vann asks.

"Can he go through walls?" I ask.

"No, he can't come into someone's house."

"Sounds like a vampire," I say.

"Miss, no one can go out there," Ousmanou whispers.

"Then you'll have to sleep here on the couch."

"Thank you, Miss."

"We'll be outside," says Vann.

"No! You can't!" Ousmanou warns.

"I doubt he'll want white meat anyway," says Vann.

Vann and I are brave at different moments. Ghosts and evil spirits terrify me, but I try to be tough and refrain from showing it. I follow her outside, and she tucks the mosquito net all the way around the bed except where we're going to enter.

With the flashlight, I take a few steps toward the latrine and stop.

"Vann, will you go to the bathroom with me?"

Vann smiles. "I'm sure glad you came today. Some birthday, huh?"

"One we'll never forget," I say.

"It's only been one day," says Vann.

"A lot can happen in a day in Africa."

Can you guess what I dream about in plus-110-degree heat at midnight?

Men!

Not just ordinary men. Chunky men. Sweet, decadent men. I dreamed about *the* men: Ben and Jerry of Ben & Jerry's Real Ice Cream.

Ben and Jerry are a big inspiration to me. I don't have to be eating Chunky Monkey, Cherry Garcia, or Coffee Heath Bar Crunch to feel inspired. Ben and Jerry are my heroes because they dream up enjoyable sweetness, then share it with others. That's what I want to do in life: dream up sweetness and share it with loved ones—even with the whole neighborhood.

This morning, I woke up in a foul mood. Yesterday, I received a card from my mother, encouraging me to "hang in there" during the eight remaining months in Guidiguis. She promised that, when I got home, she'd have a pint of the new Ben & Jerry's Chocolate-Chip Cookie Dough ice cream waiting in the fridge. Real bits of cookie dough in the ice cream. Big chunks, even. "It's to die for," she said. She underlines "die."

But eight months is years away.

It's 5:00 AM on a school day, but there will be no school. Cameroon is broke, and no one working for the government has been paid in four months. Fear and frustration are rampant, and survival is at stake. Teachers are now seriously talking about a strike happening in Cameroon.

If things continue, my colleagues doubt they'll be able to feed their families. Many have kids at home sick with either malaria, worms, or amoebic dysentery. Doc has been using his own savings to buy what medicine he can.

What makes matters worse is that the extreme north is running out of food. The millet crop is dying as a result of a long drought. Worse, the CFA has been devalued by the former French colonists. Prices have doubled. People working for the government who could once afford to pay for electricity have gone back to the traditional bush life. I feel ashamed to be the only one within miles with lights on.

Lately, when I visit neighbors, I bring along a bottle of cool water as a gift. My friends are delighted, regarding me as something like Santa Claus. Adele and the twins run to sit on my lap and be the first to drink the water. Nights are so hot now that I can put a tea bag in a cup of room-temperature water, and voilà—hot black tea! No kidding!

I'm depressed. My Peace Corps salary isn't enough to help my neighbors, and there's nothing I can do to change the political situation. It will certainly get worse before it gets better. I feel fortunate to be leaving soon; Cameroonians aren't so lucky.

I shuffle out onto my porch, plop into a stick chair, sit, and mope. Immediately, I hear a sound like someone eating Rice Crispies. Turning, I discover that the "Snap, Crackle, Pop" is coming from my chair. I poke at the legs, and dust begins to fall. I push the chair aside and see dust tunnels coming up through cracks and stretching out across the cement floor, tunnels left by tiny critters who have sniffed out the wooden aroma of my chair. Termites! Again!

I give the chair another shove, and the whole thing collapses.

I imagine my stick bed, left outside on the sand, as a pile of sawdust. I race around the corner to check it out. I close my eyes, fearing the worst. When I open them again, there lies my bed—a swarming termite feast.

Now I'm really depressed. No work. No chair. No bed. And no sweet men: Ben and Jerry. Defeated, I walk back to the front of my house and collapse onto the shaded sand. It's nearly 120 degrees, and we are all suffocating, flat on the ground, beaten and soaking with sweat. Everyone except the children. Their singing and giggling break the silence as they make their way to the water well. They stop in front of my house and stare.

Adele walks up to me and says, *"Bonbon. Bonbon."*

I shake my head. I want to tell her that it's her fault that I don't have any more sweetness to give. I'd run out of candy weeks before. Adele couldn't keep her gold mine a secret and only come with her brother and baby sister. No, she had to lead each neighborhood kid by the hand to my house, one at a time, to make certain that each got a fair share. Adele keeps pleading with her eyes, but I regretfully shake my head.

She lowers her eyes, turns, and leads the children away.

One four-year-old boy whom I haven't seen before lingers behind. He's only a skeleton, and a top layer of skin looks as if it's turning white. He sets his bucket down and approaches. Frightened, he closes his eyes and outstretches his hand to shake mine. Taking his hand, I pull him close, then pick him up. I tickle and twirl him about, and he shrieks in surprise. Startled with his screaming, I want to scream, too, for I suddenly realize he's never been tickled. I quickly slow down to turn him loose when he begins to giggle.

He throws his arms around my neck and begins to laugh. Delicious giggles cartwheel out of my throat. It's been weeks since I've laughed. I put the little fellow down, and he hugs my legs for a long time. I wish I had candy for him or a pint of Chunky Monkey we could share.

What to do about a nagging sweet tooth in the middle of the desert?

I think about Ben and Jerry and how determined they must have been when they began to pursue their dream. They had a vision, turned it into reality, and shared it with the world. I decided right then and there to make a new commitment to life. Not just to breathing, but to life with all the toppings: love, laughter, hope, charity, and chocolate.

I jump up and quickly pack for a day trip. I write a short note for Abbo and Egré, letting them know that I've gone to Maroua to buy a kitten. I want to surprise them with ingredients from the "White Man's Store" to make ice cream. Chunky Monkey is out, but cold, sweet banana splits I figure I can concoct.

I wait three hours for a bush taxi. Finally, a dump truck with a missing windshield shows up. Three well-groomed Foulbe men sit in front. Their wives are standing with the children and goats in the back. The driver nods at me and motions to the rear. I climb up and immediately step into goat shit. I feel it ooze up between my toes. As I lean over to slip off a sandal, a few children edge toward me. One reaches out and touches a strand of my hair. Another reaches out to touch, but when a mother nervously calls for her, all the children return to their mothers. Everyone stares at me as if I were a giant-screen TV. An old woman approaches with her canteen. She pours a little water over my foot as a goat looks up my skirt. Calling it by name, she shoos the goat away, then smiles at me, revealing her dark orange teeth.

Hours later, I take the last sip from my canteen. The old woman notices and offers me a drink of water. The sun is so hot and my thirst so great that I accept, not even caring if I get another intestinal disease. This ancient woman knows just how much I need that water, and I am grateful for her kindness.

As the sun sets, the corn and millet fields seem to sigh as a light breeze licks our bodies. Cold ice cream dreams dance in my head like the days before Christmas, when I was girl. We are more than halfway to our destination, and things are looking up. The truck sputters but moves slowly along. It seems possible that we might actually reach the capital before the store closes. I cross my fingers, close my eyes, and listen to the wind as if I were hearing it for the first time. My body rocks back and forth against hard-muscled women's bodies. They don't seem to be in pain, but I feel an ache in my feet. And they don't seem to notice the odor of chicken shit as my face twists in disgust.

I will never again complain about a bus ride in the States.

The vehicle wails as it slows, approaching a military checkpoint ten kilometers before a small village. Four military police sit atop their motorcycles, looking extremely smug. They chug their beer and smirk at passersby with bags of millet on their heads or transporting animals to the market. I see one bicycle carrying a live pig tied on the back. A pig? I rub my eyes. The cyclist is having a hell of a time pedaling. And the pig is squealing. I can't help giggling, which draws the attention of an enormous policeman. He grins and pinches his crotch as he staggers toward us. He asks the driver for registration. But the driver shakes his head. The policeman orders him to pull over for further questioning.

I kiss banana splits good-bye. The policeman checks our ID cards and searches luggage. All the women are hassled for not owning an ID, but their husbands, who sit comfortably in the front of the truck, pay off the police with a couple of high bills. Next, the fat policeman motions for everyone to step off the truck. He grabs my shoulder, pinching it hard, and shoves a drunken mouth in my face. My ID is no good, he says.

I want to slug him.

I don't. The trip has taken any fight out of me. He's asking for a bribe, but I don't have enough money. So I take a deep breath and pray. I know it's important not to show frustration. That will only create more delay—and even give them ammunition with which to shoot someone.

"It's a school day, teacher. Why aren't you teaching?" he asks.

Choked up, I say nothing.

His hand moves from his crotch to his rifle, which he pushes against my shoulder, separating me from the rest of the group. "Are you striking, Miss?" he demands.

I shake my head, afraid any words of mine will cave in on us.

Now that there are rumors of a national strike, the military are picking on Americans, accusing us of being politically active. What will my traveling companions do if the police decide to rough me up out here in the middle of nowhere? Will they come to the rescue? Or will they turn away? I don't like being *nasara*. I don't like all the attention. And I wish I were anywhere but here.

What can I say about the strike? That I won't cross a picket line? More ridiculous, how can I explain my sweet tooth to a pack of drunken military police? They wouldn't understand.

And besides, they've never tasted ice cream.

A different policeman returns with my Peace Corps ID. He speaks in pidgin English that I barely understand. He says something about remembering meeting me at the hospital in Guidiguis. But I don't remember him. He winks and reminds me that I am "the doctor's woman." I shake my head, thinking of Doc and dancing under the moonlight. The policeman smiles as he pats my shoulder, motioning for the others to let me go.

We arrive in the capital after eight hours of frustrating hell. In Africa, if you get one thing done while the sun's up, it's a good day.

If not, well, you've survived another day, and that's reason enough to celebrate.

This is destined to be a good day, because I reach the "White Man's Store," run by a German and his French wife, minutes before it closes. I buy all the fixings for a banana split. Everything is imported from Europe and very expensive. I spend easily half of next month's salary. I buy imported French chocolate, sweet canned cream, powered milk, almonds, peanut butter, bananas, eggs, sugar, and more chocolate. I walk out of the store feeling like a little girl with a quarter in her pocket, skipping after music soaring from an ice cream truck.

Since the Peace Corps house is full, a volunteer friend, Amy, invites me to stay at her new post within the city of Maroua. I'm thankful not to sleep on the floor and for the opportunity to spend quality time with Amy. We talk until the sun rises, and I get up and pack the ice cream ingredients in my backpack.

I leave Amy's house at 6:00 AM, but it's not until four hours later that I'm able to catch a bush taxi back to Guidiguis. It's already more than 112 degrees when seven of us pack into a VW bug. Although my supplies get a little mushy, it's a perfect day to cool off the neighborhood with banana splits.

When I reach home, Egré and Abbo are sitting outside on stools, washing our laundry by hand. Gumbo barks to welcome me and wags his tail as I pet him. I smile at the boys but tell them they aren't allowed in the kitchen. Their eyes grow wide with terror, and they begin to whisper in French and Tapouri.

"What do you think Miss is doing now?" Abbo asks.

"God, I hope she's not cooking Chinese food again," says Egré. "How can she eat that stuff?"

"And she complains that our spicy fried locusts taste bad."

"My family says I'm getting too thin living with Miss," Abbo says.

"Should we tell her?" Egré asks.

"Not yet. So far, I don't smell anything bad."

"Maybe she's making pizza. Pizza is delicious."

"Maybe she's topping the pizza with ground meat like she described."

"Maybe cat meat. Miss said something about buying a small cat," Egré says.

"She did say that. Maybe that's what she's cooking now," Abbo says.

I'm not offended that they don't like my Chinese stir-fry, but I immediately put off any thought of getting a pet kitten. I close the kitchen door and crank up Aretha Franklin as I mix the ingredients:

Suzi's Cameroonian Banana Splits

Ingredients:

1 pint sweet cream, whipped
5 eggs
1/2 gallon milk
1 1/2 cups sugar
2 tsp. vanilla
Pinch of salt
5 pounds bananas (mushy)
1 cup peanut butter (sun-melted)
10 bars milk chocolate (any candy bar will do)
1 cup almonds

Combine whipped cream, eggs, milk, sugar, and vanilla. Cook for 20 minutes on low heat, stirring quickly and constantly (eggs and milk burn easily). If too salty, add a little more milk and a touch of sugar. Then cool in a freezer for at least five hours. When solidified, melt milk chocolate and crush the almonds.

In the desert, it's difficult to keep sweat driblets from rolling off one's chin and nose and into the ice cream batter. So if you're making ice cream in the heat, then it's important to taste the batter a few times to get the right sweetness.

After slicing big chunks of dark French chocolate, I peel the bananas and place them whole in several plastic bowls. Last, I round up Adele and the neighborhood kids and invite them over. Egré and Abbo are hesitant to come into the kitchen, but they sample the ice cream anyway because I'm their mother and because I tell them they have to. (Did I say that?)

Imagine being a child of the desert and never having tasted that delicious milky coolness. Then, suddenly, a crazy white woman with a mad craving for chocolate grabs you by the hand and, smiling wickedly, marches you into her house and makes you sit on the floor. Then she hands you a banana split topped with naturally sun-melted peanut butter. You take a bite, and it's cold. But then it's sweet! Yikes!

What the hell is this stuff?

I blow their minds. A dozen kids shriek with delight and because their teeth hurt! Abbo and Egré hold their cheeks, moaning that I'm trying to make their teeth fall out. Teenagers!

Ice cream spills out of the children's mouths and onto their round bellies. The little army of children laugh, get sticky, and give me messy kisses. They get chocolate on my nose, in my hair, and on my favorite Dire Straits T-shirt. For a wonderful and glorious moment, I find sweetness in my life. I create a little joy. I hear my sons licking their fingers when I'm not looking and turn and catch them smiling.

The next day, the neighborhood ants come over to celebrate my charity, too. They march in with their trumpets, set up camp, dance a little, eat a little, and stay awhile. I don't have the heart to squish the little buggers. Maybe they're down in the dumps and need a spoonful of sugar, too.

Then the trumpets sound, and the orchestra takes its place. From the nooks and crannies, I hear an African rendition of "For He's a Jolly Good Fellow," dedicated to Ben and Jerry, our delight and our inspiration.

Dear Mom,

You finally asked how I go to the bathroom. Well, I'm in the latrine at this very moment. I've got yet another bout with amoebic dysentery. Here I am squatting over the latrine for nearly fifteen minutes, and my bowels still aren't empty. I ran here from my desk rather quickly, feeling I wasn't going to make it in time. I didn't even put the pad of paper and pen down. Well, now you're here with me, so I'll describe it to you.

The latrine is an area at the back of my house where a slab of concrete was poured and there's a small hole that opens up into a fifteen-foot bucket. I squat and aim into the hole. My aim is getting better, as I'm now able to go to the bathroom without making a mess. It took some practice, though. Talk about penis envy. I'm green.

There's no roof over my head, so my buns are getting burned this very moment. I've thought of buying an umbrella and leaving it out here or rubbing sunblock on my buns before I go, but so far I've done nothing about it yet. As you can probably guess, my butt burns easily since it's never seen the sun. Until now.

One thing I have done is put a machete out here—just in case any snakes get crazy ideas about joining me. I saw a scorpion out here once, and I've never run so fast in my life.

You thought I used a lot of paper back home. Check this out. I went through ten rolls in a weekend. I had diarrhea so bad that I ran out of toilet paper and had to use leaves. (Ouch.) Later, when I had to use the bathroom at a villager's house, I discovered how the villagers take care of business: they simply use water from a plastic teapot and soap. They say it's cleaner that way because toilet paper wipes but doesn't clean. Interesting point.

But that didn't stop me from buying three gigantic cases of toilet paper the next time I was in Maroua. Since the bush taxi stop at the *carrefour* is miles away from my house, I always hire a Muslim teenager on a motorcycle to take me home with my usual one box of groceries. This time, I had to hire four motorcycles to carry me and my cases of toilet paper. The entire village came to a standstill with their mouths hanging open as they first watched me zoom by, then another motorcycle with a case of toilet paper, then another, and another. One kid plopped down on the sand and rolled over laughing. Most of the villagers just smiled and shook their heads. I'm sure they're wondering why white people are so dumb.

Mom, sometimes it's so hot, I imagine the toilet paper bursting into flames after being left out here for hours. But Vann says it's not possible. Last time I visited her in Kaele, she told me she had talked to the carpenter in her village. She asked him to design a wooden toilet bowl in her latrine to fit perfectly on top of the hole. When I sat on the wooden box, it felt so luxurious to sit while taking a pee, I imagined myself a queen on a throne.

I liked the idea of sitting on a box so much, especially when having diarrhea, that I went to the carpenter in my village to design one for me. But he only shook his head, not understanding my Fulfulde. The next day, I was even more determined to sit on a wooden toilet bowl. I went back to the carpenter and pleaded for him to come to my house so I could show him what I meant.

He eventually made one, but it was so low to the ground that I felt three years old using my old training potty. The next one he made was too high, and my feet didn't even touch the ground. I used it for a while but couldn't get over the horrible feeling that I was going to fall into the latrine. (Did I ever fall into the toilet bowl when I was a child?) Finally, I got the guts to hire a motorcycle and carry the wooden toilet bowl across the village and return it to the carpenter. The next one's gotta be just right, right? But Mom, I wonder, what will the villagers have to gossip about when I leave?

Enclosed is a self-portrait of me squatting over the latrine—just in case you weren't able to quite picture just what I meant. Squeeze the Charmin for me.

Love,
Suz

Abbo and Egré buried Gumbo in the backyard while I was away in Maroua to receive a phone call from home and visit with Amy. The boys said that "his stomach blew up" and there was nothing they could do. When Gumbo stopped eating and drinking, Abbo biked to the hospital to ask Doc for help, but the assistant said he was away on vacation and wouldn't return for a month.

"Where did the doctor go?" I ask, fighting back the tears. I can't believe Doc is gone and Gumbo is dead. The boys shrug their shoulders and look away from my eyes. They return to scrubbing their buckets of laundry.

"What is it?" I ask. There's something they're not telling me. Abbo wrings out a towel and then moves to the clothesline to hang it to dry.

"Did you see him before he left?" I ask. They only shake their heads. Doc left Guidiguis without saying good-bye. What if I never see him again?

"The mayor's wife came to see you yesterday," Abbo says.

"And your neighbor, too," Egré says, rubbing two ends of the sheet together and making so many suds that they spill over the side of the bucket.

"Clotilde? Is she up and walking again?" I ask.

Abbo smiles. "Yes, and the tailor's children also came to greet you."

"How do they know where I live?" I ask.

"Everyone knows where the white woman lives," Egré says, and laughs.

"Oh," I say. "Well, I guess I have a lot of visiting to do. You boys want to come?"

They shake their heads: they have lots to do—finish washing the clothes, dishes, and sheets, sweep, go to the market, and fill up the water barrel.

"Miss, did you reach the bank before it closed?" Egré asks.

"Yes," I say, raising my eyebrows.

"Do you think I could get paid early?" Egré asks, looking me straight in the eyes.

"Why do you need money today?" I ask. What would Egré need to buy?

"I'd like to buy a notebook, a duck, and some mangoes," Egré says defensively.

"Mangoes are here?" I ask, excited that there's something juicy to eat.

"Yes, they've come from Dzigilou. They're sweet and enormous!" Abbo says.

"Egré, I'll give you your allowance and will add some money to buy us some mangoes. How much are they each?"

"Two hundred CFAs," Egré says.

Abbo hits Egré in the side with his elbow and says, "You know they're only 100 CFAs each, some even fifty!"

"The biggest mangoes are 200 CFAs. She wants the biggest!" Egré says angrily to Abbo, and leaps off his stool.

"You can bargain down to 100 CFAs because you know the merchants have too many!" Abbo says, and rises slowly to meet Egré's threat.

Abbo puts his face up to Egré's and says, "You're trying to make a profit! That's what you're doing!" Egré yells at Abbo in Tapouri, and Abbo retaliates. I jump in between them and strain my neck looking up at my tall boys.

"Stop! Please stop!" I put a hand on each of their shoulders. "Abbo, thank you. I appreciate how you look out for me. Egré, you were mistaken. Right?"

Egré nods, mumbling to Abbo in Tapouri, before leaving with two buckets. Abbo returns to his stool, thrusts his hands into the suds, and scrubs fiercely.

"What did he say, Abbo?" I ask.

"He said I'm trying to be your favorite and make you hate him," Abbo says dryly.

"I could never hate Egré," I say.

Abbo looks away. He rubs the soap in his right hand, turning it over and over again. He looks up at me and says, "Egré says he wants to be a priest, but I don't believe he has God in his heart."

"Abbo, what's gotten into you? Egré is a devoted Bible student. The Father tells me he's doing well in his studies."

"Egré only wants to sit at the feet of the white man to get any scraps or coins that fall from the table!"

"Abbo, I can't believe you said that! Egré is like your own brother."

"You are a mother to me. Egré is only my brother because you love him."

Egré comes back through the door with two buckets of water, and already the sweat is dripping down his forehead.

"Do you hear the music?" Egré asks.

"Yes," I say. "Isn't it coming from next door?"

Bob Marley's music comes in crystal-clear, nothing like the tapes played on the cheap Nigerian cassette recorders. I walk out the door and follow the music to Clotilde's house. I clap before entering their compound, and Alex greets me by hugging my legs. My knees are going to miss all this loving when I return to the States.

Yves, Mr. Mfoumba, LeoPaul, and Benito are sitting on chairs talking. Yves pours tall shots of whiskey in three glasses. When their hands bring it up to their lips, I say, "*Salut!*"

They knock back the glasses, then welcome me to their compound. I shake their hands and ask for Clotilde. Yves points to the mud-hut kitchen.

"The mayor can't strike, but he supports us," LeoPaul says.

Yves agrees. "Not the new commander. He's loyal to Biya and very suspicious."

"We can wait for the revolution. When they move, we move," Mr. Mfoumba says.

Yves pours another round of drinks.

When I reach the kitchen, Clotilde is squatting, sweating as if she were running a marathon. She begins stirring the millet porridge, and she's quickly out of breath.

"Clotilde, are you well enough to be cooking?"

"Of course, Suzanne. *Jam bah doo nah?*"

"*Jam core doo may, mon amie.* Please let me help you."

I squat down next to her, and she moves over to let me stir the porridge in a pot over the fire with a stick as long and thick as a baseball bat. But the porridge is so thick, it's like cement in the pot, and I can't even move it in a full circle. I shift my weight to get a better grip, and Clotilde laughs.

"Am I stronger than you, Suzanne?" Clotilde asks.

"Yes," I say. "Maybe I could stir better with my legs."

"I heard you traveled to Kaele on your bike," Clotilde says, as she gently pushes me aside so she can continue stirring. "Don't you know how dangerous it is now for a woman to travel, especially a white woman, and on her own with only a bicycle?"

"I'm still in my skin, *mon amie*."

"Let's keep it that way, *sobajo am*. But be more careful."

"What about you? Are you taking care of yourself?" I ask.

"The medication Yves bought is working. The doctor took good care of me. I'm fortunate I got sick before he left Guidiguis."

Clotilde doesn't mention losing the baby, and I'm not sure if I should bring it up. I know Yves has put pressure on her to give him another child and blames her for the miscarriage.

"Where did the doctor go?" I ask.

"To his village, I think. You mean, he didn't tell you?" Clotilde looks surprised.

"Tell me what?" I ask. Now I *know* something is being hidden from me.

"I thought he said good-bye, that's all." Clotilde turns her eyes away from me.

"No, he didn't. Is he coming back?"

"I believe so," Clotilde says, and stops stirring. "You love him, don't you?"

"No," I say, then stumble over my next few words. "I mean, yes, I care for him very much."

"We hear him at your door late at night."

"You were sleeping outside?" I ask, and immediately feel my face flush.

"Yes," Clotilde says, and smiles.

"You heard everything," I say, and realize that she knows. Everyone must know.

"Yes," Clotilde says. "He loves you."

"It could never work," I say. "I can't stay, and he'd never leave Cameroon."

"You know, Suzanne, soon his parents will be looking to arrange a marriage for him. You might want to tell him your feelings before his family finds your doctor a bride. You might want to consider remaining in Cameroon and marrying."

"I cannot stay here, *mon amie*. I do love Cameroon, but not enough to be here for a lifetime. And he cannot leave Africa. We're not meant to be."

"Somehow it feels that you are," Clotilde says, and sighs.

I stop to think about that. It's too soon to make that kind of decision or commitment. And anyway, it's not as if he must marry someone tomorrow.

Clotilde continues stirring the millet, and I pick up the spice-grinding rock. I grind garlic, onions, and spicy red peppers in a wooden bowl and pound the spices to a pulp.

I think of the first time I met Doc and how he sang for the children. I sing along to Bob Marley's "Redemption Song."

"You know the words to Bob Marley?" Clotilde asks.

"If I had known you had the tape, I would've worn it out by now."

"It's a CD. Yves just bought a new stereo and three new CDs."

"What?" I stop pounding the spices and look up at her.

"He saved up a long time. Yves was able to pay for the medication and the hospital and still buy me a stereo. Back in my village, there's music in every home, even if it's only songs from our lips."

Yves wouldn't pay for his wife's medication, but he'll go out and spend 20,000 CFAs or more on a stereo! There is talk of a strike, the drought, another salary cut, and yet he can afford a CD stereo. I can't even afford one in the States.

"My husband is a good man."

"Yes," I say, swallowing the secret of who bought her medication.

"Are you staying and eating with us?"

"No, I promised the mayor's wife I'd eat there."

Clotilde pours the millet into a big bowl and puts the top on it.

She stands up and shakes my hand, thanking me for coming to visit.

As I walk out, Yves waves for me to come and join them.

"We need to speak with you," Yves says. "Bring Miss a glass!"

Clotilde comes out of her kitchen, wiping her hands on her sarong. LeoPaul stands up and offers his chair to me.

"I'm sorry, but I can't stay. I'm expected at the mayor's house."

"Miss," LeoPaul says, "you know there's a strike about to happen in Cameroon. We expect you to support us."

I sit down, knowing that it will be tedious to explain why I can't strike.

"LeoPaul, my boss won't allow me to strike. I'll lose my job," I say.

"But, Miss! You must support us. We're all family here," Benito says.

"Yes," I say, "you're right. We must stick together."

"We need more water here," Yves says.

Clotilde, carrying Alex, dutifully pours cool water in our glasses. "Miss," LeoPaul says, then clears his throat, "the teachers need to have a meeting in order to discuss our strategy. We are asking you to be there."

"We can't have a strike meeting," I say.

"It's important to know that you are with us. If you're not, then you're against us."

"I'm with you," I say.

Leaving, I shake the teachers' hands. I thank them and return home for my bike.

"If you go to the mayor's house, please be back before dark," Abbo says.

As I get on the bike, he hands me a flashlight.

"Take this just in case. You can hit them over the head if they bother you."

"Which are you afraid of," I ask, "the Chadians or the villagers?"

"Mom, I'm afraid for you. Times are hard. It's *la crise*." Abbo hugs me good-bye, and I wonder what's gotten into him. Then I wonder if I've become blind to how bad conditions have been since I arrived.

Biking to the mayor's house, I'm chased for nearly half a mile by the children returning from Koran school. They shout my name and laugh, making me feel like a famous movie star just trying to live a normal life.

When I arrive, Calixte greets me as if she hasn't seen me in years. She kisses me on both cheeks as the French do and leads me by the hand into her home. I sit on the couch and look to the spot where Doc sat next to me the first time we were received here together. I didn't think I'd miss him so much.

"Did you hear the wonderful news of our doctor?" asks Calixte.

"What's the news?"

"He didn't tell you?"

"What would he have told me if he had had the chance?"

"Well, that he's . . . uh . . . gone away for a month on a vacation."

"Yes, I've heard that. Is there something more?" I ask.

"Oh, no," Calixte says, and begins to serve me rice at her coffee table set up for our lunch together. "Did you see your Foulbe family before coming here?"

"No, I was worried I'd be late."

"The tailor's little boy drowned."

"No!"

"Yes, the story is that he woke up during the midday nap to pee and fell into a bucket. Everyone slept right through it."

"The family must be heartbroken. Calixte, I'm sorry, but I have to go see them."

I apologize again and hop on my bicycle to race to Sali's compound.

When I arrive, there are over seventy men sitting on a mat in front of their house. I hear the women screaming in the compound. The children see me and take me by the hand through the entrance and beyond the mud-hut walls. There are even more women inside, busily preparing enough food for over a hundred people. Inside Sali's wife's hut, the women are wailing.

When Dada sees my face, she stops screaming and rushes to greet me. Her belly looks a lot less bloated, and her eyes are clearer. She takes me to her mat, and we sit holding hands, rocking back and forth. Tears fall down my cheeks, and she wipes them softly away. The children gather, and we sit silently, listening to the crying and screaming. Dada says my name, then stands to act out what happened while explaining it in Fulfulde. She found him dead and tried to breathe life back into him, but his soul had already flown away.

She sits down next to me again and joins the women wailing. I wail with her. The sounds come up from deep within me. The wails grow louder until I'm screaming with her and holding her hand tightly. The boy's death has pinched a nerve. It hit a spot I've long denied was there. I can't help but cry for the pain I've carried in my heart for so long.

Up rises sadness; I remember events in my life that I've never allowed myself to think about. Suddenly, I'm crying for the death of my childhood and the innocence that was stolen from me. I shed tears for the girl inside who aches to feel safe and loved. I let out tears for my father's several suicide attempts, beginning when I was six years old. Memories of each time I rescued him flash in my mind until it's the day of my sixteenth birthday, when his suicide was finally successful. I cry over the brutality I suffered at the hands of my stepfather. I let out tears for the memories of a failed marriage and my divorce. And on and on the events in my life unfold like the blooming of a flower suddenly touched by the sun.

I let it all out—screaming and crying and pounding my fists on the earth. This is a ceremony—this wailing of women. I think of *La Llorona*, a legendary figure in Mexican folklore, whose only protest against the cruelty of the Spanish male conquerors was to wail by the river through the night.

My wailing with the African women has become my protest against what was done to me. But I don't feel like a victim. I reach inward and with my own two hands take hold of my power. I offer my voice and wailing up to Spirit as a form of resistance. I wrestle with the pain; when I finally have it pinned down, I push it out of my belly, up through my lungs, and out my throat. Now I wail even louder and more aggressively. I wail at the top of my lungs, and it feels like justice to express the hurt and then finally to let it go.

I let it all go. The pain, the resentment, the anger, the bitterness, the shame, and the judgment for myself and others. I feel a desire to forgive, to return to my love for them and move on in a new direction. I know it's a long road to walk upon in order to go through the healing process, but I've got the *ganas*. In Spanish it means desire.

Yes, this young woman has got plenty of *ganas* and enough courage and strength to embrace her wild woman's heart with both hands and to fill it with fire. I desire to burn brightly and passionately—to really be alive, to experience it all, to taste and savor and delight in the wine.

Rumi explains in Sufism that life is a process of being in God's wine shop: opening each bottle and discovering love, desire, hate, passion, pain, suffering, bliss, and joy. Creation and destruction, life and death, we must dance for them both. They are one and the same. We are here to experience the entire range of the human spectrum.

This way of the Foulbe releases grief and is healthy for the mind, heart, and spirit. The men sit together outside to support the family; they listen and grieve in silence, while the women gather together to shout the pain out while comforting and nourishing each other.

There is only silence after the women stop wailing. Dada and I immediately stop, too. More women walk out of Sali's wife's hut and sit with us. We rock until we hear the call to prayer from the mosque—just before sunset.

They fill their plastic teapots and gather together on a mat to wash for prayer. I wash my feet, ears, face, and hands until I feel completely cleansed in mind, body, and soul. The women lay down sacred prayer carpets and begin chanting and doing prostrations. I follow Dada's lead, repeating her words in a soft whisper to my soul.

It's not important what name I call God; I know I'm heard. I say Allah's name, listening to my voice taken with the wind. I feel Mother Africa, like an eagle landing on my shoulders. I feel its claws hold my shoulders high. Its wings spread wide, and we rise together in flight into an evening sky sparkling with stars, which reflect in my eyes.

Egré and I are planting peanuts and corn in the field in front of my house. He scoops up the sand with a plow, and I drop a kernel or peanut. Egré covers it with sand, and we move on. He works diligently while I sing. "Wonderful" has become my powerful mantra: when I say it, not only the energy inside me changes, but even the scent in the air seems to turn to perfume. I breathe it in and feel life somersaulting inside me.

Egré and I work our way up and down the field until we are out of peanuts and corn. Clotilde, Alex, and Yves are bent over in their own field fifty yards from us. Alex sees me stand up and skips over, repeating "*bonjour*" like the chorus of a song. He gives me a couple of kernels from his sweaty hand as if they were a birthday present. Egré plants them, and then we're taken by the hand of our little guide to his parents' field. Just as we begin helping Yves and Clotilde, Valentine and her twins salute us with a wave and then dive into their field, directly behind us. Last night's fierce rain seems to have given everyone hope that, this year, Guidiguis may actually have a rainy season.

A yellow car speeds down the muddy street, turns right, and drives across my newly planted field. Egré and I look up, horrified to see our land being ripped apart by tire tracks. The Foulbe man driving sees me and stops his car. He yells, "*Nasara!*" and throws a letter out the window. He reverses like a madman, leaving us with our mouths hanging open. All that work ruined in an instant.

The letter is addressed to the White Woman of Guidiguis. (I guess that would be me.) How the heck did the driver know where I live? And where did he come from?

I open the envelope, wondering who would address a letter like that and send it with a crazy man. It's from Vann! She writes that letters should only be sent by bush taxi because they're being opened and read for evidence that Americans are spies. That's it, she writes; she's made up her mind. She's quitting. Please come and say good-bye.

I read the letter to Egré. He only shakes his head and says, "*Asha*, Mom."

How could Vann leave me?

I drop everything and run to the house. It'll be hard to get out of Guidiguis now that it's Ramadan and Muslims are fasting from dawn until sunset. They can't take in any food or water. Since most of the bush taxi drivers are Muslim, they'll be sleeping all day, weak from thirst and hunger. But I have to try and reach Vann before she goes, so I pack an overnight bag, then I'm off to wait for a bush taxi.

The *carrefour* looks like a ghost town. No one is selling mangoes or cooking goat meat. There aren't any eager Muslim teenagers on motorcycles waiting to taxi people around Guidiguis. There aren't even any children playing in the streets, only women and young girls journeying to the water well in the intense heat. They are the only ones with an ounce of strength in the daytime during this religious season of starvation and dehydration.

I look in both directions for any signs of bush taxis on their way but see no movement. I sit on my bag and wait.

Two hours pass.

Nothing.

Noon comes, then evening.

Nothing.

Then, out of nowhere comes a pair of headlights, and I stand up to flag the car down. It's the Italian Catholic priest, but he must not see me because he drives right on by. I sip the last of the water from my canteen and watch the sun set. I finally give up, pick up my bag, and head home. It would have been faster to have run to Kaele with my bag on top of my head. Why didn't I just pick up and start making my way there on foot? I think of Chadian bandits and drunk *gendarmes* and my promise to Clotilde to be more careful.

When I reach home, Egré wakes from his nap, surprised to see me. He hops up from his mat to fix us both a plate of the dinner he's cooked.

While he's in the kitchen, I hear the chewing and crackling of termites. When I pick up the mat from the sand, one million of them are eating the bottom layer of straw. Chills break out down my arms and legs. I pick up the mat and cast it as far away from the house as possible.

Egré returns, hands me a plate, and we sit down to eat.

"I hate termites almost as much as the roaches in the latrine."

"Termites are worse after the rains. They eat everything everywhere."

"But they've been doing that all along," I say.

Egré shakes his head. "They have a nose for anything that touches the sand. They'll even eat clothes that fall from the line. It'll get worse, Mom."

"Worse? How can it get worse? They've already cost me two beds, a chair, three mats, and hundreds of my students' tests!"

"Lucky us that they did," Egré says, and chuckles. I wonder if he led the termites to the stacks of exams while I was away in Maroua.

I dip a ball of millet porridge into the tomato sauce and pop it into my mouth.

"This is very good," I say. "Egré, you know what I should have done? At two o'clock, when there wasn't a single car that passed by, I should have just gotten up and run to Kaele."

"There's no way that you'd make it. No one could run all the way to Kaele."

My eyes light up. I sit up straight and smile at Egré.

"No, there's no way," he says, shaking his head as if he can read my mind. He gets up and says, "No way, Mom, I'm not running with you all the way to Kaele."

At four in the morning, while Muslims are feasting on water and food before dawn and the morning prayers that begin the daily fasting of Ramadan, Egré and I head out to Kaele in the darkness. Egré rides the bike with a box full of water, Kool-Aid, cut mangoes, and guavas.

The farthest I've ever run so far has been about fifteen miles, so I'm not quite sure how I'll do at twenty. Egré mumbles under his breath that he'll die before he even gets to Kaele, but I just laugh and get behind the bike and push him for a few yards. He yells out to please stop or he's going to fall, so I let go, and he says, "Some kind of Mom you are."

One foot in front of the other and I'm moving. Slowly, Egré and I are getting somewhere, making our way across the desert. My feet are more reliable than any bush taxi. From now on when transportation looks hopeless, I'll just make a point of either running or riding my bike out of Guidiguis. By the time I get back to the States, I'll be ready to run a marathon.

The sun stretches its golden arms and cradles the desert to its bosom. We watch the splendid morning stretch out before us as the stars wink and gently fade away.

Two hours later, Egré and I reach a sleepy village just off the paved road. My legs feel fine; I'm stronger now than I've ever been. Egré is holding up, and as long as I keep him singing Tapouri songs, he doesn't complain about being hot, thirsty, and that his back is tired.

No one is yet awake in the village, and not even a lizard is stirring. Egré stops singing so as not to wake anyone when, suddenly, Tapouri boys and girls jump out from nowhere like an ambush, scaring us out of our skins. The children scream and laugh at our expressions and at the sight of Egré and me traveling on bike and foot. Concerned parents appear to see what all the fuss is about. They smile, nod, and wave. They see that it's just me; they're getting used to seeing me moving through these parts. The adults yell out my name, and the children copy, rolling its unfamiliar sound off their tongues, then repeating over and over, "Suzanne." The adults disappear as quickly as they arrived, and it all seems like an illusion—for suddenly, the village is almost deserted.

I wave for the children to join in, and they rush across the street to run with us. They chase us down the road for nearly half a mile, holding out their hands for me to shake them. When they've gone far enough, they stop and scream out good-bye in Tapouri. Egré and I can hear them singing my name for almost a quarter of a mile.

I wonder, when I leave Africa, will the children remember me? Will they tell stories to their children or future Peace Corps volunteers of the crazy white woman who would cross the desert by foot or bike to Kaele?

I know I will never forget their smiles, their excited little hands holding mine, and their willingness to love me no matter what my color or nationality. It's the children I will remember the most when I leave Cameroon.

Egré complains that his legs are tired, so we stop and drink more Kool-Aid and water. Egré nearly swallows a guava and a mango whole, but I'm not hungry, just thirsty. I hope that Egré's legs are going to hold up until we get to Kaele.

Down the road a few more miles, Egré refuses to sing any longer. He's tired and wants to stop. Again, we take a short break. He gets off the bike to stretch his legs. The sun has risen higher, and the temperature is quickly soaring. Egré wonders if we could die from being out in the sun too long.

When we run out of water, Egré worries that we won't make it. I assure him that we're nearly there, but he says I told him that an hour ago. Then he reminds me that I was once detained by the military police for over two hours here and that I could have died of thirst.

"We don't have any water, Mom," he says. For some reason, I'm not worried. I try my best to reassure him that this time I have my ID card, but he shakes his head and tells me that we're in danger.

"There could be trouble. You're white, remember?" Egré says, and sighs.

I don't know why it's so hard now for me to remember how different I am. I never used to forget that I was a stranger here. There's something about being in the desert that makes me feel I'm connected to everything. I draw the life force into my soul from the Earth and the sky, and because of that, I know I am safe.

Feeling disappointed by his long absence, I look for the lizard and listen for his voice. And then I remember, like a nudge in the side to turn in another direction, that I no longer have to search outside myself for a guiding voice. Everything I need to know on this journey is right here, as it has always been. I simply need to be quiet and listen to the wind blow across the desert sky. I am my own companion, and the source of my strength doesn't come from water, food, or the body but from a peaceful place within that knows that I am more than myself: I am Spirit. I feel it moving within me.

When we see another small village ahead, Egré yelps and pedals faster.

"Water!" he cries out, and races to the well.

Women and children stop their work and offer Egré and me the spout to fill our bottles. Egré takes a calabash and fills it with water, then gulps it down quickly. As I sit on the sand to take a look at a blister on my toe, a tiny naked boy tiptoes to me and offers a full calabash of water. Instead of drinking it, I pour it over my head. He thinks it's hilarious and gets the other children to come with their calabashes. They fill them with water and offer them to me. One after the other, I pour them over my head. Then the children stop handing me the calabashes; instead, after they fill them with water, *they* pour them over my head. I feign surprise each time they do it, and they run back to the water pump for more full calabashes.

When I'm completely soaked, and when our bellies are tired of laughing, I stand up and shake all of their hands good-bye. Egré is more relaxed now that we have water, and when we resume our journey to Kaele, he starts singing again.

After four hours of running, we reach Kaele without any trouble from the *gendarmes*. They simply wave me past when they see me. I smile and wave back.

But when we reach Vann's house, she's already left for Maroua.

Egré and I look at each other long and hard. He knows I want to continue to Maroua, but I know he's hungry and tired. After a long back-and-forth argument, I convince Egré that we can make it another ten miles to Mindif, where another Peace Corps volunteer teacher lives. I explain that we can stay there, eat and sleep, then continue to Maroua, only twenty-two miles away.

Egré agrees only after a lot of arm-twisting. I tell him that, when we reach Maroua, I'll take him to this really fancy hotel that has a swimming pool and I'll teach him how to swim. The idea of sitting in a pool of water as the sun rises directly above us sounds like a miracle.

A total of fifty-two miles from Guidiguis, at eight o'clock in the morning and twenty-eight hours after we left Guidiguis, Egré and I arrive in Maroua. We both have tears in our eyes when we enter the city limits. We've made it, and our legs didn't fall off. We reach the Peace Corps house, but Vann has already left for Yaounde just two hours before. She's already half a country away. My heart drops, but my son picks it up off the floor.

"Mom, we're not running to Yaounde, OK!" says Egré, and this is a *command,* not a question. He limps across the living room holding his aching back and making a face that looks like he's dying. He pours us a glass of Kool-Aid and limps back to me. I laugh, "Of course not, it's over 400 miles; I can't run that far yet," I say, "but we've got to run back to Guidiguis. You ready, Egré? Let's go."

"Nooooooo!" Egré wails and throws his head into his hands. "My butt hurts!"

"Yeah? Mine, too. Maybe we'll take a bush taxi back."

Egré's face peeks out from behind his hands to see if I'm serious. Slowly, he flashes me a big smile.

"Come on, Son," I say. "Wanna learn how to swim?"

"Yes," he says. "Does the hotel make pizza?"

"Nelson Mandela has suffered in prison for twenty-five years, and yet he still hasn't given up hope for a new government and a free South Africa," I say to my advanced English class.

Lydie now sits in the front row and has stopped taking notes, listening as if memorizing every word. I've asked the girls to sit in the front row in all my classes. Next to her, the Foulbe girls sit, writing down as much English as they can understand from my lecture. Now, after a year and a half, the students have learned to speak most of the English they've known how to read and write for years.

Abbo raises his hand, and as I call on him, he stands.

"Does Nelson Mandela's vision include a revolution and *coup d'état?*"

The class is fired up today. For days, news of the oncoming strike has forced us to glue our ears to the radio. Within the high school, the teachers have spent time secretly educating students without the principal finding out. When he disappears behind his desk in a faraway office, the teachers stop teaching their subjects and continue explaining Cameroon's history as a former colony and the revolution's intentions. My students have heard various reports from teachers about Nelson Mandela and his vision for South Africa. Last week, my students asked me to lecture on Mandela and apartheid. Vann had helped me prepare the statistics before her departure, and I brought in a tape of Bob Marley's "Redemption Song" to teach my students.

"He envisions a peaceful liberation of his country," I reply.

"Can a country be peacefully liberated?" Abbo asks.

"Gandhi liberated India from the British using nonviolence," I say.

"What is nonviolence?" Egré asks.

"Gandhi said that nonviolence is the practice of loving those who hate us."

"That's impossible!" Abbo says, and the class agrees, talking to each other and shouting words across the room in their patois. Abbo sits down, and other students cheer for him.

"He said that loving only those who love us is not nonviolence. That's easy to do. Loving the hater is the most difficult of all actions. It's the weapon for the brave."

Egré raises his hand and then stands up when I look at him.

"Nonviolence is not a shield!" Egré says. "It will get many people killed!" He sits down and crosses his arms.

"It's true. Many people will die, but there has to be a sacrifice. Even in war, there are those who die; nonviolence is a war of love."

"But you can't kill the enemy with love!" Egré says.

"But you can appeal to their human heart, turning them toward humanitarian service. That is the goal."

Lydie raises her hand, and the class becomes very quiet.

"Yes, Lydie, what do you think?"

"Love can be a road to freedom. My teacher said that," Lydie says, and smiles as she sits back down.

Smiling at hearing myself quoted, I say, "Lydie, you're right. It's the only road."

We hear a motorcycle speeding through the grounds bringing the mail. I look up with hungry eyes. I've been dying for letters from home, and mail hasn't come for two weeks. Rumor has it that the government is reading the mail, and that's why we haven't received any.

As the motorcycle stops at my classroom door, I forget that I'm a teacher and that I have 107 students waiting. I hurry to the door. Yves turns off the engine, and Mr. Mfoumba gets off the back of the bike.

"Miss! You have five packages at the post office!" says Yves.

Packages? He shouldn't have said that. Now I won't be able to concentrate on anything else.

"We tried to get the packages for you, but you have to sign and pay for them," Mr. Mfoumba says.

"Thanks for trying," I say, and start to return to my class.

"But Miss, you have two letters here!"

He hands them to me, saying, "You should leave your class early and bike to the post office before they close at noon."

"Good idea," I say. "Thank you." I try to return to my class, which is still strongly debating our topic, but Mr. Mfoumba stops me again.

"Be careful what you teach, Miss," he says seriously.

"What are you talking about?"

"I hear the students talking about Nelson Mandela and the revolution."

I must have a question on my face because he adds, "It's not wise to teach desert children politics."

"But you—"

"We've long given up hope," he says. "They're not genuinely interested."

"But they asked me to further explain because you mentioned it in your class."

"We've stopped, Miss. And I would, too, if I were you," Mr. Mfoumba says.

I want to scream, but instead, I turn away from him. I don't understand what he wants from me. He wants me to go on strike when they do, but he doesn't want me to explain what it all means to the students.

I don't know what to do. How do you get involved and support the country you live in and at the same time stay out of politics?

I let my class out thirty minutes before lunch break and run home for my bike. I race to the post office and get there just in time. I pay 1,000 CFAs for each package, nearly four dollars—and the postman gives me two more letters. I put them in my backpack and make it home in record time.

I'm glad to see that Abbo and Egré haven't come home yet because I want to savor each word and slowly open the packages at my desk.

But when I turn the first letter over, I notice that it's already been opened. The pages have been crumpled, then stuffed back in and taped shut. When I look at the other letter, I discover that it has also been opened and looked over and then stuffed back inside.

I can only stare at the packages, afraid to open them.

The first package I do finally open has a French Bible in it instead of the tape my family recorded for me around the dinner table last Christmas. The other packages have cheap Nigerian cassettes instead of the store-bought music cassettes I asked my mom for. And the package that was supposed to have Kool-Aid is only French newspapers.

Not only have I been robbed, but the government is searching for evidence that I am an American spy.

Freedom of speech. Respect. Privacy. We never fully understand their meaning until they've been taken away from us. Before I left the United States, I'd been sickened by the Reagan administration and the Iran-contra affair. Then Bush stepped in, and we had the Gulf War. Now we have a new president. After reading Maya Angelou's poem written for Clinton's inauguration—it looks as if there might be a new hope and direction for America.

I'm beginning to understand a little of what freedom means: it's the most basic human need.

Freedom is the only thing worth fighting for.

Dear Mom,

Well, you're right. You said there were lots of things I wouldn't fully know until I became a mother myself. Now I understand why you disciplined me the way you did when I was acting like a little scoundrel. Thanks for always loving me anyway. There's certainly something to be said for unconditional love.

Mom, I'm starting to believe in karma. Absolutely. And anyone raising a teenager will agree. Karma is real. Watching how kids behave, I suddenly become aware that the scene is familiar. Only the names, places, and characters have changed. Ah ha! I'm getting back exactly what I gave to you. All that energy, negative as well as positive, returns—tenfold. Great.

Did you receive my last letter, explaining that I've adopted two of my students, Abbo and Egré? It's not official or anything, but it is an official awakening of the spirit. And it's not completely their fault that they've driven this young mother nearly crazy. After all, they're teenagers. Cameroonian teenagers. Enormous, burly teenagers. True, I may be exaggerating when I say I see eye to eye with their belly buttons. But their muscles! Since they were old enough to walk, Abbo and Egré have been old enough to carry a water bucket on their heads and plant fields of peanuts, millet, and corn.

When I'm disciplining my sons, I wonder if they look down at me and chuckle secretly to themselves. They know that this fragile American woman—who winces while killing a chicken or anything alive—could never harm a hair on their heads. Although I take my new motherhood seriously, I have doubts that the feeling is mutual. Teenagers. Mmfph!

Mom, no one told me about the expenses involved in being a mother to a pair of Cameroonian teenagers. I was barely aware of their needs—or of the Western consumer buying habits that have penetrated deep into Africa. Oh, sure, I thought they'd want the usual teenage stuff: Walkman, cassettes, designer jeans, sunglasses. And they did ask for some of these. But I really wasn't prepared for my karma to unfold in the way it did.

It all starts coming onto me one moonlit night as I'm walking home from school, after filling out 554 report cards by hand. I pass a group of mothers, stirring millet porridge over a fire and gossiping about me in low whispers. How could the little American woman allow her boys to go to school like that, they say—one in plastic sandals and the other with gaping holes in his shoes?

I stop behind a mud hut to listen. I'm stunned. Neglecting my children! I long to have enough Fulfulde to explain my financial situation. The small Peace Corps stipend is designed for a single person to live as a volunteer and at the same level as local villagers. The salary for one woman isn't adequate to raise two growing boys. Then there's the cost of school supplies—which neither the U.S. nor Cameroonian government provides—and the expense of traveling to another village to buy pens, chalk, paper, and books. The women don't realize that, by taking Abbo and Egré into my home, I'm acquiring a large debt, and that in order to feed and school my burly boys, I sometimes have to borrow from other volunteers.

The consensus around the fire is that the white woman's kids ought to be wearing Nike high-tops—not the artificial junk smuggled in from Nigeria, but quality American shoes. Housing, school, and food are simply not enough. They feel that, since I haven't given birth to either boy, I have to prove my motherhood.

(Mom, I remember that when I was a kid, you used to ask, "Do you think money grows on trees?" Some Cameroonians believe that, in America, it does.)

With the village women's words still buzzing in my ears, I take the boys to the next village market. But we don't see anything we want. Not much comes into Guidiguis from the outside because the villagers buy little other than food. So I finish my teaching at noon, take my sons out of school, and head to the capital city to shop.

When we arrive in Maroua, the market is crowded with merchants and customers. Abbo and Egré, who have never been far from Guidiguis, are stunned by the sheer size of the market as well as by the quantity of goods and the diversity of expensive garments being worn by the Foulbe men.

Abbo is impressed. Egré is disturbed.

"Look at the Foulbe, Abbo," he says. "They steal from us in the bush and bring it to the city to sell at triple the price."

"The Tapouri have always let the Foulbe control prices," says Abbo. "We are so desperate for a single franc, we don't even think of many francs."

It's easier to bargain if you follow the customs and speak the language, and it's more respectful. I'm wearing a brightly colored sarong and cape, which covers me from head to toe, but Egré and Abbo do the opposite, showing off their American jeans and T-shirts. Their hormones do the talking as they strut impressively behind girls selling mangoes and ginger from large plates on top of their heads.

The merchants are impressed with the little Fulfulde I've learned and begin to bargain reasonably with me. But when they spot the kids in their fancy clothes, the price always goes sky-high—up to four times as much. My attempts to bargain are futile.

"Mom, it's not just because of us," says Abbo. "You're white, remember?"

"Oh, yeah, thanks. I forgot again."

"Mom, I don't understand how you forget you're white," says Egré. "It's so obvious. We can spot you from a mile away!"

"It's true," Abbo goes on. "In a crowd of a thousand people at the market, we just look for the blinding white skin."

"Thanks, guys," I giggle. "But I don't feel white."

They shake their heads, unconvinced. We continue walking through the market.

"Well," I ask, "do you feel black?"

"No! Hungry is a feeling," says Egré. "Black is not a feeling."

"So why would white feel any different?" We stop at a merchant's shop to buy vegetables from the southwest, but he's not yet back from the mosque, so we wait.

"Because you are different," says Abbo. He scratches his head and closes his eyes, searching for ways to explain what he means.

"People treat you differently," adds Egré.

"How do they treat me?" I ask, folding my arms across my chest and smiling.

"People treat you with more respect," Egré says dryly.

"What people? The villagers? I don't think so," I say.

"No, the French people and all those white people who come here," says Egré.

"Oh. And how they treat people is important?" I ask, not sure what Egré means. I detect anger rising in him but don't think that much of it.

"You're treated like you're important. We're just poor black people. Our lives don't mean anything."

"Why do you say that, Egré?"

"The mayor's and doctor's TV doesn't show movies about African people. On TV, we just see white people, those who live on that farm in Dallas and that Carrington family. You said people watch that show all over the world. No one wants to know about us, about droughts or elephants. Even we don't want to see us on TV."

"This is true," says Abbo. "I like watching the white people on the TV because it seems as if they feel different—happier. Happy they aren't black."

"White people are happier because they're rich," says Egré.

"White people don't feel happier. Egré, you know that not all white people are rich. I'm not wealthy, and I'm considered to be white."

Egré mumbles that he'd be happy if he were rich. Abbo stops and points to a little shoe shop opening again after midday prayers.

On this particular day, merchants are hard-pressed for money to celebrate the end of Ramadan, the fasting season, so it isn't easy shopping. One Foulbe man refuses to even get near the real price; all he can see are dollar signs tattooed on my skin. He grins and licks his lips. I clench my hands, frustrated. Abbo and Egré jump in front of me when they see my face turn red—a phenomenon they never quite understand with white skin. But with me, they know it's bad. Abbo puts a hand lightly on my shoulder.

"Mom, I don't need new shoes. I like sandals. Anyway, my feet get too goddamn sweaty in tennis shoes."

"Where the hell did you learn that word, Abbo?" I say, feigning anger but holding back a smile. They see right through me; I can never get mad at them. (Actually, Mom, they're good kids. They never stay out late. They don't know video games exist. They're always on time for dinner or to *kill* dinner.)

As we wander away, the Foulbe man begins hissing like a snake with orange fangs and waves us to come back, saying he'll give us another price.

"I don't want to hear you cussing, Abbo," I say firmly.

"Mom, we hear you cussing all the goddamn time!" says Abbo, breaking into a grin. Then he roars with laughter.

Egré laughs, shyly at first, wondering if I'll get mad at Abbo for mimicking me. But I eagerly join in, laughing until tears roll down my cheeks.

"Do as I say, not as I do, boys," I say wickedly.

(Mom, where have I heard that before?)

My sons. My already-made, growing-up sons. How will I ever be able to leave Egré and Abbo and return to America? There is a bond between us that couldn't be any stronger. It's as if they've been waiting for me all their lives—as if I've been aching to find them and love them again.

"Mom," says Egré, "if you want, you can give us the money, and we can come back without you. The prices would be a lot cheaper."

"He's right," says Abbo. "If we come tomorrow, we'll dress like poor students."

"OK, but I want you both to get a good pair of shoes, not some cheap stuff. You understand me?"

(I can hear you in my voice, Mother.)

"We won't be able to come back to Maroua for a long time," I say. "You know that. So you need to do some clever bargaining for some great shoes."

"Don't worry, Mom," Egré says gently, "you can trust us."

(Mom, a red light flashed when Egré said that. Remember how you told me never to trust anyone who says you could trust them? I should have listened.)

I give Abbo and Egré 5,000 francs each—about thirty-five dollars and about a third of my Peace Corps salary. Thirty-five dollars really equals about $150 in Cameroon. But $150 in their pockets is about as rare as a million in my own.

Later that night in the capital, Abbo comes home to the place we're staying, wearing his new shoes. Excited, he tells me about all the discoveries he's made in town. I'm happy for him—but why is he alone?

"Where the hell is Egré?" I ask.

"We split up. I think he doesn't want me around," Abbo says.

"Maybe he just wants to be on his own for a change," I respond, trying to cover up my concern.

"He'll probably be back soon, Mom. Everything's closed."

I wait for Egré until after midnight. Nothing. I pace back and forth, imagining him lost or dead somewhere in this big city. I think about the enormous trust his real mother has placed in me and how she'll kill me if anything happens to her eldest son.

Abbo, also worried, has gotten out of bed and waits beside me.

Eventually, Egré comes in the door, empty-handed, with a tale about how someone has robbed him. He even shows us a scrape on one knee and a cut on the face that he's received while struggling to hold onto the shoe money.

Believing his story, I give him another 5,000 CFAs.

The next morning, we shop separately. When we meet again, I don't ask Egré to show me his new shoes. I want him to feel that I trust him. We ride back to Guidiguis in total silence. Something is up, and even Abbo looks pushed out of shape. It's another scorching day, and I'm exhausted, so I don't try to make conversation.

About a week later, I see Egré at school wearing his old worn-out sneakers.

"Egré, why on Earth aren't you wearing your new sneakers?"

"Last night as we were sleeping, someone stole them right off my feet!"

"Egré, please."

"Mom, I'm serious."

"Egré, you either tell me the truth or you will leave my house immediately."

Egré's face becomes pinched and out of shape. He bites his lip and then looks up at me.

"I didn't buy the shoes."

"And you didn't get robbed of the first 5,000 CFAs either," I say.

Egré shook his head. "I fell off a moto-taxi."

"Then where's the 10,000 francs I gave you?"

"I don't have it, Mom."

A knife goes through my heart. I can't speak. I simply stare at him. My son has lied to me. He's stolen from me. What else has he done that I don't know about? How much has he stolen?

(Money isn't the issue, Mom, but how many times has he betrayed my trust? And why is love so blind?)

"You'd better get that money back to me today, or we will never speak again."

"I can't get the money," Egré says flatly. I can only glare at him.

"I spent it," he says.

"You spent 10,000 CFAs? On what?"

Egré won't answer. He looks down and doodles in the sand with the toes hanging out the front of his torn left tennis shoe.

"Egré, answer me!"

He neither moves nor speaks.

"Was it a stereo? Cassettes? A French watch? What did you buy, Egré?"

Very softly, he whispers, "A cow."

"A cow! A cow?"

Egré nods, ashamed.

"You bought a cow?"

He nods again.

"A cow? One of those rather large, furry animals that says 'moo'?"

"Yes."

"Are you pulling my leg?"

"I'm not touching anything, Miss!"

"Egré, let me get this straight. You took 10,000 CFAs and bought a cow?"

"I already had another 9,000 CFAs saved up."

"How long have you been saving to buy a cow?"

"Six months."

"What are you going to do with a cow?" I ask.

"Eat it," he says.

Yes, yes. Of course. I knew that.

"What do you do with them in your country?" Egré asks.

"We eat them, too, Egré," I say, "but they don't come whole. We don't see them mooing and breathing."

"How do you see them?"

"In tiny pieces, wrapped in plastic on a Styrofoam plate."

"Do you eat Styrofoam?"

"No," I say. "Egré, where is the cow now?"

"At my father's compound. We'll fatten him up before we eat him. We're so hungry we can hardly wait."

Mom, what am I to do? How can I stay mad at Egré for trying to help his family survive in the middle of the desert? Is it against his beliefs to buy good shoes for himself? Is it in his blood to think of the greater good—to think of his family? Has he only thought of feeding them with the money I've given him—money he believes is his to do with as he wants? Am I the light at the end of his tunnel?

Mom, I've decided that motherhood is a scheme someone has designed to get you to pay off your karmic debts.

Love,
Suz

I'm bargaining for the most beautiful and luscious tomatoes I've ever seen when I see Doc's car come driving into Guidiguis. He's back!

I give Saidou my money and drop the bag of tomatoes on his lap. I jump out of my skin and thank God that Doc's returned safely to Guidiguis. I take off running down the paved road to greet Doc with a smile, a hug, and a long, welcome-back kiss.

His car turns left down a dirt road toward the post office. I'm racing now and breathing heavily while my sarong unravels and I hold it up while I run.

I'm going to tell Doc how wrong I was to have been afraid of having a relationship. I'll tell him that I love him. I'll even say that we can have many problems and solve all of them.

I turn down the dirt road and see the post office and Doc's car pulled up in front. I will my legs to go faster and hope he'll stay there a few minutes so I can surprise him.

I turn around another corner, then stop to catch my breath. I wipe my face of sweat. I calm myself down, but my smile is so big I'm afraid I'll break my cheeks.

I walk through the entrance to the post office and see Doc laughing and talking to the clerk. His back is to me, but I can see him tapping his hands on the table as if he were playing the drums. The mayor laughs with him and then turns to speak to a woman I've never seen before but who is smiling warmly at Doc.

I race across the room, and before I can reach him and surprise him, Doc turns to the woman and takes her hand in his. She looks up at him shyly, and he leans toward her and whispers in her ear.

I stop.

Doc turns around; he sees me with his peripheral vision and does a double-take.

He smiles and looks at the woman while putting his arm around her and escorting her toward me. The mayor accompanies them, and I'm doing everything I can to keep myself from falling to the floor in a million broken pieces.

"Suzanne," Doc says, "I want you to meet my wife."

I reach out my hand and shake hers softly. She's radiantly beautiful and very happy at Doc's side. They are very much in love.

"How wonderful to finally meet you," I say to her.

Then I can't help it, but I turn my hurt and betrayed eyes on Doc while saying to his wife, "The doctor has told me all about you."

The mayor takes my hand, leading me to the clerk. "You have some mail from your mother," he says.

I hold on tightly to the mayor while Doc and his wife say good-bye and leave hand in hand.

The clerk hands me several letters, and I don't even bother to look at them. My neck feels broken, and my head hangs low.

The mayor offers me a ride home, and I graciously accept.

Has Doc been married all this time and not told me? Or did his family arrange this marriage for him? Why didn't he tell me?

The mayor leads me to his jeep, and I climb inside. I don't say anything and don't ask. I don't want to know, only want to forget. When I arrive home, I thank him and close the car door. Inside my house, I curl into a ball and cry—allowing my heart to bleed.

Later, someone slips a letter under my door. I recognize the scribble. It says:

Dear Suzanne,
   As Rod Stewart sings, "You're in my heart." And you'll be in my soul always.
   It seems too soon to say good-bye. I'm going to miss you every day. In the next life, don't forget me. See you at the café in the clouds.

   Yours always,
   Doc

52. LIZARD SPEAKS

She watches Doc
As he makes heavy footprints
Upon the sand.
Each one a step farther away
From the home she had built
For him inside her heart.

She watches,
Hands defeated by her sides,
Standing in the winding dirt road until
He becomes a tiny black dot.

She looks up and sees me,
Then gets lost somewhere again.
She plunges her hands
Into a bucket of last night's dishes.
"The pain Doc caused you
Is not what is real here."

"His lies are unforgivable."

"Anyone can say that but more is required of you.
Can you recognize that what a human being has done
Is not always who he is?"

"I trusted his love. I began to believe that I could love again."

"You can choose to forgive Egré and the doctor, to let go of the anger.
It would help you to heal."

"This is crazy! I forgive Doc, and he gets off the hook?"

"He may look like a Cameroonian doctor
On the outside, but inside,
He's a spiritual guide

Giving you the opportunity to choose
To be one with love or one with fear."

"Great! Now Doc is an enlightened master as well as a liar!"

"Doc is a wonderful teacher."

"He taught me so well that now I can really love with all my heart!"

She begins to cry for everyone she's loved and lost.
"Why are you here?" I ask. She doesn't respond. I listen to her from the inside, and she wonders why her soul won't leave her alone. "What do you want?" I ask.

"Love."

"You only want to be who you are. So be it."
She doesn't respond, for it is the first time she has ever thought of aligning herself with love.

"I hadn't thought about it that way."

"God moves in mysterious ways."

"You're telling me!"

"But this lesson with Doc is not a mystery,
Merely an opportunity for you to choose.
Love is the only choice that feels any good.
Pain is an indication that you are
Out of alignment with your soul."

"Am I in sync again?"

"Yes. You are exactly where you need to be."

"Thank God."

"You're welcome."

Inside the mud hut, my colleagues huddle together to privately discuss my penalty for teaching during Cameroon's national strike. They exclude me from their circle as if I were a prisoner of war. I sit and watch their body language in an attempt to decipher what will happen. The heat of our anger and differences is so thick I can hardly breathe. I remain still in the heavy darkness, which flies through an opening of the mud wall and perches on my shoulder.

It's difficult to believe that their voices are contained inside the hut where we're cleverly hiding our illegal political meeting from the *gendarmes*. Our nerves cause a loud static as fear moves quickly through our veins. We know what happened to protesters in Bamenda. Though death is a consequence of a meeting, our differences create a haziness we can't see past.

The stool I'm sitting on is a tree stump carved to be a woman's chair. Such chairs usually remain in the kitchen, a place where Cameroonian men are used to finding their women, where peanuts are shelled and corn flour sifted for the night's *fou-fou* and sauce. As far as my colleagues—LeoPaul, Mr. Mfoumba, Laurence, Mr. Ndo, and Benito—are concerned, the stump chair is the proper place for me, and my disobedience is intolerable.

"If you continue to teach, you are against us!" LeoPaul shouts as he towers over me, then paces around the stool. The muscles in his forearms spasm, and he restrains himself by tightening his fists at his sides.

If I were a man, they'd douse me with kerosene and set me on fire as revolutionaries have done to teachers and government employees who are out of compliance in the northwest. But a woman, a white woman, is simply a nuisance.

I stare back at LeoPaul, my eyes burning with held-back tears. Inside, I'm a coward, but on the outside, I hold my head high, demonstrating that I cannot be bent. As LeoPaul steps back to stand beside his colleagues, I concentrate on gathering strength.

What LeoPaul refuses to admit to himself is that his verbal bullets aren't going to destroy the color of white. My skin is not the enemy, and battling a Peace Corps volunteer is futile. The enemies

LeoPaul wants to fight are the French politicians, who, he believes, still manipulate their puppet, President Paul Biya, with clenched teeth and devious hands.

I'm the only white in sight, the only one at whom to fire his loaded words. The real war is hundreds of miles away in the northwest. And LeoPaul is stuck in the desert with a group of angry male colleagues and a single American woman.

"Gentlemen, if I strike, I will be sent home immediately. The Peace Corps won't allow us to get involved in politics. We are volunteers, not activists," I say.

"If you continue to teach during the strike, then you must have no interest in the welfare of Cameroon. If you admit it, you must return!"

"Miss, you're only a tourist here," says Mr. Ndo. "This is your vacation."

Some vacation, I think to myself.

"*C'est la vérité. Elle fait du tourisme!*" It's true, she's a tourist!

"*Le tourisme? Le tourisme? Ça c'est fou!*" I say. A tourist? That's crazy!

They laugh together and say, "*Elle fait du tourisme au Cameroun!*"

The teachers nod and whisper in agreement, purposely speaking their language so I won't know what they're saying. Their quick, sharp voices feel like blows across my face. I watch their angry eyes fixed on me.

Doc had once told me that teachers in Guidiguis were prisoners, enemies of a government that didn't know what to do with them. Killing them would only start a war against a rising political party, so they isolated the activists from friends and family. Most important, they were not to have contact with any of their colleagues.

These prisoners of the desert were being punished for previous political acts, and if found gathered together, the consequence could be that they would disappear without a trace—as had the 200 others in the 1991 civil disobedience general strikes.

"Yes, go back to America!" LeoPaul spits. "What do whites know about human suffering?"

What am I doing here?

"They steal natural resources and then leave us without honor or dignity," Benito adds. "You should never have gone against us!" he yells.

"This is not my strike," I say softly. "I understand your cause. But I also believe that students need to be provided with information in order to learn to think for themselves."

Mr. Mfoumba approaches me, hissing, "Better for you to go back to your comfort in America than to stand up for a cause you believe in!"

"I believe in Cameroon!" I say. I stand up and stretch myself five feet taller than my normal size and expand my hips and thighs while taking a step toward these men, whom I refuse to allow to frighten me any longer. "But this is not my fight!"

"You purposely went against the strike and taught school without even consulting us!" Mr. Mfoumba shouts. He paces around the hut.

"But this strike could last for months! Years! How are students going to become involved in Cameroon's struggle if they remain isolated and ignorant?" I ask. The teachers stand in silence and disbelief, their eyes jumping from one to another, in shock that a woman would disregard her place and raise her voice to question a man's actions as well as his politics.

"You are their only door to the outside world," I say, and I'm surprised now that they're really listening. "And the only key to the university of Yaounde. You've shared your dreams, but now you turn your backs on them!"

Their eyes show a flicker of tender fire as they reflect on their attempts to motivate changes in students. In their eyes, I see a longing for justice and peace. Mr. Ndo sighs. "Their dreams of the university are meaningless. That's why the government sent us here, to be as useless as possible."

"But you inspire them! They believe in you. They want to be part of Cameroon's struggle!" I try to remind them of their own hopes, which are fading in the sun like a child's decorated paper flower.

"No," Laurence interjects, "you're wrong. They don't know

anything other than their tribe. They've never seen land thirty kilometers from their compounds. They learn French because they're lazy and don't want to break their backs working in the fields as their parents do. Dreams of the university are disguised as dreams of the city. When they stand at windows to watch TV, they see Yaounde on the news. They want what they see—an easier modern life, not a political struggle."

"I don't understand. You fault them for believing what you told them."

"We were once like you," LeoPaul replies, leaning forward. "Don't you think we came here thinking we could make a difference? We thought we could carry on our resistance by teaching Cameroon's history. It was a waste of time!"

I feel his lost passion rising like a tide inside me. The lantern flickers as if disturbed by an evil spirit passing through the hut.

"But the students deserve to be respected, not lied to by their teachers," I say.

"What do you mean?" Benito snaps.

"It's a lie to say you're striking when you're playing sick and sitting in your houses, terrified to be discovered by the *gendarmes!*"

LeoPaul spins, then surges toward me, until I'm leaning against the wall.

"I haven't been playing sick! I've been striking!" LeoPaul shouts.

"The principal told me you had malaria," I shout back.

"I am striking, Miss!" says LeoPaul. He turns his back to me.

"Striking doesn't mean lying about being sick when you're not! It takes strength!"

"You have no right! I am not weak! You, Miss, you have no idea what it is like to be black in Africa! It's easy to preach when you're white among us blacks! How can you tell me how to strike! Your laws protect your skin from even a single puncture! Imagine being black and the military captures you. Imagine them peeling your skin like a root until you're nothing but a crippled animal screaming for the beating to stop and you'll tell them anything they want to know. Anything, just stop."

"Imagine yourself African, imagine it back to America!" Mr. Mfoumba says.

"Get out of this country! You are not wanted here!"

"You have insulted us enough! Go home!"

The teachers nod in agreement, and a whisper passes among them like a wave returning to the sea and smashing into an oncoming wave.

In their eyes, I can no longer see my friends. Instead, I see enemies who wave their flags as they march over me like a ripped-down banner.

I move slowly toward the door, hoping they'll allow me to leave. The teachers are huddled again, talking in their language, seeming to be unconcerned with my departure. When I reach the door, I raise the latch, then stop when we hear the sound of a car. A jeep is speeding along the dusty road toward the school. That could mean only one thing: it's the commander.

I turn around, my eyes filling with tears, and look to my colleagues for help.

LeoPaul leaps across the room and puts the latch over the door. Benito blows out the lantern. Laurence reaches for the stick that holds open the metal covering of the window. He locks it shut.

I lean against the wall and wonder what will happen to us.

No one moves. No one swallows. No one dares to breathe.

I can't see the teachers in the darkness, not even the whites of their eyes.

We hear the jeep quickly returning from the school and approaching our alley. It slows down and seems to be sniffing for our scent like a police dog.

As the jeep rolls closer, we're as stiff as statues. I think of the Lamedoh, whom I saw earlier today on my way to the meeting. I knew I smelled trouble when our eyes met. The king was sitting on his wooden stick throne and watching me closely as I quickly walked through his neighborhood to LeoPaul's mud hut. I bet this is the king's revenge on me for not sleeping with him and for insulting his integrity. I bet he told the commander that he saw me and other teachers on our way to a strike meeting.

The commander's jeep stops in front of the entrance to Leo-

Paul's compound. We hear the door open. Then we hear another car pull up.

The mayor greets the commander warmly. I hear the faint humming of the chorus to "Stand by Me." Doc is here, and his singing is a signal that he's aware I'm in here. Doc describes to the commander three women drinking cold sodas at the bar as they wait for a bush taxi to fill up and take them to Yagoua. The mayor quickly adds that the bar's refrigerator is finally up and running, and at last he has an opportunity to buy the commander a cold drink. The commander is easily persuaded and they make arrangements.

Then we hear the commander jump in his jeep. He speeds off, and we hear the mayor's car follow. We all breathe. That was too close.

When they've driven away, I unlatch the door and open it.

"In this country, Miss, you have to watch yourself. People disappear, and we never see them again. You have no fear because you are American."

"I am scared. I'm afraid to stay, and I'm afraid to go home."

"If you can't fight with us, then go home."

As I walk out of LeoPaul's hut shaking, I think about what he said. I turn on my flashlight, careful not to step on any scorpions. Tonight, I'm afraid to walk home alone. My flashlight becomes weaker and quickly fades. I shake it and hit it, but the batteries are dead. My house is nearly a mile away.

I don't have African eyes. I cannot see in the dark.

I creep down the sandy path in the dark, holding my arms out like wings by my sides. I take one cautious step after another as if I'm tiptoeing on a thin wire in the circus. I imagine snakes scurrying below waiting for me to run past. I pray that these wings will lift me above this black, moving sand, lift me above politics and government corruption, lift me so high above it all that I can cross the Atlantic Ocean and fly home.

But instead of soaring high, I crash to the ground, my foot catching in the gnarled root of a tree. The impact of the fall stings like sandpaper rubbing across my chin, hands, knees, and elbows. I try to yank my foot free, but I can't shake it loose. As I squirm away, I feel the hold becoming tighter around my ankle. I imagine the branches coming alive and a claw pulling me backward into the belly of a hungry, growling tree.

As I stand up, I see swirling lights in the distance. It looks like a pack of fireflies dancing toward me. I've never seen such a thing. I sit up, turn to the tree, and pull my foot out of its grip. I quickly turn back to gaze again at the beautiful lights. I think of Christmas and my family back in the States. Then I hear the lights singing as they approach, the music so sweet it's as if someone were putting a child to sleep. I remain still on the sand, not wanting to awaken from this lovely vision.

I imagine these lights are my fairy godmothers, coming to save me from the scorpions, dragons, and the wicked witch.

When I finally stand up, I can see the glow of the lights illuminating the beautiful faces of six young girls walking home from Koran study school with tin oil-burning lanterns in hand. They are singing prayers and asking for blessings.

Even though they aren't fairies, they are still my angels, sent to rescue me and guide me back home.

When the children come near, the lanterns give us vision, and one of the girls recognizes me and runs toward me, shouting, "*Suzannedee! Suzannedee!*"

The rest of the girls giggle and follow, singing my name like a mantra.

My eyes fill with tears. When adults get lost in their "shoulds" and "should haves," in their politics so thick that they can't see the light—it's the children who are there to guide us into the future.

The girls gather around me. One whom I recognize now is Aïssatou's little sister. She hugs my legs as she looks up smiling. I pick her up in my arms and twirl her around. The other girls shout, *"Hokeeam, Suzannedee! Hokeeam!"*

I pick each of the six girls up in my arms and twirl them about, my heart singing that the night has had a happy ending.

The girls take me by the hands, three hands holding my left hand and three holding my right.

The stars are twinkling brightly, as if God were watching and winking at us.

55. WEEKENDS OF HOPE

I was the only teacher who arrived at school on Monday. I felt like Judas betraying his friends with a kiss. Most of the students had continued to show up every day after the strike had begun, not knowing what else to do and wanting in some small way to keep hope alive.

I started class the usual way, with the roll call and then my announcements. But then I stopped. I looked into the eyes of my students. I thought of the angry, passionate, and hopeful eyes of my colleagues in LeoPaul's hut. These students are tomorrow's teachers and perhaps leaders of Cameroon. I feel that what I do concerning the strike will have at least a remote impact on them in how they will choose to live their lives. They are the future of Cameroon.

I stopped the class. I couldn't do it. I couldn't cross a strike line. With tears in my eyes, I apologized to my students for not being able to teach, and I told them that I had no choice but to support the strike.

They clicked their tongues against the back of their throats, showing that they strongly disagreed with my decision.

Lydie's sister, Hervine, looked into my eyes. She, too, had tears but raised her hand to speak. When I called on her, she stood up, her eyes never leaving mine. Even if only subtly, perhaps some things have changed within the school.

"Who is going to teach us?" Hervine asked.

"After the strike, all your teachers will be back," I said, not knowing if that were really true. I felt I was drowning in their sorrow; I wanted so much to be the one to see them through to their exams in June.

Defeated by my look of hopelessness, she sat down. Another student raised his hand and stood up. He, too, looked straight into my eyes, as if the pleas in their African eyes would melt my resolve.

"But, Miss, they might send you back to America if they discover you're striking."

"Yes, it's a risk I'm taking," I said.

"You promised you wouldn't abandon us!" Hervine cried.

"I'm not going to abandon you," I said.

"You said that you didn't know how long the strike would last and that we must continue with our studies."

I looked at all of them looking back at me. This is my chance, I thought to myself, to make a difference and to show them that, when there is the desire, there is always a way to manifest the dream. I paced up and down the aisles, and they held their breath waiting for my reply. I spun around in front of the class: I had an idea.

"What would you think about studying English on the days we don't have class: Wednesday afternoons, Saturdays, and Sundays? Would you come?"

Hervine stood up.

"I will be here, Miss."

Another student stood up.

"I will, Miss."

Another stood up.

"Yes, me, too, Miss!"

Like dominoes, one after another stood up and told me they would come. Soon the whole classroom was standing in front of me. They know that their education is their only hope of having a better life.

"Thank you," I said. I had goose bumps over every inch of my body. This was a moment that would live on in my heart.

"Be here at seven sharp on Saturday," I added.

After announcing my plan to all of my classes, I went home and took a bucket bath. I felt clean again.

SATURDAY

I got up early and ran. There are only four months left of Peace Corps service, and now that the strike is in full force, I'm mentally and emotionally preparing to leave. I've started to cross out the days that go by and count down the rest. I'm glad I still have time in Guidiguis. It will take me a month to say good-bye to everyone.

On my run, I prepared myself for my departure. I went over the last two years in my mind and experienced it all over again. I went over the first night I arrived in Guidiguis and how frightened I was. I thought of the women who helped me survive—especially Clotilde and Calixte. I thought of the first time I lifted a water bucket over my head—how each time it got easier and how the women at the well grew to accept me. I thought about teaching Lydie to ride a bicycle and Aïssatou's smile and then her sudden death. I remembered Sali's family with their open arms and the first time my Foulbe mother looked at me. I thought of little Adele and Ahmadou and how they taught me to come out and play. I remembered my neighbors coming over to my house the night François was killed and how I knew that I had become a part of the village. I thought about Egré and Abbo, and of course, there will always be Doc and his music playing everywhere I go. And then there's the lizard, whom I will take with me when I leave Africa. How will I possibly be able to say good-bye to the family I've made here?

Returning to Guidiguis after my run, I noticed that there weren't any students making their way to school. Maybe no one would show up. But I thought, if only five show up, maybe I will have made a difference in someone's life while I was here.

I walked to school prepared not to see anyone, but a little hopeful that maybe thirty students would show. My classes had looked excited and committed when I told them that I'd be here. I wanted to be optimistic, but I was also afraid my hopes were too high.

I walked into a classroom and wrote instructions on the board. I thought we'd write plays about life in Cameroon and act them out the following day. I brought a lot of paper and pens for my students to write their scripts.

As I was writing on the board, a few students drifted in. I welcomed them and was so happy that at least someone showed up. I was surprised to see them in uniform.

I heard more students talking and laughing in the distance. Maybe I'll have at least fifteen, I thought.

I stopped writing a moment and just stood still. I listened to the students and let their laughing fill my heart like a song. I felt the morning breeze come through the window. I drank in the smell of the dry desert and its sweet innocence. This might be the last time that I'd be a teacher in Cameroon, and I wanted to remember these final moments and savor what it's like to be here—fully present right now. *Jam core doo may!* I am truly in my skin.

It was five minutes after seven, and I saw more students across the field and in uniform on their way to school.

Ten minutes later, the classroom was completely full, with almost a hundred students in it. I filed students into the classroom next door, and I saw many more on their way.

Greeting each of them by name, I asked them to please be patient because I'll be running back and forth between classrooms.

Fifteen minutes later, three classrooms completely filled up. Tears blinded my vision; I couldn't believe that over 300 students had showed up for my English class.

What better gift could I have asked for at the end of my Peace Corps service in Cameroon? That moment told me everything I needed to know about my future.

I knew then that I wanted to be a teacher for the rest of my life.

I raced between the three classrooms. I divided the students into small groups to write their plays. Most of them used English, but for the low-level English students, I allowed them to write their plays in French, and we'd translate them into English later.

There were some startling ideas for plays. One play is about a Cameroonian English teacher who bribes a young female Cameroonian student with good grades for sexual favors. I was shocked to hear that it happens quite frequently.

Another idea for a play is about a husband whose four wives get jealous and angry with each other. Three of the wives join together to kill the favorite wife, who is getting pregnant every year. The story is chilling and gruesome, but they tell me that it's a true story and that often there is a problem among the wives.

I am still so naive about the reality of the daily lives of Cameroonian girls and women.

The boys wanted to play women, but I asked the girls to try to take female roles, even though I know they're shy and would rather not.

We practiced the plays and pledged to come back tomorrow.

SUNDAY

Eighty percent showed up, and we selected play ideas we liked and regrouped. We wrote, rehearsed, and rewrote all day. Finally, at the end, we watched three scenes of a play. The students laughed at the parts when the Cameroonian teacher is bribing his female student. So often humor shows us what the truth really is, even if it's sometimes disturbing.

Egré stopped by in the late afternoon but remained in the audience. Our eyes met a few times, but he didn't approach me. I wanted him to come and say hello. Once, I nearly waved him over, but he looked away. I wanted to ask him about his family and the cow.

WEDNESDAY

There were a hundred students who arrived at school to rehearse. Lydie, Abbo, and Hervine were among the troupers. We decided on three plays, and we committed to seeing this through until school resumes again.

While they were writing their plays, I wrote a short story from an entry in my journal. I called it "Mango Elephants in the Sun."

SATURDAY

Thirty students arrived with their scripts and lines memorized.

Lydie suggested that we perform for the mayor and the doctor of Guidiguis.

Abbo suggested that, after we perform in Guidiguis, we head to Maroua and perform for Amy's high school class. Maroua's high school is huge, having fifty teachers compared to our ten in Guidiguis. The word is, fifty percent of the teachers in Maroua are too afraid of striking and losing their jobs and salaries forever.

SUNDAY

The same thirty showed up, and we wrote letters to Amy with our proposal. We asked her if she'd also like to start a theater company, and then we could perform for each other. The students suggested that we spend the weekend in Maroua and that Amy's students could each take one student into their homes. We made a list of Tapouri students and Foulbe students and indicated male and female and sent it off with a bush taxi.

We rehearsed all day and then went over to my house and had a party. We drank ice-cold Kool-Aid and cold water, ate pounds of peanuts, and listened to Bob Marley on my tape recorder.

Will American students be so pleased with a cold drink, peanuts, and only music that their teacher loves? I imagine the answer is no. Teaching in the States will be more of a challenge—especially since I can't tell a student in America to kneel in front of the class (I might be sued) or walk a mile down the road and bring back five buckets of water in 125-degree heat. Perhaps I've been spoiled in Cameroon.

I'll have to learn how to discipline all over again.

Still, a decent chalkboard will be nice. So will only one student per desk, a book for everyone provided by the school, and the class size limited to thirty-four.

But I'll really miss my students here in Guidiguis.

Journal, April 1994

FRIDAY

We arrived in Maroua standing in the back of the dump trunk with the missing windshield. The driver promised no cows or goats in the back with us, but on the way there, he tried to go back on his word and wanted to buy twenty goats at a tiny village between Maroua and Guidiguis. We all protested with shouting and demands for our money back. He knew better than to force it. The students would have aided me in mutiny since I told them I could drive a vehicle and was ready to hijack the truck.

Amy's students warmly welcomed us at the high school. The school was over half empty. Each of Amy's theater company students took a student home, with the agreement that everyone would show up on Saturday to rehearse and then perform at ten o'clock sharp.

Amy took my hand and led me to Maroua's market. We bought enough food and drinks for the celebration party after the play. We felt lucky to have each other during this dark time. Most of the volunteers who were assigned to the extreme north had quit and gone back to the United States. Sometimes I felt that the reason I was still in Cameroon during the strike was because I had Amy to support me and see me through these difficult times. She and I had become the best of friends.

When we arrived at Amy's house, she told me the news. She heard that Peace Corps teachers were dropping out like flies all over Cameroon. The strike has made it difficult for many volunteers to work and not to work. Working is why we're here. She showed me a bulletin from headquarters that offered volunteers other countries to which to transfer for a third year of service. Botswana, China, Morocco all sounded interesting, but Amy and I agreed that some traveling in Europe sounded like fun after our service ended, and anyway we were now ready to get home.

We broke out the maps and planned on seeing Turkey, Greece, Italy, France, Spain, Belgium, and Holland, in that order. We were excited to get on a subway, rent a car, use telephones, take a hot shower, and see a movie. I reminded her about ice cream, and we agreed that we'd gain at least twenty pounds on our way home.

SATURDAY

The plays were a delightful success! I only wish that I had brought a video camera to Cameroon. Amy took pictures, but it wasn't anything like we had ever dreamed of: the students were absolutely brilliant.

At the party, Amy and I learned to dance the Makosa with our students, and they performed a special song in tribute to their teachers. The party lasted until midnight, and by the time we cleaned up, it was after one o'clock.

The only problem was that Amy and I had drunk so much Coke that, when it was time to get ready for bed, we were so wide awake we couldn't even close our eyes and try to sleep.

We lay awake and stared at the stars.

What would the future hold for us?

Will we remember what is really important when we get back home?

We promised each other to remain aware of the jewels in life—clean water, good health, a happy tummy, a comfortable temperature, electricity, an indoor toilet—and if you have at least one person in your part of the world who understands you, you are an extremely wealthy and fortunate human being.

We talked until the sun came up, and I can't remember what topic we were on when we finally drifted to sleep.

It's Sunday morning, and my die-hard students from the theater company arrive for their English lesson. The textbook mandates that I go over city life and show a picture of London. Although it seems senseless to teach words for the city life, the vocabulary will inevitably be on the national exam, which could gain them entrance to the university. Since not a single student owns the textbook, I move around the room with the picture. The students ask what various things are on the page, and one of them is a Coke machine.

A student stands up. "What is a Coke machine?" He sits down.

I draw it on the chalkboard. They just stare at me.

How the heck do I explain it? I don't even know how a Coke pops out of a machine! And why am I so grumpy and tired today? It doesn't make sense because I must have slept over twelve hours last night. Abbo had a hard time waking me up, even after the sun came up and brushed my face.

"You put two coins in," I say while holding my pounding temples, "push a button for the soft drink you want, and out comes the cold Coca-Cola can. You pick it up, open the can, and drink. Modern technology."

They don't get it. My students stare at me as if I'd come from Mars. Imagine what they'd do if I gave them an overview of the United States—Disneyland, a computer, Nintendo, or a Laundromat. Geez. They'd get a headache from all the stimulation.

A student stands up. "Who is standing in the box?" He scratches his head and then sits down.

Why in the world do I have a splitting headache?

"What box?" I ask.

He stands up. "The Coke box." He sits down. He stands up. "*Pardonnez-moi*, Miss." He sits down.

Why do we have to follow this stand-up, sit-down routine anyway? I keep telling my students that they don't have to do it in my room, but their tradition is so strong, they can't seem to break it even when they try. Then they apologize to me because they don't know any other way of being.

Oh! The box is the Coke machine! He wants to know who works inside the machine!

"No one," I say. "The machine works by itself. All you have to do is push a button, and the machine will do what it's told."

"Ohhhh," they all say.

Understanding American life isn't easy. Most of the time, even I don't get it. How does a microwave work, anyway? Or a car? And why do nylons run? How did they send a man to the moon? I don't know how the TV, radio, VCR, or any of it really works, not enough to explain it. I just sometimes know which buttons to push. I'm sure that by the time I get back home, they'll have developed telephones like the Jetsons had, where you can see the person you're talking to.

Another student raises his hand and stands up. "Where does the sun go when it's night? Where does the moon go when it's day?"

"Good questions," I say. My vision gets blurry, then goes black. I stumble to the left and right, then backward, until I find the wall behind me and lean against it. My vision comes back, but everything is still blurry. I feel as if I'm going to vomit. Why am I now shivering and cold?

Abbo jumps out of his seat, climbs over the students sitting between the aisles on cement bricks, and puts his arm around my shoulders to hold me up.

"Miss, I think you are getting sick now," he says.

I can see my students stand up out of respect for me as Abbo walks me out of the room.

"Abbo, I don't feel so well."

Abbo escorts me to the latrine, and then waits behind the straw wall. Diarrhea shoots from one end of me while I vomit from the other. Could I possibly be more miserable? My head hurts so badly I feel it will crack open.

Abbo leads me across the school grounds and back home.

When we get to my house, I'm burning up, and my body feels as if there were a terrible internal itch or as if my blood were on fire.

Abbo opens the door and helps me into bed. He leaves the

room, and I get scared that I'm dying and start to cry. My body is aching, and my fever is soaring higher. In moments, the sheet below me is drenched.

Abbo comes back with a bucket of water, my canteen, and a sarong. He makes me drink a sip from my canteen even though I don't want it. He wets the sarong and rubs my forehead, arms, and legs with the cool water.

"Abbo, I'm so hot."

"Miss, you have a fever. It's malaria."

"Abbo, do you know where my Peace Corps medical kit is?"

He jumps up and brings it to my side.

"What medicine cures malaria?" Abbo asks, as he rummages through the kit.

"Look for the Fansidar. It's in a yellow box."

I'm fading. Everything is becoming blurry again, and my bones have caught on fire. I want to get out of my skin. I begin to drift off as if sailing into the fog and out to sea.

When Abbo finds it, he has to shake me awake. I can barely hear his voice or see his face. I feel myself leaving this place, and everything is becoming dark.

"Miss! Miss! Please! Can't you hear me? Is it this one, Miss? Mom! Mom!"

I can't see the writing, but I can see the yellow on the box.

"Yes, Abbo. That's the one," I say.

I close my eyes, but Abbo shakes my shoulders. He rips open the box and takes the pills out. He lifts up my torso and hands me a glass of water. I drink down the pills and sink down into the bed. I fall asleep, but when I awake again, I feel as if there were a million needles piercing my skin and making me bleed all over.

"Abbo, I'm so cold," I say. I'm shivering, shaking, and my teeth are chattering. Abbo puts a towel and a sarong over me.

"Isn't there a blanket?" I ask.

"There isn't a blanket in all of Guidiguis, Miss."

Abbo touches my forehead. "Mom, your fever is higher."

"How long has it been, Abbo, since I've taken the pills?"

"Two hours."

"It'll come down, you'll see. When the medicine takes effect, it'll come down."

I fall into a delirium, half awake and half asleep. I dream I'm in a burning pit and there are tarantulas crawling over me and digging underneath my skin. I feel thousands of them stinging me and releasing their poison into my skin. I try to dig them out with my nails, but once I get to one black tarantula, I find another burrowing its way inside. Then scorpions come out of the nooks and crannies of the walls and walk over me. They keep multiplying and multiplying until I am completely covered by scorpions.

I hear Abbo's voice, and I can almost feel his hand on my head, but I sink into the flames and disappear. The next time I wake, I yell for Abbo, but no one comes. I cry out his name, but he's not there. I just want to say good-bye to someone before I die. Someone please tell my mother I love her.

When my eyes open again, I think I'm in heaven because I see Doc's beautiful eyes, and he's carrying me in his arms. I can hear him singing Rod Stewart's "Heart and Soul." I want to say, "I love you," but my lips and tongue aren't working. I fall into darkness.

Later, I feel Doc's hand on my forehead. My eyes won't open. I keep trying to open them, but they're glued shut. He tries to put something in my mouth, but I shake my head and try to say "no." My mouth still isn't working. Doc grabs my tongue and holds it up, puts a metal thing under and closes my mouth. I fall back to sleep.

I can hear Abbo and Doc arguing, but I can't tell what they're saying. I open my eyes and see Abbo walk angrily out the door. Doc sees that my eyes have opened, and he smiles at me. I try to make my mouth smile back, but I'm not sure what it looks like.

"The Fansidar didn't work, Suzanne. Your fever is 105.4. I gave you some Halifan, and I'm praying your body will react. You need to hold on, my love. You need to stay here with me, OK?"

Doc looks at me tenderly, and I see all his love for me in his eyes. Then he puts on his doctor's eyes as he takes off my shirt and skirt, then picks me up in his arms. He squeezes me tight, and I feel his tears on my cheeks. He kisses my forehead, and then ever so softly, he kisses my lips.

"Don't leave me, Suzanne. Please don't leave us."

He takes me into the kitchen and sits me on his lap in a pool of water in my largest bucket that we once used to wash my hair. He puts my arms around his neck and then pours cool water from a teakettle over my body. Again my heart is squeezed by the pain of too much tenderness in his love for me.

"Abbo is so worried about you. He's telling your friends to come see you. He didn't want to leave your side, but I wanted people to come and give you some of their strength. You have so many reasons to live your life, Suzanne. Don't you give up. I'm not going to let you break your mom's heart, OK?"

I close my eyes. The water being poured over my body feels like medicine that Doc is using to make me well again. The water caresses my skin and cools me down. But I fall back into the darkness and discover the body to be too hot to live in. I want to jump out and fly in my own direction.

I long to be free of my skin, to break out of myself. Suddenly, a voice tells me I can, I know how. I instinctively crack open the eggshell that surrounds me from all directions and catch only a glimpse of this other dimension. I push my head out into the world.

Am I dreaming?

A part of me is in some other place and time, but I can still faintly hear the doctor's singing and slightly feel the water being poured over my feverish body. The cool water falls in drops over my skin, but I feel it touching me, falling over my bones, my muscles, my cells, all on the inside. The water becomes a river flowing inside of me, running through each part of my body and taking me across stretches of valleys and forests of the earth, until I am somewhere far away from the bucket of water and my body.

I am getting further and further away from my lifetime—going back and forth across future time periods and past lifetimes lived on the planet. As if tuning in to one channel of the many on a radio, I tune in to a place and time of my many souls' incarnations.

In this star-form of myself, I see vast galaxies dancing and swirling across the endless sky above. I watch as stars push out from blue dust and are born as dazzling light making sweet music, calling to my soul to fly through inner space and in this direction.

I hear the solar system moving to a pulse. Recognizing that it's the beat of my own heart, I pull my head back inside the shell.

This is scary. Suddenly, I'm not bound to the only reality that is familiar.

Is this dream my own creation?

Next, I notice the blood along the broken bits of the eggshell, and directly above me are my lungs, heart, and blood streaming through my veins. Like a river under the moonlight, there is a radiant sparkle upon the red river shooting life through my body. I see my heart as a gorgeous supernova beating and pulsing. I am inside the universe that exists within myself, as if having an inner-body experience.

I feel as light as an egg yolk. It births itself out between my legs and falls like rain down to the dirt ground, sliding along and then diving into a river. I can hear the raw silence that echoes within this universe. I'm floating in a medicine river inside myself. Above the water, I sit weightless and free. Then, suddenly, I become heavy and sink underwater. When I open my eyes, I see emerald green water surrounding me as if I were being pulled down to a bright golden light.

As I breathe in, the emerald water expands in my lungs. I feel the water filling my body with solid existence and form. I've taken the shape of a human body once again. I feel I am now at the center of an earth, but unlike the planet I'm familiar with, unlike home. I'm being pulled farther down until I've crossed through the water-filled sphere.

I come up to the surface and find myself in an ancient stone bath. The emerald water runs in front of several enormous pyramids. I can see galaxies in the sky like moons and suns. Something tells me to jump out of the bath and walk through the entrance of the pyramid. There I see a temple sitting upon a sparkling green sea. I am greeted by someone who looks familiar.

"Hello," he says. As he comes closer, I see that it's a Navaho medicine man dressed in traditional ceremony attire. He puts a blanket around me and guides me into a room.

"Welcome home," he says.

The man indicates for me to lie down on a stone table.

"The way here is like being born," I say.

"You always find your way home," he says.

"I know your name. Your name is Windchanting. I've heard your voice before."

"Yes," he says. As he's rubbing an ointment on my forehead, a woman walks in the room and lights incense and candles.

"And that's Amanda," I say, "the tree spirit who talked to me in my childhood, projecting light shows into the darkness."

"Yes, you remember well," Windchanting says. "You want answers." Amanda joins him by my side.

"Who are you?" I ask.

"You. We are all aspects of who you are," Amanda says.

How can I be in this room, in Guidiguis, in Amanda, in Windchanting, and in several different lifetimes all at once?

"Just like the lizard," Windchanting says, and I immediately understand when he looks in my eyes, but I don't know why.

"So what do we do? How do we—" I ask.

"Do what comes naturally," Amanda says.

I close my eyes and ask my question: "Why do horrible events happen to children?"

Windchanting steps forward and moves his hand over the top of my head as if he were adjusting something above, because the light in the room changes.

"Why things happen to us," Windchanting starts to answer my question, "and what's going to happen next are sometimes not appropriate for us to know. The soul chooses for reasons even we don't understand. But we can always choose to grow or shrivel up and die. Relinquishing all attachments to trying to figure it all out and what it's going to look like will give you peace."

"I don't know what's going to happen next. Am I going to live? Will I ever find a soul mate?"

"You've never wanted someone to give the movie plot away before you've seen it," Amanda adds.

"You're right," I say, but I am really interested in the possibility of meeting the love of my life.

"Knowing the answers to all of those questions would ruin the surprise, wouldn't it? Then where would the adventure be?" Windchanting smiles at me, and then he winks. I have this sudden feeling that I will meet my soul mate after returning to the States. This feeling floods me with love for everyone I've ever let into my heart. And I now see that I can go on loving Doc. For love, real love, is unconditional, and it doesn't matter whether you are in a physical relationship with that person or not—he can still live inside your heart.

"I don't know what's going to happen," I say, "but I know it's going to be good, and I know it's going to be interesting."

"Sometimes it might not be so good," Amanda reminds. "But that's OK. It doesn't mean you've done anything wrong. It doesn't mean anything. It means only what you want it to mean."

"If you identify more with the Divine within, then you know it's going to be OK. You'll be taken care of because nothing that happens is really real anyway." Windchanting winks at me.

"This isn't real, either," I say.

"No, it's like a video you put in the VCR. It's real as long as you are deeply engrossed in the film. As soon as you turn on the lights, you've chosen to partake in some other reality."

"This sounds like the 'café in the clouds' theory, the idea that we are souls up at this café in heaven, writing our scripts together for our next lifetime."

"Yes, it'll be a good movie if you ever decide to write it."

"So in the meantime, what can I do to make life easier?"

"Set your intent. Be clear with that. The universe only knows how to say yes to everything that you declare to be true. Pray. Pray a lot. Keep the vision alive. Align yourself with Spirit. Then let it roll."

"OK," I say, "let it roll."

Windchanting and Amanda put their hands on my chest and lift my soul out of my body.

I am now a brilliant golden ball, which takes off at a speed faster than light.

Up I go, flying so fast that I have no control. I see the cord that connects me with my body down in Guidiguis. It pulls me back to my galaxy and down to the Earth. In a split second, I am falling down to Africa and leap into my body. My body shakes, and I open my eyes.

Thank God, I am back in my skin.

I am alive!

Jam core doo may!

Me donne!

When I open my eyes, the first person I see is Dada. My heart knows I'm home. She doesn't see that I've awakened, and I catch a glimpse of her tears. She rocks back and forth, holding my hand tightly; her lips whisper her prayers to Allah. She says in Fulfulde, "God is great. God is good."

Yes, life is good. It is so very, very good.

I turn my head and see Doc, Abbo, and Egré sitting on the pillows on the floor; their heads are resting against the wall, and their eyes are closed. How long have I been sleeping? I turn my head in the other direction, and Lydie is standing at the window looking up at the sky.

Dada continues her prayer but then sees that I've awakened and jumps in her skin with surprise and delight.

"*Suzannedee! Suzannedee!*"

Tears flow out of my eyes when I feel all the love from Dada pouring into me. She takes both my hands into hers, and I cry, too. I'm so happy to be alive.

"*Jam bah doo nah?*"

"*Jam core doo may, Dada am!*"

Dada pats my hand hard and laughs. She rubs both my arms up and down until my skin is tingling. No doubt about it, now I am *really* in my skin.

Abbo and Doc are at my side in an instant, but Egré only stands back behind them, not sure how I'll react.

"Hello, everybody," I say. "What's going on here?"

They just stare at me because, really, there are no words for how wonderful life is. They can only smile.

"Come on, you guys, you look as if you'd lost your best friend," I say, hoping to take the weight off the moment. I had no idea when I stopped taking the malaria prophylaxis that it could possibly be deadly.

"I almost did," Doc says, and kisses me on the forehead. He brushes my cheek softly with his fingertips, and I smile at him.

Lydie sits on the bed next to Dada, who repeats my name over and over. I smile at them both, thinking to myself that they *are* my soul mates. I don't have to go looking for love or wonder if it'll ever show up. Love is right here, right now, looking straight at me. What could be better than this?

"You saved my life, Doc! 'Doc operates, and nobody dies!' Nobody!"

"A promise is a promise," Doc says. He laughs and touches my shoulder.

"I was hoping you'd return to us, Miss," Lydie says, taking my hand and squeezing it.

"Remember the little ant, Lydie? That was some crumb I had to carry!"

"Yes, Miss, and you made it."

"Thanks to you, to all of you. You were strong for me. Thank you."

I reach out my hand to Abbo, and he comes closer and kneels at the bed.

"How are we going to go on without you when you leave?" Doc asks, and looks at Abbo.

"Mom," Abbo says, "I was so afraid that you were never coming back. God answered my prayers."

"He answered mine, too," I say. I look at Egré, who stands still not knowing if I've forgiven him about the money. "Egré, come and give your mom a hug," I say. I open my arms, and Egré rushes into them. He squeezes me so tight I yell out, "Hey! Be careful there!"

Egré laughs and lets go.

"Hey, Egré, I'm so hungry, I could eat termites!"

Egré laughs again, and we all join in. We know that the past is behind us now. We are a family, and no matter what happens, we will always remain so.

"Do you think we will ever meet again?" Doc asks me, and takes my hand. He is trembling and I long to hold him this one last night. We are saying good-bye to each other, our hearts feeling smashed by the weight of it all.

"Maybe not in Africa, but perhaps we'll meet again somewhere up in the clouds in a little outdoor café. We'll sit together, sip coffee, and write our scripts for our next life." I squeeze Doc's hand and then let it go. I don't want him to see me cry. Now would be the time for him to go, when I can still hold each part of me together and keep them from running off in all directions and acting out the years pent up inside me.

I stand up and move to the window. Looking up at the stars, I remember the nights that Doc and I made wishes upon them and dreamed of what our lives would be like. Tears fall, and I know that I'll never be able to stop them now.

"Do you really believe in your café in the clouds?" Doc asks, and crosses the room, standing behind me. I can feel his breath on my cheek, and I close my eyes, drinking in these last moments together.

I am silent a long time, and Doc takes another step toward me. I push myself up against the wall to keep us from touching, but he steps even closer and wraps his arms around me. I let go, leaning my head back on his chest, and cry—for me, for him, for both of us.

"Perhaps the café doesn't exist, but it comforts me at moments like this when nothing much makes any sense."

"I wish your departure wasn't tomorrow. How will we be able to fill this empty space you've left in our hearts?"

"Watch over Abbo, Egré, Dada, Lydie, Calixte, and especially Clotilde for me."

"I promise I'll look out for the ones you love."

"Doc, why do you suppose we wrote our scripts up like this? What was our plan when we were up there in that café?" I ask and although I know that we can't really invent an answer to soothe the pain, I hope he'll give me one to take with me back home.

"We learned that we can love even when there is no logical reason to love, or even a safety net to catch us from experiencing pain."

"I love you, Doc," I say to him for the first time. "I always have, and I will even when I'm on the other side of the world." I smile and am glad I remembered to say these words back to him.

"Me too," he says, and I turn around and hug him tight. "You have been my best friend," says Doc, and I smile.

"We always will be," I say, and my heart feels lighter. Somehow I needed to tell him that I loved him without any expectations or needs or promises or anything of the like. My love for him feels pure and simple, the way real love should be.

"I have a feeling that you will soon meet your husband, and he is the one you had plans to meet from your café in the clouds."

I nod my head. I realize that I can't see the big picture. I also see that now I don't want to. I want life to seize me by surprise. I want to be delighted by the thrill and sheer madness of taking risks and allowing my heart to love again.

Doc hugs me tight one last time and then slowly and sweetly kisses me on the lips. He pulls back, and we're both smiling. This is right; somehow I know it's meant to be.

"Have a safe journey. Tell your mom that I kept my promise."

I nod my head and walk Doc to the door.

"Doc, see you up at that café in the clouds sometime."

He squeezes my hand and then turns quickly and leaves, whistling "Stand by Me."

I won't be afraid, I say to myself, because this time I am standing beside me. I look up at the moon and just like in the song, it's the only light I see. But now I can feel the light within shining bright, too.

All of Guidiguis has known that today is the day. It feels like doomsday the way we are all walking around with our hearts so heavy we can barely lift a foot.

The villagers have cried and pleaded with me to stay another year. It's as if my departure were a tragedy. We can't believe that it's over so soon. In three hours, the mayor and Calixte will pick me up to take me to Kaele. From there, I'll catch a bush taxi to Maroua, where I'll meet up with Amy. Tomorrow, we'll travel together to Yaounde and meet up with other volunteers who are closing their service and taking a plane out of Africa. When I woke up this morning, I decided not to say good-bye but to say "thank you" to everyone in Guidiguis.

When I walk out the front door, I see the women at the well. They were there before I ever showed up, and they'll be there tomorrow for sure. Will it be as if I'd never pumped water there before? Life will go on as usual, but I will never be the same.

"Oh say ko jour," I say to the women at the well, and I raise both hands up in the air. Here is where I learned to walk through my fear and still have the ability to laugh at myself, no matter how ridiculous and weak I feel inside. Will I take those lessons I learned with me back home?

I stop at Lydie's house. She rushes into my arms, and we cling to each other desperately—as if we'll die if someone tears us apart. We cry in each other's arms, and then suddenly, she pulls away from me.

When I ask Lydie to come with me to say good-bye to everyone, she refuses and slips away from my embrace, saying it's better this way. As I leave her compound, I feel my heart tearing apart.

Valentine and the twins stand in front of their field. This is harder than I thought. Valentine is already crying, and the boys start, too, but when they see me, it hurts too much, and they turn away from me to cling to their mother. I hug Valentine and tell her thank you for everything.

When I try to say thank you to Clotilde, Alex, and Yves, Clotilde stops me by embracing me. She tells me that real friends never have to say thank you. It is already known in the heart. Clotilde gives Alex to Yves and leaves them behind to take my hand and walk me through the village and to the last moment. She was the first friend I made in Guidiguis and the last face I want to see as I'm driven away. Clotilde is right, because even if she had let me continue and say it, thank you is not nearly enough appreciation for having taught me to embrace the unknown, to plant, harvest, and survive in the desert. I suddenly stop walking for a moment and turn and hug Clotilde tight. Friends don't have to say it; sometimes you show more when you don't say anything at all.

"*Oh say ko jour,*" I say to Saidou and his mother. His mother offers me another chicken, but I tell her that I don't have anywhere to put it on the airplane. She insists that I take it, so I grab it by the feet and plan on giving it to Dada.

"*Oh say ko,*" I say to Aïssatou's mother and father, who have come out into the dirt road to greet and receive me. The children come running out of the house and beg for airplane rides. Clotilde and I pick each child up and take them for a spin. When everyone's had their turn, I tickle them and chase them back into their compound. I only say that I will see them later.

When Clotilde and I turn the corner, we see Dada walking toward my house. This is only the second time in her life that she has left her compound. We call her name, and she runs and embraces me. She takes my other hand and leads me down the dirt road and to her compound.

"*Oh say ko jour,*" I say to Sali and his family. Real love needs no words. We sit together for a long time. Sometimes we cry; sometimes we are silent. Dada brings out bowls of food for Clotilde and me, but we can't eat. Our hearts are too heavy.

When Dada and I say good-bye, I know that I will never see her smile again. She holds my hand with both hands, and we are still and without words for a long time. We can only stare into each other's eyes and gaze into each other's soul. We hold each other there for a long time. I will never forget her; for me, she *was* Mother Africa.

I say thank you to all the villagers at the *carrefour,* and then Ahmadou races out of his compound, crying and screaming for me not to leave. He holds onto my legs and won't let go. I swing him around until we get so dizzy we both fall to the sand laughing and crying at the same time.

When I finally return home, Egré is there. We say thank you to each other and nothing else. We know we will always be together in our hearts.

When the mayor and Calixte come for me, my tears flow the hardest when I say good-bye to Abbo. Abbo reminds me that we will always be a part of each other. Neither time nor distance will ever change that.

As I leave my house for the final time, I fall completely apart and have to stop and lean against a tree to regain my balance. I need to let it out, as if I were a Foulbe woman mourning, screaming and crying over the death of a loved one. I need to let go of the immense sadness that is sufffocating my heart. The rituals of the Tapouri and Foulbe are now a part of me. I was theirs and they were mine. We were a family joined by faith and trust and hope.

Clotilde rushes to my side and sweeps me up in her arms. She soothes me by whispering in my ear, but I can hear her voice cracking and soon we are sobbing together.

"It's not good-bye," she reminds me. "Africa will call you to come back. I know this."

Someone *has* died. The young American woman I was before I came to Africa no longer exists. I am looking at the world from a new perspective. I have never felt so alive and free. Now wherever I go *is* home. I am already there because home is where the heart is.

I did what I thought I couldn't possibly do—I survived two years in Africa. I made it. I discovered the heroine inside, and she is all me.

"I am my own best thing," I say, "And I'm still alive! I'm still here!"

I see the orange and black lizard zip up the tree in my front yard. He races toward the end of a branch and watches me leave Guidiguis for some other unknown adventure. I thank him for leading me to my very soul.

Oh say ko, oh say ko jour, sobajo am.

"*Oh say ko jour*, Guidiguis," I say, as my village fades away in the distance and we head toward Africa's horizon for the very last time.

I pluck my hopes, ripe and succulent, out of the African sky and fill my woman's heart with visions for the future.

ACKNOWLEDGMENTS

Thanks to you who walked with me for a while and reached out for my hand when I was about to stumble and fall; to you who listened when I was afraid, lost, lonely, heartbroken; to you who saw something in me when I didn't see it in myself; to you whom I will never have an opportunity to meet but whose souls thirst for simple, genuine human kindness; to you who've traveled to foreign countries and seen magnificent beauty and atrocities, but who remain committed to peace in the world and within your own homes; to you who find the courage to love again and again and again.

I would like to express my love and gratitude to the following people for enabling me to create this book: to my mom, Yvonne Herrera, for her constant support, faith, and love, and for never letting me give up on the Peace Corps, on myself, or on this book; to Dionette Kelton for embracing me in her heart and for always reminding me why we must live our lives at the level of our own integrity; to Jeanne Willis, my friend, guide, and editor extraordinaire, whose healing and recognition of my soul's calling has manifested my dreams into reality; to Reverend Deborah Johnson for her teachings, celebrations of spiritual laws, and reminders that each of us is perfect, whole, and complete, no matter what may have happened to us in the past.

To Neil Brown, my "miracle worker," whose commitment to my vision, healing, and writing has inspired me; to Anne Brown, mentor and kindred spirit, who has walked with me every step of the way, from Africa to publication; to Anne Hale Selby, who has fed and listened to me until weary long after midnight; who holds my hand, lets me cry on her shoulder, and corrects my grammar, pronunciation, and vocabulary; who makes me laugh until I cry because my cheeks hurt (thank you); to Betsy Schwartz, who taught me to walk through my fear, who listened until we worked it all out, who gave me the most wonderful room in a very cozy house in which to write my book, and—most of all—whose friendship with John, Jordan, and me made all the difference in the world; to Rose Martillano, who believes in mangoes and elephants and chocolate and who never let me compromise my vision or myself; to Amy Johnston, who was an answer to my prayers in the desert of Cameroon, who quenched my thirst for a true friend and who brought me out of my shell to a place I could walk freely and happily in the sun; to Catherine Louise, Kim Mosely, Debby Ginner, Tami Brown, Sara Corfield, Cyrus Armajani, JeanAnne Seago, and Haruo Kuartei for their amazing and endless well of love and support throughout this inward and outward journey from Africa back to my soul.

To the teachers and staff at E. A. Hall Middle School, who always support me and believe that anything is possible, especially Liz Hiltz, who believes in my dreams and helps to make them happen and who reads me the best children's stories ever written—you inspire me. To Ximena Ospina, who is the beautiful sister I always wanted to have; to Janet Johns, my mentor and master teacher, who reminds me what in life is really important—children, dancing, and chocolate. And of course to my students, who are always teaching me that dreams are worth every ounce of courage it takes to reach them. I love you all. Special thanks to Ben Harper for coming to my classroom and singing at the request of my students. You proved that miracles can indeed happen.

To Peace Corps Volunteers in Cameroon in 1992–94 and all volunteers in the past, present, and future—especially Gwen and Reid Bates and Celia and Keith Sandbloom, who taught me that true love is real.

To Jordan Guillory, who teaches me to see the world from a three-year-old's perspective and love all of it with all my heart.

To Morton Marcus, Linda Kitz, Sue Moore, and Pete Newell, who were the best teachers I've ever had and made me fall madly in love with literature, writing, and teaching.

To Maya Angelou, Alice Walker, Toni Morrison, Gloria Anzaldua, and SARK, who inspired me to reach into my soul and to write.

To Emily Hilburn Sell and all the others at Shambhala Publications who encouraged me in my early work and made all my dreams come true.

And most especially to my friend Dan Bessie, who saw my letters from Cameroon as the beginnings of *Mango Elephants* and never let me lose sight of the vision. Thank you for pushing me and working so hard on this project. I love you.